NON-CIRCULATING

THOMAS MERTON:
PROPHET IN THE BELLY OF A PARADOX

THOMAS MERTON:
Prophet in the Belly
of a Paradox

Edited by
Gerald Twomey

PAULIST PRESS
New York/Ramsey/Toronto

Library of Congress
Catalog Card Number: 78-61717

ISBN: 0-8091-0268-4

Jacket Photograph: Edward Rice

Published by Paulist Press
Editorial Office: 1865 Broadway, New York, N.Y. 10023
Business Office: 545 Island Road, Ramsey, N.J. 07446

Printed and bound in the
United States of America

Acknowledgements

Selections from *Mystics and Zen Masters* by Thomas Merton, copyright © 1961, 1962, 1964, 1965, 1966, 1967 by The Abbey of Gethsemani, from *The Secular Journal* by Thomas Merton, copyright © 1959 by Madonna House, from *Seeds of Destruction* by Thomas Merton, copyright © 1961, 1962, 1963, 1964 by The Abbey of Gethsemani, from *Thoughts in Solitude* by Thomas Merton, copyright © 1956, 1958 by The Abbey of Gethsemani, from *The New Man* by Thomas Merton, copyright © 1961 by The Abbey of Gethsemani, from *Disputed Questions* by Thomas Merton, copyright © 1953, 1959, 1960 by The Abbey of Gethsemani, are reprinted with the permission of Farrar, Straus & Giroux, Inc. Selections from *Thomas Merton/Monk*, edited by Brother Patrick Hart, including the poem "A Man: T.M." by Brother Patrick Ryan, are copyright © 1974 by The Abbey of Gethsemani and are reprinted by permission of Sheed and Ward, Inc. Selections from *The Seven Storey Mountain, The Sign of Jonas*, and *No Man Is an Island*, all by Thomas Merton, are reprinted by permission of Harcourt Brace Jovanovich, Inc. The poem "By His Death" by John Moffitt first appeared in *America*, Dec. 9, 1972, copyright 1972 by America Press, and is reprinted by permission of the magazine. The excerpt from "Coplas on the Death of Merton" by Ernesto Cardenal from *Apocalypse and Other Poems*, translated by Donald D. Walsh, is copyright © 1975, 1976, 1977 by Ernesto Cardenal and Donald D. Walsh and

Contents

Editor's Note

I wish to acknowledge my debt to the following persons, whose interest and support ensured the progress and completion of this work: first, John Eudes Bamberger and Patrick Hart, whose initial encouragement fostered my desire to undertake this project; my friends and mentors Bill Cook and Ron Herzman, who taught me to share the fruits of learning; Anthony Weber and the monks of the Abbey of the Genesee, whose lived witness instilled in me a love of Cistercian monasticism and an appreciation for Thomas Merton; my brother Paulists of the Washington community, especially Jim Brenny, Jay Kenney, and Mark Fischer; and my friends and colleagues at the Paulist Press, Don Brophy, Bob Heyer, and Kevin Lynch.

For
John B. Sheerin, C.S.P.—
A prophetic voice

A MAN: T.M.

Prophets never age
They live too strong
To prolong
Their days
Pure heart
Friend
Your words remain
To test our heart
You, word,
Will never age.

Patrick Ryan, O.C.S.O.

Thomas Merton: An Appreciation

Gerald Twomey, C.S.P.

In an early journal entry, Thomas Merton reflected: "... like Jonas himself I find myself traveling toward my destiny in the belly of a paradox."[1] Even in his younger monastic life, Merton recognized the paradoxical elements that had converged in him and impelled him toward the Abbey of Gethsemani in Trappist, Kentucky. Paradoxes marked his entire life, and cling to him in death, as his poet-friend Ernesto Cardenal muses:

> Our lives are rivers
> that go empty into the death
> that is life
> Your rather amusing death Merton
> (or absurd like a koan?)
> your General-Electric-brand death
> and the corpse back to the U.S.A. in an Army plane
> with that sense of humor so much your own you must
> have laughed. . . . [2]

As paradoxical and complex a figure as Merton was, his significance for our contemporary society cannot be overstated. Theologian David Tracy ranks Merton as "perhaps the most significant Christian figure in twentieth-century America."[3] The eminent scholar and monk Jean Leclercq extends even beyond that appraisal: "Merton was the man Christianity needed in a time of transition which began not with Vatican II, but with World War II. . . . "[4] He concludes:

1

"I am not given in to an ingenuous, admiring expression of friendship when I rank Merton with the Fathers of the Early Church and of the Middle Ages. . . . Just as they drew from the culture of their own times in order to make it a part of their inner experience, so did Merton work in our times toward bringing the 'Good News' to the world, less by converting individuals than by Christianizing cultures."[5] This insight neatly captures the religious genius of Thomas Merton. He emerges clearly as a seminal figure in the history of contemporary Christianity.

The present volume seeks to commemorate the essence of the man and his work, and to further their impact upon the American Church and larger society. Upon appraisal it is apparent that there are painfully few figures evident in the wake of his death who begin to approach the stature of Thomas Merton. This work was undertaken because its contributors agreed that Merton's legacy is too crucial to be allowed to fade away or become obscured. His "voice in the wilderness" needs to be expressed again, with clarity and conviction. The contributors to this volume explore the key areas in which Merton exerted significant influence, assess his impact in that area, and gauge the legacy that remains in the wake of his death. The purpose of this essay is to shed some light on the underpinnings of Merton's social witness, to provide an "umbrella" under which the subsequent essays will fall.

In one of his "cold war letters," Merton wrote: "When speech is in danger of perishing or being perverted in the amplified noise of beasts, perhaps it becomes obligatory for a monk to try to speak."[6] He felt a deep compulsion to undertake a mission to assist in the great task *"to restore man to a state of fitness for God"* (to use the phrase of the Jesuit Alfred Delp, whom he greatly admired). He soberly perceived the condition of humankind today: "As he now is, alienated, void, internally dead, modern man has in effect no capacity for God."[7] He echoes this concern strongly throughout his monastic experience: "In an age when totalitarianism has striven, in every way, to devaluate and degrade the human person, we hope it is right to demand a hearing for any and every sane reaction in favor of man's inalienable solitude and his inner freedom. The murderous din of our materialism cannot be allowed to silence the independent voices which will never cease to speak: whether they be the voices of Christian Saints, or the voices of Oriental sages like Lao-Tse or the Zen Masters, or the voices of men like Thoreau or Martin Buber, or Max Picard."[8]

By his own account, Merton never made any serious effort to convert anyone or anything. Toward the end of his life, he expounded upon the core of his monastic charism: "I have sought only to speak the truth as I see it, and to bear witness to what I have discovered by living in the world of the twentieth century, both without the light of Christ and with it. There is a difference, and I have experienced the difference, and I have endeavored to say so. That is all."[9] The demands of the twentieth century weighed heavily upon this monk, who perceived his role in the modern world "to keep alive the contemplative experience and to keep the way open for modern technological man to recover the integrity of his own inner depths."[10] Patently aware of the reality that our culture faces crises which ultimately may result in our self-destruction, he asserted: "We have to make ourselves heard. Christians have a grave responsibility to protest clearly and forcibly against trends that lead inevitably to crimes which the Church deplores and condemns. Ambiguity, hestitation, and compromise are no longer permissible."[11] Perhaps the finest capstone of the Merton legacy is contained in the "Statement Concerning the Collection in the Bellarmine College Library" which he issued on November 10, 1963: "Whatever I may have written, I think all can be reduced in the end to this one root truth: that God calls human persons to union with himself and with one another in Christ....It is certainly true that I have written about more than the contemplative life. I have articulately resisted attempts to have myself classified as an 'inspirational writer.' But if I have written about interracial justice, or thermonuclear weapons, it is because these issues are terribly relevant to one great truth: that man is called to live as a son of God. Man must respond to this call to live in peace with all his brothers in the One Christ."[12]

Merton gained instant notoriety through the astonishing success of his autobiography, *The Seven Storey Mountain*,[13] which finished the year 1948 as the number three non-fiction bestseller.[14] Unfortunately, despite its genius, the book became for Merton something of an albatross. A journal entry in the middle of 1951 reflects the genesis which Merton underwent in the intervening years from the time of *The Seven Storey Mountain*'s first appearance: "I became very different from what I used to be. The man who began this journal is dead, just as the man who finished *The Seven Storey Mountain* when this journal began is dead, and what is more, the man who was the central figure in *The Seven Storey Mountain* was dead over and over ....*The Seven Storey Mountain* is the work of a man I never even heard of."[15] Fifteen years later, he stated, with candor and annoyance: "I notice that for nearly twenty years my society—or those in it who read my books—have decided upon an identity for me and insist that I continue to correspond perfectly to the idea of me which they found upon reading my first successful book. Yet the same people simultaneously prescribe for me a contrary identity. They demand that I remain forever the superfically pious, rather rigid and somewhat narrow-minded young monk I was twenty years ago, and at the same time they continually circulate the rumor that I have left my monastery. What has actually happened is that I have been simply living where I am and developing in my own way without consulting the public about it since it is none of the public's business."[16] As Daniel Berrigan[17] quips, judging Thomas Merton solely on the basis of *The Seven Storey Mountain* would be a little like judging Thomas Aquinas by his playpen graffiti.

Nevertheless, this dynamic continued to plague Merton. In 1967, he told an interviewer: "I left the book behind many years ago....It is a youthful book, too simple, in many ways, too crude. Everything is laid out in black and white....Since those days I have acquired a little experience, I think, and have read a few things, tried to help other people with their problems—life is not as simple as it once looked in *The Seven Storey Mountain*. Unfortunately, the book was a bestseller, and has become a kind of edifying legend or something. That is a dreadful fate. I am doing my best to live it down."[18] Merton was well aware of the stereotype of the world-denying contemplative that he had acquired ("the man who spurned New York, spat on Chicago, and tromped on Louisville, heading for the woods with Thoreau in one pocket, John of the Cross in another, and holding the Bible open at the Apocalypse"[19]), and recognized that it was something he would have to try to demolish on occasion.

This development process is best captured by Merton's friend and confrere, John Eudes Bamberger: "When in the Sixties he emerged as one of the most prominent and effective social critics of the political and racial policies pursued by our country, it came as a surprise to some who knew him as a poet and a 'monk.' But he had been gaining experience in the genre over the years in his monastery. Few of us were similarly surprised. If it was a prophetic calling . . . it was one he was suited for by nature, training, and preference."[20] Merton's prophetic calling was indeed something he was suited for by nature and preference, but it was the flow of experience that he underwent over the years at Gethsemani that enabled him to shoulder the prophet's mantle.

This genesis is reflected throughout his writings. In a journal entry composed in 1941, he notes: ". . . this is the New Year. . . . I tried to tell myself: a year of terrors, but the sun was out. It may well be, just the same. I am the worst of all prophets: prophecy is the one thing, besides mathematics and being a soldier, that I am certain I have no gift for."[21] As he grew in the monastery he initially retained this attitude. In the mid-1950's he wrote of "the worst and most insidious despair, which can mask as mysticism or prophecy, and which intones a prophetic answer to a prophetic question. That, I think, is likely to be a monk's professional hazard. . . ."[22] Merton was extremely wary of what he dubbed the "prophetic illusion," which he sensed as so prevalent in our time. Even by 1961, he could shrug in relation to the modern scene and say, "I am no prophet, no one is, for now we have learned to get along without prophets."[23] Toward the very end of his life, he would still note: "I certainly do not think I have a 'task' of social commentator, or preacher, or pseudo-prophet, or what you will. My only task is to be what I am, a man seeking God in silence and solitude, with respect for the demands and realities of his own vocation, and fully aware that others too are seeking the truth in their own way."[24]

Nevertheless, Merton became keenly aware that every believing person must, "whether he likes it or not, fulfill in the world the role of a prophet. If he does not face the anguish of being a true prophet, he must enjoy the carrion comfort of acceptance in the society of the deluded by becoming a false prophet and participating in their delusions."[25] He was acutely aware of the individual responsibility that confronts each Christian in the modern world: "Creativity has to begin with me and I can't sit here wasting time urging the monastic institution to become creative and prophetic."[26]

It is essential that we achieve an understanding of Merton's notion of prophecy. He notes plainly: "To prophesy is not to predict, but to seize upon reality in its moment of highest expectation and tension toward the new. This tension is discovered not in hypnotic elation but in the light of everyday experience."[27] In an essay treating William Blake, a figure who captivated Merton in his youth,[28] he describes Blake in terms which could easily be applied to himself: "...Blake can be read as a 'prophet' not of course in the sense of one who exactly predicts future events, but in the more traditional sense[29] of one who 'utters' and 'announces' news about man's own deepest trouble—news that emerges from the very ground of that trouble in man himself."[30] For Merton, a prophet in the traditional sense "is not merely a man who foretells the future under spiritual inspiration. That is in fact quite accidental. He is above all a 'witness.'...The prophet shoulders the 'burden' of vision that God lays upon him."[31] He extended upon this to stress that "a prophet is one who lives in direct submission to the Holy Spirit in order that, by his life, actions and words, he may at all times be a sign of God in the world of men."[32] In later life he came to view this prophetic dimension as integral to the monastic vocation: "The monastic life must maintain this prophetic seriousness, this wilderness perspective, this mistrust of any shallow optimism which overlooks the ambiguity and the potential tragedy of 'the world' in its response to the Word. And there is only one way for the monk to do this: to live as a man of God who has been manifestly 'called out of the world' to an existence that differs radically from that of other men, however Christian, however holy, who have remained 'in the world.' "[33]

Merton keenly sensed that a monk must be able to identify and understand the crucial problems of the world today (race, war, genocide, starvation, injustice, revolution), and to see his or her own monastic vocation in the light of these problems. He noted the need for a sufficient understanding of the wider context of social conflict, and cautioned that great care and discrimination are necessary: "Openness to the 'world' must not come to mean a merely uncritical and superficial acceptance of everything that is said in the mass media of one's particular country. A monastic community can entirely lose its prophetic sense and witness when it identifies itself with some particular party or nation."[34] He lamented: "We are not prophets. We are failing in the prophetic aspect of our vocation. Why? Perhaps because we belong to a Christianity so deeply implicated in a society which has outlived its spiritual vitality and yet is groping for a new expansion of life in crisis. Our monasteries are not fulfilling any kind of prophetic vocation in the modern world."[35] This became one of Merton's prime concerns. In the letter that he wrote to Jean Leclercq in which he accepted the invitation to speak at the Bangkok conference where he died, he emphasized this point: "Those who question the structure of contemporary society at least look to monks for a certain distance and critical perspective, which alas is seldom found. The vocation of the monks in the modern world, especially Marxist, is not survival, but prophecy. We are all busy saving our own skins."[36]

Merton's prophetic sense could be exasperating to many. The renowned American theologian Martin Marty,[37] for one, bristled at Merton's audacity in donning the prophet's robe and predicting the outbreak of racial violence in the nation's cities in the mid-1960's. Later, Marty was compelled to retract his criticism and admit that from his vantage point among the gently sloping knobs of Kentucky Merton understood the climate of the country more deeply and fundamentally than he did from the streets of Chicago, and he wrote a public apology for his rash criticism. In the wake of Merton's death in 1968 (the same year which saw the horror of the Tet offensive in Vietnam, the assassinations of Robert Kennedy and Martin Luther King, the political ascendency of George Wallace and Richard Nixon, and the outbreak of urban violence in Washington, Watts, Newark, and scores of American cities), peace activist Gordon Zahn ruefully reflected: "The shocking news of his death came to most of us last December as the fitting final note of a spiritually disastrous year for this nation and for the world. If the amplified sound of beasts seems louder now with his voice stilled, it is the duty of each of us who loved and honored Thomas Merton, monk and prophet, to do what he can to fill the void that he left."[38]

The essential paradox of Merton was that he was able to occupy himself critically with the world only after he found his own solitude. As John Eudes Bamberger notes: "Spiritual maturity, liberty, solitude, the deepening of human experience, protest against infringements of man's dignity— all these terms are constants in the Merton glossary. All are elements, present from the beginning and closely bound together, in his monastic spirituality."[39] Of these, the key element is solitude. In his early monastic life, Merton wrote: "It is clear to me that solitude is my vocation, not as a flight from the world—but as my place in the world...."[40] He experienced the desert of the monastery not as a place to escape from other men and women, "but in order to find them in God."[41] He perceived the special work of solitude as "a deepening awareness that the world needs a struggle against alienation. True solitude is deeply aware of the world's needs. It does not hold the world at arm's length."[42] Merton believed that the contemplative must assume "the universal anguish and the inescapable condition of mortal man. The solitary, far from enclosing himself in poverty, becomes every man. He dwells in the solitude, the poverty, the indigence of every man."[43] Merton concluded that "it is the solitary person (whether in the city or the desert) who does mankind the inestimable favor of reminding it of its true capacity for maturity, liberty, and peace."[44] In the quiet of his heart Merton discovered the power of God's love, the light of the Holy Spirit which burns within men and women. As he remarked, "It is deep in solitude that I find the gentleness with which I can truly love my brothers."[45]

In Merton's view, the monk is a "marginal person who withdraws deliberately to the margin of society with a view to deepening fundamental human experience."[46] He knew well that he was very much an involved member of our age: "That I should be born in 1915, that I should be the contemporary of Auschwitz, Hiroshima, Vietnam and the Watts riots, are things about which I was not first consulted. Yet they are also events in which, whether I like it or not, I am deeply and personally involved."[47] His notion of separation from the world while remaining intimately involved in it congealed in the latter phase of his life: "To choose the world is to choose to do the work I am capable of doing, in collaboration with my brothers, to make the world better, more free, more just, more liveable, more human. And it has now become transparently obvious that mere 'rejection of the world' is in fact not a choice but the evasion of choice. The man who pretends that he can turn his back on Auschwitz or Vietnam and act as if they were not there is simply bluffing. I think this is getting to be generally admitted, even by monks."[48] The key to the evolution of Merton's social consciousness was his ability to look on the world with a sense of compassion that was rooted in his life of solitude, his prayerful communion with the Father and Son, through the power and love of their Holy Spirit.

It was not so much Merton's keen intelligence that afforded him such ready insight into the social and political problems of our time, but rather his sense of *compassion*. John Eudes Bamberger feels that since Merton never felt completely at home anywhere in his lifetime, he could readily identify and empathize with those who were oppressed, uprooted, or neglected.[49] In the Preface to the Japanese edition of *The Seven Storey Mountain*, Merton reflected: "Twenty years ago I left the world. . . . Since that time, I have learned, I believe, to look back on the world with greater compassion, seeing those in it not as alien to myself, not as particular and deluded strangers, but as identified with myself. In breaking from 'their world,' I have strangely not broken from them. In freeing myself from their delusions and preoccupations, I have identified myself, none the less, with their struggles. . . ."[50] His outlook grew in his later years, as his journal entries reflect: "Perhaps the things I had resented about the world when I left it were defects of my own that I had projected upon it. Now, on the contrary, I have found that everything stirred me with a deep and mute sense of compassion."[51] In the same preface cited above, he notes: "My monastery is not a home. It is not an environment in which I become aware of myself as an individual, but rather a place in which I disappear from the world as an object of interest in order to be everywhere in it by hiddenness and compassion. To exist everywhere I have to be No-one."[52]

Compassion is the wellspring of Merton's social concern. As Henri Nouwen notes, Merton enfleshed the kind of compassion that comes out of a deep experience of solidarity," in which one recognizes that the evil, sin and violence which one sees in the world and in the other, are deeply rooted in one's own heart. . . . Precisely because Merton had discovered this non-violent compassion in his solitude, could he in a real sense be a monk, that is to say, one who unmasks through his criticism the illusions of a violent society and who wants to change the world in spirit and truth."[53]

Merton's prophetic concerns were a logical outgrowth of his monastic vocation. As a result of his monastic experience, he came to understand and enflesh the conviction of Gandhi (who influenced him so markedly): "I could not be leading a religious life unless I identified myself with the whole of mankind, and that I could not do unless I took part in politics. The whole gamut of man's activities today constitutes an indivisible whole. You cannot divide social, economic, polit-

ical and purely religious work into watertight compart-
ments."[54] Merton, the contemplative, perceived his mission
to work for unity and peace, which meant involvement in the
world.

He was, indeed a paradoxical figure. Above all, he was a
person seeking God in silence and solitude, though deeply
and personally involved in the world of men and women. By
his life, action and words, he was a sign of God in the world,
enabling human persons to recover the integrity of their own
inner depths. He was a man of compassion and vision, who
remained in the world as a prophetic voice, "crying in the
desert as a sign of contradiction."[55] His approach to the
monastic life was both traditional and revolutionary, at times
contradictory. But he had been growing as a result of his
monastic experience, and knew well:

> What choice remains?
> Well, to be ordinary is not a choice:
> It is the usual freedom
> Of men without visions.[56]

The ancient Hebrews fostered a proverb whose wisdom
has endured to the present day: "Where there is no vision,
the people perish" (Proverbs 29:18). How paradoxical that in
our age, when at times the very fabric of human society seems
rent and many question our prospects for survival, a prime
source of hope, compassion and vision pointing to the recovery of the integrity of our inner depths is "a voice crying out
in the wilderness," the voice of Thomas Merton.

NOTES

1. Thomas Merton, *The Sign of Jonas* (N.Y.: Doubleday Image
Books, 1952), p. 11.
2. These are the opening verses of Cardenal's epic poem "*Coplas a la
Muerte de Merton*" ("Verses on the Death of Merton"), translated by Kenneth Rexroth and Mireya Jaimes Freyre and revised by Donald Walsh. I am
grateful to Mr. Walsh for making the original poem and its translation
available to me. The poem appears in Cardenal's *Apocalypse and Other*

Poems (N.Y.: New Directions, 1977), pp. 45-57, and refers to Merton's electrocution in Bangkok, Thailand on December 10, 1968 (twenty-seven years to the day after entering Gethsemani), while attending a conference on Christian Monasticism in Asia. It is a masterful eulogy to Merton. Its opening lines echo the verses of Jorge Manrique's *"Coplas en la Muerte de su Padre"* ("Verses on the Death of His Father"), written in 1476, and one of the greatest poems in all of Spanish literature. It laments not only the death of Manrique's father, but sounds the death knell of a whole era, the Spanish Middle Ages. In his tribute to Merton, Cardenal consciously echoes Manrique's opening lines: "Our lives are the rivers/that go to empty into the sea,/which is death."

3. Cited by Elena Malits, C.S.C., "Thomas Merton: Symbol and Synthesis of Contemporary Catholicism," *The Critic* (Spring, 1977), p. 26.

4. Jean Leclercq, O.S.B., Preface to *Contemplation in a World of Action* by Thomas Merton (N.Y.: Doubleday Image Books, 1973), p. 17.

5. *Ibid.*, p. 18.

6. Merton, *Seeds of Destruction* (N.Y.: Farrar, Straus and Giroux, 1964), pp. 170-171.

7. Merton, Introduction to *The Prison Meditations of Father Alfred Delp, S.J.* (N.Y.: Herder and Herder, 1963), p. xiii.

8. *Merton, Thoughts in Solitude* (N.Y.: Doubleday Image Books, 1968), p. 12.

9. Merton, *Contemplation in a World of Action*, p. 245.

10. Merton, *The Asian Journal of Thomas Merton* (N.Y.: New Directions, 1973), p. 317.

11. Merton, cited in *Commonweal*, February 9, 1962, p. 513.

12. Merton, "A Statement Concerning the Collection in the Bellarmine College Library," *The Thomas Merton Studies Center* (Santa Barbara, Cal.: The Unicorn Press, 1971), pp. 14-15.

13. Merton, *The Seven Storey Mountain* (N.Y.: Harcourt, Brace, 1948).

14. Ironically, behind *The White Collar Zoo* and a book on canasta.

15. Merton, *The Sign of Jonas*, p. 328.

16. Merton, *Raids on the Unspeakable* (N.Y.: New Directions, 1966), p. 172.

17. Daniel Berrigan, *No Bars to Manhood* (N.Y.: Mentor Books, 1970), p. 139.

18. Cited in Colman McCarthy, "The Wide World of Thomas Merton," *The Washington Post*, December 25, 1976, p. 16.

19. Merton, *Contemplation in a World of Action*, p. 159.

20. Cited in *Thomas Merton/Monk*, edited by Br. Patrick Hart (N.Y.: Sheed and Ward, 1974), p. 44.

21. Merton, *The Secular Journal of Thomas Merton* (N.Y.: Doubleday Image Books, 1968) p. 148.

22. Merton, *No Man Is an Island* (N.Y.: Doubleday Image Books, 1967), p. 11.

23. Merton, *Emblems of a Season of Fury* (N.Y.: New Directions, 1963), p. 86.

24. Merton, *Contemplation in a World of Action*, p. 245.

25. Merton, Introduction to *Delp*, p. xxvi.

26. Merton, *Contemplation in a World of Action*, p. 350.

27. Merton, *Raids on the Unspeakable*, p. 159.

28. His Master's thesis at Columbia was on "Nature and Art in William Blake."

29. He follows in the tradition of the great prophets of Israel, whose life and words influenced him profoundly. At the conclusion of *The Seven Storey Mountain* he wrote: "...you shall taste the true solitude of My anguish and My poverty and I shall lead you into the high places of My joy and you shall die in Me and find all things in My mercy which has created you for this end and brought you from Prades to Bermuda to St. Antonin to Oakham to London to Cambridge to Rome to New York to Columbia to Corpus Christi to St. Bonaventure to the Cistercian Abbey of the poor men who labor in Gethsemani. (One might add: to Santa Barbara to Alaska to Tokyo to Calcutta to Bangkok—Ed.) 'That you may become the brother of God and learn to know the Christ of the burnt men' " (p. 423). In *The Sign of Jonas*, he adds: "Isaias, Moses, Matthew, Mark, Luke, and John are all part of my life. They are always about me.... They are more a part of my world than most of the people actually living in the world. I 'see' them sometimes more really than I see the monks I live with. I know well the burnt faces of the Prophets and Evangelists, transformed by the white hot dangerous presence of inspiration, for they looked at God as into a furnace and the Seraphim flew down and purified their lips with fire.... They are solemn and dreadful and holy men, humbled by the revelation they wrote down. They are my Fathers. They are the 'burnt men' of the last line of *The Seven Storey Mountain*" (p. 224).

30. Merton, "Blake and the New Theology," *The Sewanee Review* (Fall, 1968), p. 673.

31. Merton, *Disputed Questions* (N.Y.: Farrar, Straus and Cudahy, 1960), p. 209.

32. *Ibid.*

33. Merton, *Contemplation in a World of Action*, p. 29.

34. *Ibid.*, p. 217.

35. *Ibid.*, p. 343.

36. I am grateful to Dom Jean Leclercq for making this correspondence available to me.

37. Martin E. Marty, "To Thomas Merton Re: Your Prophecy, "*The National Catholic Reporter*, August 30, 1967, p. 8.

38. Gordon Zahn, cited in *Continuum* (Winter, 1969), p. 273.

39. Cited in Hart, *Thomas Merton/Monk*, p. 53.

40. Merton, *The Sign of Jonas*, p. 251.

41. Merton, *New Seeds of Contemplation* (N.Y.: New Directions, 1961), p. 53.

42. Merton, *Conjectures of a Guilty Bystander* (N.Y.: Doubleday Image Books, 1968), p. 10

43. Merton, *Raids on the Unspeakable*, p. 18.

44. *Ibid.*, p 22.

45. Merton, *The Sign of Jonas*, p. 261.

46. Merton, *The Asian Journal of Thomas Merton*, p. 305.

47. Merton, *Contemplation in a World of Action*, p. 164.

48. *Ibid.*, p. 165.

49. From an oral history interview with Fr. John Eudes from my files,

conducted at the Abbey of the Genesee on November 14, 1974.

50. Cited in Gordon Zahn (ed.), *Thomas Merton on Peace* (N.Y.: McCalls, 1971), p. 116.

51. Merton, *The Sign of Jonas*, p. 91.

52. Cited in Hart, *Thomas Merton/Monk*, p. 132.

53. Henri J. M. Nouwen, *Pray To Live: Thomas Merton, Contemplative Critic* (Notre Dame, Ind.: Ave Maria Press, 1970), p. 66.

54. Mohandas Gandhi, cited in *Gandhi on Non-Violence*, edited by Thomas Merton, (N.Y.: New Directions, 1964), p. 64.

55. Merton, *Disputed Questions*, p. 190.

56. Merton, "When in the Soul of the Serene Disciple..." from *Collected Poems of Thomas Merton* (N.Y.: New Directions, 1977).

Thomas Merton's Struggle with Peacemaking

James H. Forest

In *The Sign of Jonas*, Thomas Merton wrote: "Like Jonas himself I find myself traveling toward my destiny in the belly of a paradox."[1]

Paradox was a word Thomas Merton appreciated and often used, perhaps because there were so many paradoxes within his vocation. He was, for example, a monk belonging to a religious order with a particular tradition of silence—and yet millions of people were to become familiar with his life and convictions. He had a noisy vocation in the silent life. It was a paradox he often wished would end, in favor of silence, but it wouldn't.

He was also a pacifist—someone who has renounced violence as a means in peacemaking—yet he often said he was against war only in practice, not in theory. He accepted what Catholic doctrine knows as the "Just War Theory," a post-Constantinian Christian inheritance which holds that war, within certain defined circumstances, may be justified (if it is declared by lawful authority, after all non-military means have been fully exhausted, if the violence is focused on those criminally responsible for the war while the right to life of non-combatants is protected, if its destructive consequences are not worse than the injustice otherwise suffered, and if it seems probable the just side can win the war: and it must be all these things simultaneously).

Whether one's basis of reasoning was the Sermon on the Mount or the Just War Theory, Merton pointed out, military technology and practice in this century brought one to the same location. In words Merton quoted on occasion, Pope John put it quite succinctly in *Pacem in Terris:* "It is irrational to argue that war can any longer be a fit instrument of justice."[2]

In an existential and temperamental sense, Merton was one of the most committed pacifists I have ever met. He saw war as one of the clearest examples of human estrangement from sanity and God. He was appalled by war in an intense and personal way and saw response to war as a major element in the religious life. Some of the most lethal irony to be found in his writings is reserved for the subject: his anti-war novel, *My Argument with the Gestapo*,[3] his "devout meditation" on the court-certified "sanity" of Adolf Eichmann,[4] his "chant" to be used in procession around "a site with furnaces"[5] (Hitler's death camps), and his *Original Child Bomb*[6] on Hiroshima's atomic destruction complete with such military codes borrowed from Christian thought as "Papacy" and "Trinity."

So deep was his revulsion regarding war and its premeditated terrors and cruelties that, when World War II was bursting its European seams and men like Merton's brother were volunteering for the Royal Air Force, Merton was one of the rare Catholics to declare himself a conscientious objector. At the time Catholic bishops in America, England and Germany were as busy as other religious leaders in offering their unqualified support for lay compliance with "legitimate authority," including military service and killing under orders. Merton, though a thoroughly devout Catholic, walked to a different drummer, away from battlefields and into a weaponless Trappist monastery.

Twenty years later, increasingly conscious of the monk's responsibility *for* the world rather than against it, he established deep and continuing ties with several strongly pacifist groups, including the Catholic Worker, the Fellowship of Reconciliation and the Catholic Peace Fellowship.

It was while visiting the Catholic Worker's New York house of hospitality, St. Joseph's, that my own friendship with Merton began. I was still in the Navy, freshly a Catholic, still too fragile in my newly acquired pacifism to have begun finding a way out of the military and into a vocation that had something to do with the peace of God. But I was looking. Hence my inquiring presence at the Catholic Worker, a religious community whose commitment to non-violent social change was an outgrowth of its hospitality to social rejects.

Merton's letter (arriving just before Christmas 1960) began with a reference to the Catholic Worker's main peace witness in those years—its annual refusal to take shelter in the subways as a compulsory dress rehearsal for nuclear war with the Soviet Union. It was, really, a bad joke, as the subways offered protection only from conventional weapons, but the ritual had the effect of making nuclear war seem realistic and even survivable. Dorothy Day, the Catholic Worker founder, had been imprisoned several times for her civil disobedience, until the crowds that gathered with her in City Hall Park became so large that the war game was abandoned. But that end was still not in sight when Merton wrote:

> I am deeply touched by your witness for peace. You are very right in doing it along the lines of *Satyagraha* [literally "truth-force," Gandhi's word for what Western people often call non-violence]. I see no other way, though of course the angles of the problem are not all clear. I am certainly with you on taking some kind of stand and acting accordingly. Nowadays it is no longer a question of who is right but who is at least not a criminal—if any of us can say that anymore. So don't worry about whether or not in every point you are perfectly all right according to everybody's book; you are right before God as far as you can go and you are fighting for a truth that is clear enough and important enough. What more can anybody do?...It was never more true that the world cannot see true values.

I don't suppose anyone can readily appreciate the value of this and similar letters that were arriving at the Catholic Worker from Merton in those days.(Personally, they helped form a determination in me that led to my discharge from the

Navy as a conscientious objector and becoming a member of
the Catholic Worker staff.) Partly due to Merton, the Catholic
pacifist was to become far more common in the years ahead
and to receive open and unambiguous official support from
the highest levels of the Church. But at that time the Catholic
Worker, viewed with considerable suspicion for its talk of
"the works of mercy, not the works of war," was tolerated
because of its orthodoxy in other respects and its direct,
simple and unpretentious commitment to the humanity of
impoverished people who were ignored by everyone else.
New York's Cardinal Spellman, certainly no pacifist and no
religious innovator, was often under pressure to suppress the
Catholic Worker, or at least its pacifist newspaper, but he
never did. Perhaps he felt that, in Dorothy Day, he had a saint
in his diocese and that he had better not play the prosecutor's
part in a modern-day trial of Joan of Arc. Maybe he just
sensed, puzzling though it was, that the Church needed the
Catholic Worker movement.

At this time, Merton was hardly a controversial figure.
His books were all over the place, in churches, drugstores and
bus terminals, and each bore the *Imprimatur* ("let it be
printed," a bishop's certification that the book was orthodox). Thousands owed their faith, and millions its
deepening, to the stimulus of Merton's writings—his continuing pilgrimage from non-belief to the depths of faith.
His books were read by the convinced and the unconvinced,
from the Pope's apartment in the Vatican to prostitutes'
apartments near New York's 42nd Street. His writings had
been published in more languages than we had staff members in our Catholic Worker house of hospitality.

Yet here he was, often writing to the Catholic Worker
community, taking our lives and vocations with utmost seriousness, and even encouraging us in those aspects of our
work which were the most controversial.

If it is hard now to appreciate what those letters meant, it
may be harder still to understand our world view. To put it
simply, few of us expected to die of old age. Nearly twenty
years later, at the time this is written, many people have
gotten used to living in a world heavily stocked with nuclear

weapons. In the short measure of human life and memory, and in a century crowded with other disasters, Hiroshima is a long way off. We have begun to count on generals and terrorists restraining themselves. So now there is a certain complacency about the arms race and where it is headed. We imagine that, for the first time in human history, weapons are being produced and disbursed and mounted on delivery vehicles that will never be used. *May it be so.* Yet it didn't seem to us that human nature has changed very much since Hiroshima or that those who see reality in purely abstract ideological terms, a mentality not uncommon in political and military leadership, no matter what their nationality or slogans, could be counted on to leave nuclear weapons on the shelf if other methods fail or someone gets an itch for "decisive action."

In 1961, when even one monastery had set up a fallout shelter, we expected to be blasted to radioactive particles every time we heard the air raid sirens being tested. Somehow we never noticed the advance newspaper warnings beforehand. The sirens would begin their coordinated howling, the blasts being punctuated by silences so severe the city suddenly seemed desert-like in stillness. Stunned, momentarily paralyzed by the significance of the noise, I would stop whatever I was doing and wait at the Catholic Worker's front window, gathering a final view of the battered neighborhood with its few scarred trees struggling for light and air: even here, a kind of beauty. Shortly it would all be consumed by fire. No need to think about a hiding place. Even were there a massive barrier against the blast and radiation, the blast's fire storm would consume all the oxygen. Last moments are too important to be wasted. We were Catholics. We had done our best to take Jesus at his plain words, in our awkward Catholic Worker way. We hoped in God's mercy and, young though many of us were, we were better prepared to die than many others. And we believed in the resurrection: that the fate of God's creation would not finally be decided by the owners of nuclear weapons. It was a faith that seemed bizarre if not insane to many others who believed in human progress and technology and the wisdom of experts, but it was clear to us, and gave these moments before death a certain tranquility, despite the sadness for this immense funeral we humans had so laboriously brought upon ourselves.

But each time the "all clear" sounded. The sirens ended their apocalyptic shrieks. There was no sudden explosive radiance "brighter than a thousand suns." Then we felt like airline passengers setting shaking foot upon the ground after a no-wheels landing in emergency foam spread out across the runway. We were a flock of Lazarus folk risen from our shrouds. Our lives had ended, and then been given back: another chance for this odd experiment on planet earth; another chance for our curious two-legged breed to find a saner way to live, to free ourselves from a "security" founded upon the preparation of slaughters. Another chance for figs to grow from thistles.

It was in these days of fallout shelters and air raid sirens that we received Merton's first submission to the paper we published, an essay—"The Root of War Is Fear"—that was later to appear in *New Seeds of Contemplation*.[7] The piece as a whole had gone through the normal if often rigid channels of Trappist censorship, but Merton had tacked on a few prefatory paragraphs which briefly expressed a message that eventually led to his silencing on "political" issues:

The present war crisis is something we have made entirely for and by ourselves. There is in reality not the slightest logical reason for war, and yet the whole world is plunging headlong into frightful destruction, and doing so *with the purpose of avoiding war and preserving peace!* This is true war-madness, an illness of the mind and spirit that is spreading with a furious and subtle contagion all over the world. Of all the countries that are sick, America is perhaps the most grievously afflicted. On all sides we have people building bomb shelters where, in case of nuclear war, they will simply bake slowly instead of burning quickly or being blown out of existence in a flash. And they are prepared to sit in these shelters with machine guns with which to prevent their neighbor from entering. This in a nation that claims to be fighting for religious truth along with freedom and other values of the spirit. Truly we have entered the "post-Christian era" with a vengeance. Whether we are destroyed or whether we survive, the future is awful to contemplate.[8]

In fact, just as we were going to press with Merton's article, *The New York Times* gave front page attention to an essay that had been published in a Jesuit magazine justifying just such a shelter "ethic." No doubt, as Merton commented later on, "the case could be made for St. Peter to kill St. Paul if there was only enough food for one of them to survive winter in a mountain cave." But Merton's approach was drastically different, calling for a rejection of "mere natural ethics." He wanted to know whether Christian responsibility involved more than getting to the front of the line into the fallout shelter:

What is the place of the Christian in all this? Is he simply to fold his hands and resign himself for the worst, accepting it as the inescapable will of God and preparing himself to enter heaven with a sigh of relief? Should he open up the Apocalypse and run into the street to give everyone his idea of what is happening? Or, worse still, should he take a hard-headed and "practical" attitude about it and join in the madness of the war makers, calculating how, by a "first strike," the glorious Christian West can eliminate atheistic communism for all time and usher in the millennium? I am no prophet and seer but it seems to me that this last position may very well be the most diabolical of illusions, the great and not even subtle temptation of a Christianity that has grown rich and comfortable, and is satisfied with its riches.

What are we to do? The duty of the Christian in this crisis is to strive with all his power and intelligence, with his faith, his hope in Christ, and love for God and man, to do the one task which God has imposed upon us in the world today. That task is to work for the total abolition of war. *There can be no question that unless war is abolished the world will remain constantly in a state of madness and desperation in which, because of the immense destructive power of modern weapons, the danger of catastrophe will be imminent and probable at every moment everywhere.* Unless we set ourselves immediately to this task, both as individuals and in our political and religious groups, we tend by our very passivity and fatalism to cooperate with the destructive forces that are leading inexorably to war. It is a problem of terrifying complexity and magnitude, for which the Church itself is not fully able to see clear and decisive solutions. Yet she must lead the way on the road to non-violent settlement of difficulties and toward the gradual abolition of war as the way of settling international or civil disputes. Christians must become active in every possible way, mobilizing all their resources for the fight against war. First of all there is much to be studied, much to be learned. Peace is to be preached, non-violence is to be explained as a practical method, and not left to be mocked as an outlet for crackpots who want to make a show of themselves. Prayer and sacrifice must be used as the most effective spiritual weapons in the war against war, and like all weapons, they must be used with deliberate aim: not just with a vague aspiration for peace and security, but against violence and war. This implies that we are also willing to sacrifice and restrain our own instinct for violence and aggressiveness in our relations with other people. We may never succeed in this campaign, but whether we succeed or not, the duty is evident. It is the great Christian task of our time. Everything else is secondary, for the survival of the human race itself depends upon it. We must at least face this responsibility and do something about it. And the first job of all is to understand the psychological forces at work in ourselves and in society.[9]

In January 1962 Merton proposed a visit. The next month, after getting the paper to press, I began to hitchhike to Kentucky with a poet-friend, Bob Kaye, bringing along nothing except the latest issue and a few loaves of bread fresh from a Spring Street Italian bakery. It was an exhausting three-day pilgrimage—long waits in remote places in ferocious weather. When we arrived and were shown to our "cells" in the guest house, Bob collapsed on his bed while I found my way through fire-doors and connecting passageways to a loft in the back of the monastery's barn-like church. Surviving the trip, a prayer of thanksgiving came easily. But it didn't last long because the church's silence was broken by distant laughter, laughter so intense and pervasive that I couldn't fail to be drawn to it, such an unlikely sound for a solemn Trappist abbey. It was coming from the guest house, in fact from Bob's room: a kind of monsoon of joy. Well, that's the difference between Bob and me, I thought: I pray, and he gives way to laughter; God probably likes the laughter better. I pushed open the door, and indeed Bob was laughing, but the sound was coming mainly from a monk on the floor in his black and white robes, feet in the air, a bright red face, hands clutching the belly. A shade more than Robin Hood's well-fed Friar Tuck than I imagined any fast-chastened Trappist could be. Thomas Merton, author of so many books about such serious subjects, laughing half to death on the floor.

And laughing about what? The answer came with my first gasp of air. The smell! What would have offended so many others delighted him. The room was like a fish market in a heat wave. Bob, after three days of rough travel without a change of socks, had taken off his shoes. Had there ever been so rude a scent in this scrubbed monastery's history? It was, in a way, the Catholic Worker's social gospel incarnate—its unwashed, impolite vocation such as the Church in all its cathedral glory had seldom seen since the first Franciscans seven centuries before. The Catholic Worker, in stocking feet, had arrived indeed, announcing its sweaty message to the most non-attentive nose.

It made the monk roar with pleasure until the need to breathe took precedence and there could be a shaking of hands and a more traditional welcome.

Still smiling as he left, telling us when we could get

together later, I realized why his face, never seen before even in photos as none of his books carried the usual author picture, was nonetheless familiar: it was like Picasso's, as I had seen it in David Duncan's books—a face similarly unfettered in its expressiveness, the eyes bright and quick and sure suggesting some strange balance between mischief and wisdom. The face still haunts me in its many moods—such unremarkable features on their own, but so remarkable all together.

Those were wonderfully renewing days. There was much talk of the Catholic Worker and the difficult business of making headway as peacemakers of some kind, but there were also long walks in the woods, rambling conversations on the porch of his cinder-block hermitage looking out over rolling Kentucky hills. Shaggy guests that we were, we submitted to the abbot's proposal that we have haircuts, but then going from one extreme to the other, masses of hair falling to the floor leaving only stubble behind while the novices watched and laughed. I marveled at the huge white wool cowl that the monks wore when in the abbey church. Merton lifted his off and dropped the surprising weight of it on my shoulders—more laughter at the sudden monastic sight of me. We noticed that the several Japanese calendars in this hermitage were all for the wrong years and months.

We talked of the Catholic Mass and its many levels, the Eucharist being a kind of crossroads, not only of every condition of people and every degree of faith, but an intersection between time and eternity—the most nourishing place in the world.

Merton spoke plainly but with contagious feeling. He reminded me of a particularly good-natured truck driver— the kind of people who had sometimes given us rides on the way down.

One of the things we talked about was a possibility that nibbled at my imagination of becoming a monk myself and even joining this community. "Man, right now the Church needs people working for peace in a way that's impossible here—the kind of things you're doing at the Catholic Worker. If you want to try the life, it's possible. But wait a while. I think the Holy Spirit has other things in mind."

Merton was very much a monk and committed to his community and his monastic vows, but he didn't romanticize the problems. He had struggled for years to have a greater opportunity for solitude than was normal in the Trappist life, and had only lately gotten the hermitage; he was only a part-time hermit, as yet, still hoping for permission to live full-time in the hermitage.

Many of his fellow monks didn't understand or appreciate his leading in this direction, and even less did they welcome his recent involvement with the Catholic Worker. I recall another author-monk of the community looking at a copy of *The Catholic Worker* as Merton and I were walking down a passageway in his direction; it was an issue full of peace-related material, including a letter of Merton's prominently displayed. The monk heard our footsteps, looked up, scowled at us, crumbled the *Worker* into a ball of waste paper, threw it into a trash can and stormed away.

By this time I was getting used to Merton's laugh at unlikely times. He laughed when many others in the same situation would have abruptly looked as pompous, offended and grave as a puritan judge forced to walk past nude statues in the Vatican Museum. Then he said, "You know, when I first came here, he used to denounce me for being too hung up with contemplation and not concerned enough with the world. And now he denounces me for being too hung up with the world and not busy enough with contemplation."

One morning a telegram arrived from New York telling us that, the Soviet Union having earlier decided to renew atmospheric testing of nuclear weapons, President Kennedy had now announced the U.S. would do the same. We Catholic Worker visitors were being asked to hurry back to New York to take part in a protest action at the offices of the Atomic Energy Commission. Before leaving, we attended one last class with the novices, presented Merton with a peace button which he put on his monk's robes with mischievous satisfaction, and then we were on our way—on a bus this time, the abbey having contributed the fare. A few days later, we were in jail—a very different sort of monastery.

During the next two years or more, censorship was often a subject in Merton's letters. It became increasingly difficult for him to get his peace-related articles in print, since his Trappist superiors generally considered war an inappropriate subject. Even prior to the visit, one letter spoke of the need "to work out something sensible on this absurd censorship deal." As usual, he discussed the subject with jarring candor:

> [The censorship] is completely and deliberately obstructive, not aimed at combing out errors at all, but purely and simply preventing the publication of material that "doesn't look good." And this means anything that ruffles in any way the censors' tastes or susceptibilities. . . .

But such considerations were never the end of the line in Merton's thinking. And it was in this area that his nonviolence was put to its hardest personal test. His nonviolence, like Gandhi's, implied "enduring all things" that transformation might occur in which adversaries were convinced and won over rather than defeated but left unconvinced. Perhaps he recognized in the fears of his superiors the same fears that existed elsewhere in the world, the fears which give rise to war. What would be the sense of calling others to patience in the labors of fostering life when he could not be patient with those close at hand? Certainly many others have stormed away from committed relationships, muttering about betrayal, the abuse of authority, the Inquisition, the death of God, the hypocrisy of this institution or that—with the net result that the world was only a bit more fractured and embittered, more estranged by those who were so furious in their advocacy of truth. Merton's letter went on:

> That is the kind of thing one has to be patient with. It is wearying, of course. However, it is all I can offer to

compare with what you people are doing to share the lot of the poor. A poor man is one who has to sit and wait and wait and wait, in clinics, in offices, in places where you sign papers, in police stations, etc. And he has nothing to say about it. At least there is an element of poverty for me too. The rest of what we have here isn't that hard or that poor. (January 5, 1962)

A few months later came a harder test. It was no longer a matter of enduring the delays of censorship, or the watering down or qualifying that might involve. Now it was a matter of being silenced. The date included the notation that it was "Low Sunday":

I have been trying to finish my book on peace [*Peace in the Post-Christian Era*], and have succeeded in time for the axe to fall....

Now here is the axe. For a long time I have been anticipating trouble with the higher superiors and now I have it. The orders are, no more writing about peace. This is transparently arbitrary and uncomprehending, but doubtless I have to make the best of it....[In] substance I am being silenced on the subject of war and peace. This I know is not a very encouraging thing. It implies all sorts of very disheartening consequences as regards the whole cause of peace. It reflects an astounding incomprehension of the seriousness of the present crisis in its religious aspect. It reflects an insensitivity to Christian and Ecclesiastic values, and to the real sense of the monastic vocation. The reason given is that this is not the right kind of work for a monk, and that it "falsifies the monastic message." Imagine that: the thought that a monk might be deeply enough concerned with the issue of nuclear war to voice a protest against the arms race, [this] is supposed to bring the monastic life into *disrepute*. Man, I would think that it might just possibly salvage a last shred of repute for an institution that many consider to be dead on its feet. That is really the most absurd aspect of the whole situation, that these people insist on digging their own grave and erecting over it the most monumental kind of tombstone.

The problem, from the point of view of the Church and its mission, is of course this. The validity of the Church depends precisely on spiritual renewal, uninterrupted, continuous, and deep. Obviously this renewal is to be expressed in the historical context, and will call for a real spiritual understanding of historical crises, an evaluation of them in terms of their inner significance and in terms of man's growth and the advancement of truth in man's world: in other words, the establishment of the "kingdom of God." The monk is the one supposedly attuned to the inner spiritual dimension of things. If he hears nothing, and says nothing, then the renewal as a whole will be in danger and may be completely sterilized. But these authoritarian minds believe that the function of the monk is not to see or hear any new dimension, simply to support the already existing viewpoints precisely insofar as and because they are defined for him by somebody else. Instead of being in the advance guard, he is in the rear with the baggage, confirming all that has been done by the officials. The function of the monk, as far as renewal in the historical context goes, then becomes simply to affirm his total support of officialdom. He has no other function, then, except perhaps to pray for what he is told to pray for: namely the purposes and the objectives of an ecclesiastical bureaucracy. The monastery as dynamo concept goes back to this. The monk is there to generate spiritual power that will justify over and over again the already pre-decided rightness of the officials above him. He must under no event and under no circumstances assume a role that implies any form of spontaneity and originality. He must be an eye that sees nothing except what is carefully selected for him to see. An ear that hears nothing except what it is advantageous for the managers for him to hear. We know what Christ said about such ears and eyes.

Now you will ask me: how do I reconcile obedience, true obedience (which is synonymous with love) with a situation like this? Shouldn't I just blast the whole thing wide open, or walk out, or tell them to jump in the lake?

Let us suppose for the sake of argument that this was not completely excluded. Why would I do this? For the sake of the witness for peace? For the sake of witnessing to the truth of the Church, in its reality, as against this figment of the imagination? Simply for the sake of blasting off and getting rid of the tensions and frustrations in my own spirit, and feeling honest about it?

In my own particular case, every one of these would backfire and be fruitless. It would be taken as a witness *against* the peace movement and would confirm these people in all the depth of their prejudices and their self-complacency. It would reassure them in every possible way that they are incontrovertibly right and make it even more impossible for them ever to see any kind of new light on the subject. And in any case I am not merely looking for opportunities to blast off. I can get along without it.

I am where I am. I have freely chosen this state, and have freely chosen to stay in it when the question of a possible change arose. If I am a disturbing element, that is all right. I am not making a point of being that, but simply of saying what my conscience dictates and doing so without seeking my own interest. This means accepting such limitations as may be placed on me by authority, and not because I may or may not agree with the ostensible reasons why the limitations are imposed, but out of love for God who is using these things to attain ends which I myself cannot at the moment see or comprehend. I know He can and will in His own time take good care of the ones who impose limitations unjustly or unwisely. That is His affair and not mine. In this dimension I find no contradiction between love and obedience, and as a matter of fact it is the only sure way of transcending the limits and arbitrariness of ill-advised commands. (April 29, 1962)

Very strong stuff. Very few in the peace movement then or now could understand or appreciate that kind of stubborn continuity. Marriages often end over much less. But it is the kind of decision that would be respected and valued by Francis of Assisi or Gandhi or Dorothy Day.

He appealed the order to the Abbot General in Rome, but it was affirmed. He wrote to me:

I was denounced to him by an American abbot who was told by a friend in the intelligence service that I was writing for a "communist controlled publication" (*The Catholic Worker*). You didn't know you were Communist controlled, did you? Maybe George [a hospital visitor on the Worker staff] is really Khrushchev's nephew. Meanwhile, though I look through all my pockets, I cannot find that old [Communist Party] card. Must have dropped out when I was mopping my brow in the confessional. (June 14, 1962)

The "silenced" Merton wasn't altogether silent. The suppressed book was circulated in substantial numbers in a mimeographed form, not unlike the *samizdat* literary underground in the USSR. He collected his war-peace letters (under the title *Cold War Letters*) and self-published two editions; his recognition of the larger dimensions of the Cold War and its pervasive and destructive effects in every quarter, including even the monastery, led him to include the "Low Sunday" epistle.

In 1963, the Trappist freeze on his peace writing slowly began to thaw, at least in part, no doubt, because Pope John was saying in encyclical letters to the entire Church and world the kinds of things Merton was formerly saying in *The*

Catholic Worker and, more recently, in *samizdat* (or, on occasion, in writings published under pseudonyms—Benedict Monk was almost a giveaway, but my favorite was Marco J. Frisbee).[10] The Pope having declared flatly in *Pacem in Terris* that war could no longer be considered "a fit instrument of justice," Merton wryly mentioned that he had just written to the Order's Abbot General once again:

> I said it was a good thing that Pope John didn't have to get his encyclical through our censors: and could I now start up again. (April 26, 1963)

While the silencing order was not removed, some of Merton's peace concern began to reach at least fractions of the reading public again, and under his own name. One of these was a short statement in response to the award in 1963 of the Pax Medal, given by the American Pax Society, a mainly Catholic peace group of which he was a sponsor that later grew into the American branch of Pax Christi. His message was read aloud at the Pax annual meeting at the Catholic Worker Farm in Tivoli, N.Y., and then published in the Pax magazine. In his message, after apologizing for his inability to be present and noting that his inability might suggest he ought not to receive such an award, he went on:

> A monastery is not a snail's shell, nor is religious faith a kind of spiritual fallout shelter into which one can plunge to escape the criminal realities of an apocalyptic age.

> Never has the total solidarity of all men, either in good or in evil, been so obvious and so unavoidable. I believe we live in a time in which one cannot help making decisions for or against man, for or against life, for or against justice, for or against truth.

> And according to my way of thinking, all these decisions rolled into one (for they are inseparable) amount to a decision for or against God.

I have attempted to say this in the past as opportunity has permitted, and opportunity has not permitted as much as I would have liked. But one thing I must admit: to say these things seems to me to be only the plain duty of any reasonable being. Such an attitude implies no heroism, no extraordinary insight, no special moral qualities, and no unusual intelligence.[11]

He proceeded to offer brief quotations, "perfectly obvious and beyond dispute," from Pope John's *Pacem in Terris:* that "the arms race ought to cease, that nuclear weapons should be banned, that an effective program of gradual disarmament should be agreed upon by all nations."[12]

These propositions... are... obvious, and clear as daylight.... If I said it before *Pacem in Terris,* that still does not make me terribly original, because the same things were said long ago by Popes before Pope John, and by Theologians, and by the Fathers of the Church, and by the Gospels themselves.

...I don't deserve a medal for affirming such obvious and common sense truths. But if by receiving the medal I can publicly declare these to be my convictions, then I most gladly and gratefully accept.[13]

This same year he wrote a preface to the Japanese edition of *The Seven Storey Mountain,* in which he drew the reader's attention to changes that had occurred in his attitudes and assumptions since writing the autobiography:

...I have learned... to look back into [the] world with greater compassion, seeing those in it not as alien to myself, not as peculiar and deluded strangers, but as identified with myself. In freeing myself from their delusions and preoccupations I have identified myself, none the less, with their struggles and their blind, desperate hope of happiness.

But precisely because I am identified with them, I must refuse all the more definitively to make their delusions my own. I must refuse their ideology of matter, power, quantity, movement, activism and force. I reject this because I see it to be the source and expression of the spiritual hell which man has made of his world: the hell which has burst into flame in two total wars of incredible horror, the hell of spiritual emptiness and sub-human fury which has resulted in crimes like Auschwitz or Hiroshima. This I can and must reject with all the power of my being. This all sane men seek to reject. But the question is: how can one sincerely reject the effect if he continues to embrace the cause?[14]

Merton goes on to say that he has always regarded his conversion to Christ "as a radical liberation from the delusions and obsessions of modern man and his society" and that religious faith alone "can open the inner ground of man's being to the liberty of the sons of God, and preserve him from surrender of his integrity to the seductions of a totalitarian lie."

He speaks of his present understanding of the monastic life:

...the monastery is not an "escape from the world." On the contrary, by being in the monastery I take my true part in all the struggles and sufferings of the world. To adopt a life that is essentially non-assertive, non-violent, a life of humility and peace is in itself a statement of one's position. But each one in such a life can, by the personal modality of his decision, give his whole life a special orientation. It is my intention to make my entire life a rejection of, a protest against the crimes and injustices of war and political tyranny which threaten to destroy the whole race of man and the world with him. By my monastic life and vows I am saying *No* to all the concentration camps, the aerial bombardments, the staged political trials, the judicial murders, the racial injustices, the economic tyrannies, and the whole socio-economic apparatus which seems geared for nothing but global destruction in spite of all its fair words in favor of peace. I make monastic silence a protest against the lies of politicians, propagandists and agitators, and when I speak it is to deny that my faith and my Church can ever seriously be aligned with these forces of injustice and destruction.[15]

He notes regretfully that others who believe in war also invoke the faith, as they support racial injustices and engage in "self-righteous and lying forms of tyranny."

My life must, then, be a protest against these also, and perhaps against these most of all.[16]

The problem for contemporary Christians, he continues, is to end the identification of Christian faith with those forms of political society that dominate Europe and the West, much as did the early Christian monks of the fourth-century (Post-Constantine) Church.

The time has come for judgment to be passed on this history. I can rejoice in this fact, believing that the judgment will be a liberation of Christian faith from servitude to and involvement in the structures of the secular world. And that is why I think certain forms of Christian "optimism" are to be taken with reservation, in so far as they lack the genuine eschatalogical consciousness of the Christian vision, and concentrate upon the naive hope of merely temporal achievements—churches on the moon!

If I say NO to all these secular forces, I also say YES to all that is good in the world and in man. I say YES to all that is beautiful in nature, and in order that this may be the yes of a freedom and not of subjection, I must refuse to possess anything in the world purely as my own. I say yes to all the men and women who are my brothers and sisters in the world, but for the yes to be an assent of freedom and not of subjection, I must live so that no one of them may seem to belong to me, and that I may not belong to any of them. It is because I want to be more to them than a friend that I become, to all of them, a stranger.[17]

"God writes straight with crooked lines," offers a Portuguese proverb. No doubt Merton's silencing had been unjust and unwarranted and something his Trappist superiors came deeply to regret, not simply because it came to be embarrassing but because it was wrong. Yet the crisis it occasioned in Merton's life, if a friend dare make guesses about the "stranger" within his friend, more deeply purified his understanding and compassion, his vision of the Church and its mission, his sense of connection with all who suffer. It also made him more astute in the pastoral role he took on, mainly via mail but on occasion through visits at the monastery, with those active in work for peace, social justice, and renewal of the Church. Merton did not view the peace movement through rose-colored glasses. He knew how difficult it was for those in protest movements to grow in patience and compassion. Thus he offered us his support, but it was a critical support that sought to prod us to become more sympathetic toward those who were threatened or antagonized by our efforts. Thus he noted (Jan. 29, 1962) "the tragedy" that the majority of people so crave "undisturbed security" that they are threatened by agitation even when it protests something—nuclear weapons—which in reality is the real threat to their security. But it wouldn't help to get in a rage over this irony:

We have to have a deep patient compassion for the fears of men, for the fears and irrational mania of those who hate us or condemn us.

[These are, after all, he said in the same letter] the ordinary people, the ones who don't want war, the ones who get it in the neck, the ones who really want to build a decent new world in which there will not be war and starvation....

On this crucial matter of managing patience while being aware of the desperate urgency of responding to immediate crises, he spoke of the special attitude we were going to depend upon if we hoped to continue in such immensely difficult and frustrating work:

We will never see the results in our time, even if we manage to get through the next five years without being incinerated. Really, we have to pray for a total and profound change in the mentality of the whole world. What we have known in the past as Christian penance is not a deep enough concept if it does not comprehend the special problems and dangers of the present age. Hairshirts will not do the trick, though there is no harm in mortifying the flesh. But vastly more important is the complete change of heart and the totally new outlook on the world of man....

The whole problem is this inner change...[the need for] an application of spiritual force and not the use of merely political pressure. We all have the great duty to realize the deep need for purity of soul, that is, the deep need to possess in us the Holy Spirit, to be possessed by Him. This has to take precedence over everything else. If He lives and works in us, then our activity will be true and our witness will generate love of truth, even though we may be persecuted and beaten down in apparent incomprehension.

A week later he was at once pleased with, yet worried about, a demonstration in New York in which pacifists, from several groups including the Catholic Worker, had blocked the main doorways of the Atomic Energy Commission. He was pleased that the action had been, in planning and execution, thoroughly Gandhian—so determined to realize "openness and truthfulness" that police observers received (and accepted) invitations to be present at the planning meetings for that demonstration so there could be no doubt regarding exactly what was to happen and in what spirit. Nor was he surprised that, despite the physically unthreatening nature of a quiet sit-in before doors when other entrances were unimpeded, some of the AEC staff had kicked through our carpet of bodies in order to pass through the front doors. But he was worried that we weren't seeing deeply enough into the subtle dangers that exist even in non-violent action:

> One of the problematic questions about non-violence is the inevitable involvement of hidden aggressions and provocations. I think this is especially true when there are a fair proportion of non-religious elements, or religious elements that are not spiritually developed. It is an enormously subtle question, but we have to consider the fact that, in its provocative aspect, non-violence may tend to harden the opposition and to confirm people in their righteous blindness. It may even in some cases separate men out and drive them in the other direction, away from us and away from peace. This of course may be (as it was with the prophets) part of God's plan. A clear separation of antagonists. . . .

Even so, he went on, driving people in the opposite direction can never be seen as a goal of such actions:

> [We must] always direct our action toward opening people's eyes to the truth, and if they are blinded, we must try to be sure we did nothing specifically to blind them. Yet there is that danger: the danger one observes subtly in tight groups like families and monastic communities, where the martyr for the right sometimes thrives on making his persecutors terribly and visibly wrong. He can drive them in desperation to be wrong, to seek refuge in the wrong, to seek refuge in violence.

In words that should be carefully read and pondered by anyone hoping to defuse a bit of the world's explosive potential, Merton continued:

The violent man is, by our standards, weak and sick, though at times he is powerful and menacing in an extreme degree. In our acceptance of vulnerability, however, we play on his guilt. There is no finer torment. This is one of the enormous problems of the time, and the place. It is the overwhelming problem of America: all this guilt and nothing to do about it except finally to explode and blow it all out in hatreds—race hatreds, political hatreds, war hatreds. We, the righteous, are dangerous people in such a situation. (Of course we are not righteous; we are conscious of our guilt; above all, we are sinners: but nevertheless we are bound to take courses of action that are professionally righteous and we have committed ourselves to that course.)

...We have got to be aware of the awful sharpness of the truth when it is used as a weapon, and since it can be the deadliest weapon, we must take care that we don't kill more than falsehood with it. In fact we must be careful how we "use" truth, for we are ideally the instruments of truth and not the other way round. (Feb. 6, 1962)

As the weeks and months went by, Merton often had reason to notice that very few peace activists were deeply attuned to some of these insights, and he expressed his anguish with the peace movement's "terrible superficiality," as he summed it up in a letter of August 27 that same year. Yet he was as committed to his relationship with us, for all our immaturity and immense limitations, perhaps in a way analogous to his commitments to others in the monastic life and the wider Church who found some of his concerns so discordant and out of step. Thus he kept articulating a vision of what we might become—something more helpful in the world than a new brigade of two-legged loudspeakers joining the political shouting match:

...the basic problem is not political, it is a-political and human. One of the most important things to do is to keep cutting deliberately through political lines and barriers

and emphasizing the fact that these are largely fabrica-
tions and that there is another dimension, a genuine
reality, totally opposed to the fictions of politics: the
human dimension which politics pretend to arrogate
entirely to themselves. This is the necessary first step
along the long way toward the perhaps impossible task
of purifying, humanizing and somehow illuminating
politics themselves.

Was such a thing possible, he wondered, noting that
some had accused him of being "too ready to doubt the
possibility":

At least we must try to hope in it, otherwise all is over....

Hence the desirability of a manifestly non-political witness, non-aligned, non-labeled, fighting for the reality
of man and his rights and needs in the nuclear world in
some measure against all the alignments.

He warned against the importance of all movements
with such aims taking care not to be exploited, manipulated
or taken over by Communists whose peace, it turns out, isn't
so peaceful:

The prime duty of all honest movements is to protect
themselves from being swallowed by any sea monster
that happens along. And plenty will happen along. Once
the swallowing has taken place, rigidity replaces truth
and there is no more possibility of dialogue: the old lines
are hardened and the weapons slide into position for the
kill once more. (Dec. 8, 1962)

The years 1963 and 1964 saw America's quiet war in
Vietnam suddenly begin to bulge in size and devastation;
these events helped prod the Catholic Peace Fellowship into
existence, first as a part-time officeless project initially involving Daniel Berrigan and myself with support from John
Heidbrink of the Fellowship of Reconciliation (which Merton

had joined formally, not hesitating over its explicitly pacifist statement of purpose, in September 1962: "a rather obvious thing to do," he mentioned in a letter of Sept. 22). Merton, while mentioning his increasing discomfort at being "a name," agreed to be one of the sponsors. The CPF, with roots both in the Catholic Worker and the Fellowship of Reconciliation, took an unequivocally pacifist stand, emphasizing in its membership brochure the sweeping rejections of war by Popes John and Paul.

In November 1964, several weeks before the CPF was to have an office and, in myself, a full-time staff person, a small group of CPF- and FOR-related individuals came together for a three-day retreat with Merton to consider, in Merton's phrase, "the spiritual roots of protest."[18] Those taking part included Daniel and Philip Berrigan, W. H. Ferry (an FOR leader and vice-president of the Center for the Study of Democratic Institutions), John Howard Yoder (FOR member, prominent pacifist theologian), Tony Walsh (of the Catholic Worker house in Montreal), A. J. Muste (long-time executive secretary of FOR, founder of the Committee for Nonviolent Action, pacifism's "elder statesman" in the U.S.), Tom Cornell (of the Catholic Worker, later CPF co-secretary), myself and several others: a small crowd that had been brought together largely by John Heidbrink, the FOR's Church Work Secretary—though, due to illness, not at the retreat himself.

This was my second meeting with Merton in person. There was still laughter, but less of it. The times were deadly serious and so was much of the conversation. Merton spoke in earnest, listened with a quick and critical ear, and at times launched us into silence. I remember him best in those days not with us in his hermitage, though he was present with the group as much as anyone, but rather walking alone outside, pacing back and forth in a state of absorption in thought so complete and compelling that it brought home to me the gravity of what he was going to say in the conference that followed more than the words themselves.

Merton's contribution was to impress on us, often more with questions than answers, that protest wasn't simply an almost casual human right, but rather a terribly dangerous calling that, if it lacked sufficient spiritual maturity, could contribute to making things worse. Thus his Zen *koan* of a question that hit us like an arrow in the back was: *"By what right do we protest? Against whom or what? For what? How? Why?"*

Questions. The whole retreat was more a questioning and an answering experience. We considered the momentum of technology in the modern world: technology's implied *credo* being summed up in a few apocalyptic words—"If it *can* be done, it *must* be done."In the context of technology, whether on its battlefields or in its almost monastically-sheltered laboratories, the human being was coming to be seen as (quoting from a scientific paper) a "bio-chemical link": a shaky bridge between the solid-circuit perfection of cybernetic systems and moodless computers, and not a being little less than the angels.

By way of counter-point to man as "bio-chemical link," we repeatedly turned back to a man whose head was chopped off by the Nazis on August 9, 1943—Franz Jaegerstatter, an Austrian Catholic peasant with modest education and a wife and three young daughters to worry over who, despite strong opposition from his pastor and bishop, refused military service in Hitler's armies, even in a non-combatant capacity. Uncanonized though he was, he struck us as a saint for our moment when many would refuse to join in a war with no more justice than Hitler's. We were struck by an isolated peasant's ability to see clearly—expressed in letters written from prison (later collected and published by Gordon Zahn)[19]—what bishops and theologians couldn't see or didn't dare see. We had every reason to expect the same from our own Church leadership as the Vietnam war worsened. But we had to hope for something better than that in our situation, and not waste a minute in working toward that end—toward a Church that would put its weight behind those who refused to wage war and who refused to see other humans simply as "bio-chemical links."

"If the Church," said Merton, "could make its teachings alive to the laity, future Franz Jaegerstatters would no longer be in solitude but would be the Church as a whole reasserting the primacy of the spiritual."

With such a sense of purpose, the Catholic Peace Fellowship began its work, focusing on the right—and, in the present situation, possible duty—not to take part in this killing of Vietnamese. A booklet of mine, written with advice from Merton, even received the Imprimatur of the Archdiocese of New York—with the censorship process, to my astonishment, only weeding out a few errors of fact that weakened the text; thus *Catholics and Conscientous Objection*[20] was readily accepted for use in Catholic schools where previously anything along these lines would have landed in the wastebasket next to *Lady Chatterly's Lover*. In time, we were counseling Catholic conscientous objectors in droves—as many as fifty a week wrote for help or came to see us. Chapters were springing up across the country, as Tom Cornell and I went forth on speaking trips. A number of theologians and many clergy gave support, signed statements, and joined in demonstrations.

All the time, however, the war was getting worse and thus the pressures were on us to do more than "just" educate. David Miller, one of the Catholic Worker staff, unable to find words to adequately express his dismay with the war, its casualties and the conscription of young Americans to fight in it without their consent or understanding, lifted up his draft card at a rally in front of Manhattan's military induction center and burned the card to an ash—an event on the front page of American newspapers the next morning. A few months later, Tom Cornell of the CPF staff felt obliged to do the same, responding to a newly passed law that provided heavy fines and long jail terms for anyone mutilating or destroying these tiny forms that noted one's draft status. Tom reasoned it was an idolatrous law, making sacred a scrap of paper, and decided to burn his publicly as well. He did so at the beginning of November. The event attracted substantial national attention. A week later Roger LaPorte, a young volunteer and former Cistercian novice, burned not his draft card but himself. Sitting before the U.S. Mission to the

United Nations, he poured gasoline on his body and struck a match.

The two events hit Merton like a bolt of lightning. On November 11, 1965, we received a telegram:

JUST HEARD ABOUT SUICIDE OF ROGER LAPORTE WHILE I DO NOT HOLD CATHOLIC PEACE FELLOWSHIP RESPONSIBLE FOR THIS TRAGEDY CURRENT DEVELOPMENTS IN PEACE MOVEMENT MAKE IT IMPOSSIBLE FOR ME TO CONTINUE AS SPONSOR OF FELLOWSHIP PLEASE REMOVE MY NAME FROM LIST OF SPONSORS LETTER FOLLOWS THOMAS MERTON

We were already in a state of shock, still trying to absorb the event of Roger's action. He was still alive, dying in Bellevue Hospital. Tom Cornell had been indicted and was awaiting a trial date. Merton's telegram, and the letter which arrived a few days later, added to a sense of exhaustion and despair.

In his letter he recognized that we were as shocked as he by Roger's action. Such actions would harm rather than help the peace movement. So would draft card burnings, he went on. Such things were so disturbing, Merton said, that he was led to the "regretful decision that I cannot accept the present spirit of the movement as it presents itself to me." Not questioning anyone's sincerity, still he couldn't see in such actions the qualities of a genuinely non-violent movement, and he even sensed "there is something demonic at work in it." In fact such actions seemed to echo rather than oppose the direction of violent America:

The spirit of this country at the present moment is to me terribly disturbing. . . . It is not quite like Nazi Germany, certainly not like Soviet Russia, it is like nothing on earth I ever heard of before. This whole atmosphere is crazy, not just the peace movement, everybody. There is in it such an air of absurdity and moral void, even where conscience and morality are invoked (as they are by everyone). The joint is going into a slow frenzy. The country is nuts.

Merton's vulnerability to such events had been heightened by a major event in his own life that began only ten weeks before: on August 21, after nearly two decades of prayers and petitions, he was finally allowed to be a hermit. By this was meant not life in a hollow tree out of human reach but a life based in his cinderblock hermitage, involving considerably more solitude than had been possible before. Finally, as he put it in a Christmas letter to friends, "I am...trying to do the things I came here for." A less cluttered life, fewer chores and responsibilities, less correspondence. This more hidden and seemingly sheltered life was in reality, as surely Merton knew it would be, much less defended against the world as a whole, for better, for worse. He felt the events involving Catholic pacifists in New York like an earthquake under his feet.

In the exchange of letters that was to follow, as he heard details about what had happened and began to learn not only of the legal and political basis of Tom's action but more of the human dimensions of Roger LaPorte, he decided not to withdraw his CPF sponsorship after all. He expressed apologies, asking us to understand that, in a way, he had just begun a new life, and it presented problems:

> I am, so to speak, making my novitiate as a "hermit" of sorts and I have my hands full with this. It is a full time job just coping with one's own damn mind in solitude without getting wrought up about what appear to be the vagaries of others. (Nov. 19, 1965)

He added that some of his fellow monks held him responsible for anything that happened with Catholic pacifists anywhere: "It is...mere gossip, but they are associating the card burning with my ideas about peace. This certainly does not make life simple for me since I am not quite sure that I agree with card burning (though I accept Tom's arguments for his own position)." [A year later, in fact, while not seeing draft card burning as an appropriate tactic for big campaigns, he said, in a joint letter to Tom and me, "The more I think about the card burning, the more I think that you, Tom, are utterly right before God." (Nov. 16, 1966)]

John Heidbrink's letters to Merton at this time prompted a long reflection on the intersection of his redefined vocation with the recent events in New York:

> Roger's immolation started off a deep process of examination and it will lead far. Wrong as I did think his act was objectively, I believe it did not prejudice the purity of his heart and I never condemned him. What I condemned and... still... question is a pervasive "spirit" or something, a spirit of irrationality, of power seeking, of temptation to the wrong kind of refusal and impatience and to pseudo charismatic witness which can be terribly, fatally destructive of all good....[There is] a spirit of madness and fanaticism [in the air]...and it summons me to a deep distrust of all my own acts and involvements in this public realm....

> ...the real road [for me] lies...with a new development in thought and work that will, if it is what it should be, be much more true and more valid for peace than any series of ephemeral gestures I might attempt to make. But anyway, now is a time for me of searching, digging, and if I mention *angst* it will not be to dramatize myself in any way but to assure you that I conceive my real and valid union with you all to make this form of silently getting ground up inside by the weights among which you are moving outside.

> It is to be understood that if I get any word, I hope reasonable word, to utter, I will not hesitate to utter it as I have always done before. But this word has to come from here, not from there. That is why I worked it out with Jim that I will remain a sponsor of CPF provided it is understood that in political matters and other questions of

immediate practical decision I remain independent and autonomous.... (Dec. 4, 1965)

Merton changed his mind. This isn't a trait one takes for granted. Not only did he change it, but he decided to make a public statement about the new shape of his vocation and at the same time to mention the reasons he would remain a CPF sponsor even while pruning his life severely. The CPF released his statement a few days before Christmas and it was widely reported in the press. Beginning with a denial of the ever-current rumors that he had left the monastery and abandoned the contemplative life, he said,

> In actual fact, far from abandoning the contemplative life, I have received permission to go into it more deeply. I have been granted an opportunity for greater solitude and more intense prayer, meditation and study. As a result of this, I am even less involved in various activities than I was before.... I am not keeping track of current controversies.... I am not taking an active part in [the peace movement] . . . .

> However, I certainly believe it is my duty to give at least general and moral support to all forms of Catholic Action.... In particular, I continue to give... moral support to those who are working to implement the teachings of the Council and of the modern Popes on war and peace. If my name remains among the sponsors of the Catholic Peace Fellowship, it is because I believe that this dedicated group is sincerely striving to spread the teachings of the Gospel and of the Church on war, peace, and the brotherhood of man. However, my sponsorship does not imply automatic approval of any and every move made by this group, still less of individual actions on the part of its members acting on their own responsibility.... I personally believe that what we need most of all today is patient, constructive and pastoral work rather than acts of defiance which antagonize the average person without enlightening him. (Dec. 3, 1965; released Dec. 22)

Paradoxically, the final effect of Merton's short-lived resignation was that he decided to become more directly involved. He helped the CPF carefully define its "pastoral"
work which, by December 29, he saw as being of immense
importance. While the Council and Popes had spoken
"clearly and authoritatively," few if any Catholic prelates
were going to get the message out in a way that could be
clearly understood by the average churchgoer; the Vietnam
war would continue on its murderous course, with Catholics
as busy in the killing as any other group. The Popes'
encyclicals and the Council's *Constitution on the Church in the
Modern World* would be dead letters, unless the CPF effectively got out to the colleges, the seminaries and the clergy.
"This is a big job...it is what you are called to do now."
While in some ways the task was "colorless" and
undramatic—"simply reaching a lot of people and helping
them to change their minds"—it could have a "transforming
effect on the American Catholic Church." For his own part he
offered to write a leaflet spelling out the Church's teaching on
war—and in time this emerged as a CPF booklet, *Blessed Are
the Meek*, not only presenting the Church's teaching but
spelling out what non-violence is all about—a meekness that
has nothing to do with passivity, that involves selflessness
and considerable risk, and that is liberating rather than murderous. "The chief difference between violence and nonviolence," he remarked, "is that violence depends entirely on its
own calculations. Nonviolence depends entirely on God and
His Word."[21]

One of the helpful events for Merton in the last few years
of his life was the arrival at his hermitage of a brown-robed
monk from Asia: Thich Nhat Hanh, a Vietnamese Zen master, a leader of the non-violent movement in Vietnam, one of
the monks most responsible for the "engaged Buddhism"
which had led Vietnamese Buddhists—at immense personal
risk—to resist the war and to work toward a neutral "third
way" solution, getting rid of American soldiers and ending
the civil war that had so worsened with their involvement.
Like Merton, Thich Nhat Hanh was a poet. Because of the
horrors of the war, he had temporarily given up many of the
externals of the monastic life, though the reality of his monk's

identity remained unimpaired. "A perfectly formed monk," Merton marveled to his novices the next day, saying Nhat Hanh's arrival was really the answer to a prayer.

Merton's interest in Eastern spirituality, especially Buddhism and Zen, had long since been established. *The Way of Chuang Tzu*[22] had already been published and he was at work on *Zen and the Birds of Appetite*.[23] But he had known almost nothing of Vietnamese Zen Buddhism until Thich Nhat Hanh's arrival. The two stayed up into the night, sharing the chant of their respective traditions, discussing methods of prayer and meditation, sharing experiences in approaches to monastic formation—and talking of the war.

"What is it like?" Merton asked.

"Everything is destroyed."

This, Merton later commented, was a monk's answer. Not long-winded, carefully qualified and balanced explanations—just the essence of the event, its soul. "Everything is destroyed."

Afterward Merton wrote a kind of letter for his newly found "brother" that John Heidbrink had brought to the abbey. (Thich Nhat Hanh, a member of FOR, was on an FOR-sponsored speaking trip in the U.S.) Merton's major statement in the text was as simple and direct as Thich Nhat Hanh's comment about the war:

Thich Nhat Hanh is my brother.

This is not a political statement. It has no "interested" motive, it seeks to provoke no immediate reaction "for" or "against" this or that side in the Vietnam war. It is on the contrary a human and personal statement and an anguished plea for the Vietnamese Buddhist monk Thich Nhat Hanh who is my brother. He is more my brother than many who are nearer to me in race and nationality, because he and I see things exactly the same way.[24]

Merton went on to speak of their shared rejection of the war for "human reasons, reasons of sanity, justice and love." He underscored the fact that neither of them was political in the word's ordinary sense, not supporting any ideology of conquest and war.

He emphasized that Nhat Hanh had risked his life in order to present the war's reality to Americans. Neither armed side would readily tolerate a spokesman for toleration—with one message, he betrays both sides. He does so simply because he speaks for compassion:

> Nhat Hanh is a free man... moved by the spiritual dynamic of a tradition of religious compassion. He has come among us as many others have, from time to time, bearing witness to the spirit of Zen. More than any other he has shown us that Zen is not an esoteric and world-denying cult of inner illumination, but that it has its rare and unique sense of responsibility for the modern world. Wherever he goes he will walk in the strength of his spirit and in the solitude of the Zen monk who sees beyond life and death. . . .
>
> I have said that Nhat Hanh is my brother, and it is true. We are both monks, and we have lived the monastic life about the same number of years. We are both poets, both existentialists. I have far more in common with Nhat Hanh than I have with many Americans, and do not hesitate to say it. It is vitally important that such bonds be admitted. They are the bonds of a new solidarity and a new brotherhood which is beginning to be evident on all the five continents and which cuts across all political, religious and cultural lines to unite young men and women in every country in something that is more concrete than an ideal and more alive than a program. The unity of the young is the only hope for the world. In its name I appeal for Nhat Hanh. Do what you can for him. If I mean something to you, then let me put it this way: do for Nhat Hanh whatever you would do for me if I were in his position. In many ways I wish I were.[25]

Their conversations strengthened Merton in the conviction that the peacemaker is one who rejects victories by "sides" but is one, instead, committed to the formation of community that protects the economic, cultural, political and spiritual rights of every person and group within the disciplines of non-violence. This was the goal of the "third way" Buddhists in Vietnam. It meant an alternative to the absolutist claims and the military "solutions" of the competing sides. This had immense implications not only for the Vietnamese but for the entire world and its fragile future.

But the encounter with Nhat Hanh was also an illumination, an encounter with a hermit who carried his hermitage invisibly around him, a contemplative wandering the face of the earth bearing his own silence within the surrounding noise.

This was one of the preparatory steps for Merton's own journey to Asia. His last letter (August 5, 1968) ended with a request for Nhat Hanh's current address.

During these last years of correspondence, while there continued to be much that was of a practical nature relating to the work of CPF and FOR, there continued to be much that reminded me again that my first encounter with Merton was with a man of outrageous laughter.

I suspect his sense of humor had a great deal to do with his ability to persevere, not only with his monastic community, but also with his peace community.If he spoke grumpily about his fellow monks, it tended to be in a way that occasioned at least a smile. When a friend designed a letterhead that featured the words "the monks are moving," he asked if I could send him some blank sheets for some of his own correspondence, then added:

Only thing is I wonder if the monks are moving. Everything I do gives me scruples about being identified with this stupid rhinocerotic outfit that charges backward into the jungle with portentious snuffling and then bursts out of the canebrake with a roar in the most unlikely places. (June 26, 1967)

When his old friend and mentor Dan Walsh was ordained in Louisville, Merton wrote of the celebration that followed afterward at the home of Tommie O'Callaghan:

> ...there was a lot of celebrating. In fact I celebrated on too much champagne, which is a thing a Trappist rarely gets to do, but I did a very thorough job. At one point in the afternoon I remember looking up and focusing rather uncertainly upon four faces of nuns sitting in a row looking at me in a state of complete scandal and shock. Another pillar of the Church had fallen. (June 17, 1967)

The following spring a letter arrived that began with a mysterious Yiddish proverb, all in capitals: SLEEP FASTER WE NEED THE PILLOWS.

Another letter arrived with a color snapshot of, Merton announced, "the only known photograph of God." In most respects it was just a view of the Kentucky hills, fold upon fold of green under a brilliant blue sky. But hanging down from the top, dominating the whole scene, was an immense sky hook, the kind used in construction for lifting substantial objects. It looked like an overgrown fishing hook.

If Leon Bloy was right—"Joy is the most infallible sign of the presence of God"—God was very present in Merton, for all his hard times in a hard century. That joy and that laughter were a major element in what he had to say about peacemaking and many other things as well. He was at times a scandal to his brothers in the monastic life, and to pacifists too—the kind that can't admit a smile in These Difficult Times.

It was in that laughter that I best understood his seriousness. One discovered the connection that necessarily exists between a profound and attentive silence and words that have truth in them. A monk who could see God in a giant hook dangling above the Kentucky woods and who could roll on the floor with joy over the stench of unwashed feet was the same one who could consider war in its human dimension, with all its agony and sense that God was obliging us not to make a peace with such peacelessness.

With prayer and with word, he was able to help others to

do the same, to keep going when continuity seemed impossible. His letters did that for me on a number of occasions. But perhaps one letter was to you no less than me. Let me end by giving it to you. It was written February 21, 1966:

> Do not depend on the hope of results. When you are doing the sort of work you have taken on, essentially an apostolic work, you may have to face the fact that your work will be apparently worthless and even achieve no result at all, if not perhaps results opposite to what you expect. As you get used to this idea, you start more and more to concentrate not on the results but on the value, the rightness, the truth of the work itself. And there too a great deal has to be gone through, as gradually you struggle less and less for an idea and more and more for specific people. The range tends to narrow down, but it gets much more real. In the end, it is the reality of personal relationships that saves everything.

> You are fed up with words, and I don't blame you. I am nauseated by them sometimes. I am also, to tell the truth, nauseated by ideals and with causes. This sounds like heresy, but I think you will understand what I mean. It is so easy to get engrossed with ideas and slogans and myths that in the end one is left holding the bag, empty, with no trace of meaning left in it. And then the temptation is to yell louder than ever in order to make the meaning be there again by magic. Going through this kind of reaction helps you to guard against this. Your system is complaining of too much verbalizing, and it is right.

> ...the big results are not in your hands or mine, but they suddenly happen, and we can share in them; but there is no point in building our lives on this personal satisfaction, which may be denied us and which after all is not that important.

> The next step in the process is for you to see that your own thinking about what you are doing is crucially im-

portant. You are probably striving to build yourself an identity in your work, out of your work and your witness. You are using it, so to speak, to protect yourself against nothingness, annihilation. That is not the right use of your work. All the good that you will do will come not from you but from the fact that you have allowed yourself, in the obedience of faith, to be used by God's love. Think of this more, and gradually you will be free from the need to prove yourself, and you can be more open to the power that will work through you without your knowing it.

The great thing after all is to live, not to pour out your life in the service of a myth: and we turn the best things into myths. If you can get free from the domination of causes and just serve Christ's truth, you will be able to do more and will be less crushed by the inevitable disappointments. Because I see nothing whatever in sight but much disappointment, frustration, and confusion....

The real hope, then, is not in something we think we can do, but in God who is making something good out of it in some way we cannot see. If we can do His will, we will be helping in this process. But we will not necessarily know all about it beforehand....

Enough of this...it is at least a gesture....I will keep you in my prayers.

All the best, in Christ,

Tom

NOTES

1. Thomas Merton, *The Sign of Jonas* (N.Y.: Harcourt, Brace, 1951), p. 21.

2. Pope John XXIII, *Pacem in Terris* (N.Y.: America Press, 1963), p. 39.

3. Merton, *My Argument With the Gestapo* (N.Y.: Doubleday, 1969).

4. Merton, *Thomas Merton on Peace*, edited by Gordon Zahn (N.Y.: McCall's, 1971), pp. 160-165.

5. Merton, *Emblems of a Season of Fury* (N.Y.: New Directions, 1963), pp. 47ff.

6. Cf. Zahn, *TMOP*, pp 3-11.

7. Merton, *New Seeds of Contemplation* (N.Y.: New Directions, 1966).

8. *Ibid.*, pp. 112ff.

9. *The Catholic Worker*, October, 1961, p. 1.

10. Cf. Edward Rice, *The Man in the Sycamore Tree* (N.Y.: Doubleday, 1970), p. 79, where this and a litany of other Merton pseudonyms appear, signatures of his correspondence with Rice (editor's note).

11. Merton, cited in Zahn, *TMOP*, p. 257.

12. *Ibid.*

13. *Ibid.*, p. 258.

14. Merton, "Author's Preface to the Japanese Edition," *Nanae No Yama (The Seven Storey Mountain)*, trans. Tadishi Kudo (Tokyo: Chou Shuppansha, 1966).

15. *Ibid.*

16. *Ibid.*

17. *Ibid.*

18. Cf. Zahn, *TMOP*, pp. 259-260.

19. Gordon C. Zahn, *In Solitary Witness* (N.Y.: Holt, Rinehart, Winston, 1964).

20. James H. Forest, *Catholics and Conscientious Objection* (N.Y.: Catholic Peace Fellowship, 1966).

21. Cited in Zahn, *TMOP*, p. 216

22. Merton, *The Way of Chuang Tzu* (N.Y.: New Directions, 1965).

23. Merton, *Zen and the Birds of Appetite* (N.Y.: New Directions, 1968).

24. Cited in Zahn, *TMOP*, p. 262.

25. *Ibid.*, p. 263.

Thomas Merton:
Reluctant Pacifist

Gordon Zahn

I

I begin this assessment of Thomas Merton's contributions to the reawakened awareness of the pacifist implications of Catholicism with some modest reservations as to the
appropriateness of the editor's choice. After all, I have already
had the opportunity to do just that in the lengthy introduction to an earlier volume devoted entirely to Merton's writings on peace which I had the pleasure of editing.[1] It might
have been better, then, to give someone else a chance, especially since what follows is to some extent a summary of that
more detailed "appreciation." Be that as it may, I welcome
the opportunity to bring that earlier assessment up to date
and judge for myself how well it and Merton's writings on
peace have held up in the newer context of the changes in
world and Church affairs that have taken place since his
death in 1968. My judgment that both have held up very well
indeed is perhaps foreordained, but some of the themes that
were dominant when those writings first appeared have sur-
rendered much of that dominance to themes that excited
considerably less attention or discussion at that time.

My reticence can be traced, too, to recognition of the fact
that others may have a stronger claim upon the task assumed
here. Foremost among them are the many who were Merton
"converts" in the sense that previous to their encounter with
one or another of his books or articles they had given little
serious thought to their responsibilities as Christians to actively promote peace and oppose war and policies that might

lead to war. Such converts, it is safe to say, must be legion given the vast and highly receptive audience that was his. If I do not include myself among their number, it is only because my own commitment to pacifism extends back to my days as a Catholic conscientious objector to World War II and ante-dates his emergence as a spokesman for the cause in the early 1960's. This is not to say, of course, that I was (or am!) any less an admirer than those whose lives and outlook he would change. The appearance of "Nuclear War and Christian Responsibility" in the February 9, 1962 issue of *Commonweal*, the first of his articles dealing with war and peace to come to my attention, was a tremendous source of encouragement and inspiration for those few of us who had more or less reconciled ourselves to the fact that most Catholics—if, that is, they took any notice of us at all—regarded us as a kind of "lunatic fringe" and our activities for peace as dangerously close to heresy. Now, all of a sudden, we had one of the foremost Catholic writers of the time on our side!

To be sure, Merton's position and mine were not identical in every respect. Thus, although he would at one point describe himself as a "modified" pacifist in World War II, he never endorsed or accepted for himself the more thoroughgoing pacifist commitment some of us espoused. But we were in complete agreement on the question of nuclear war and its eschatological (in both the theological and literal senses) implications for the Christian, and that was the most important thing as far as we were concerned. At a time when the "better dead than Red" mentality characterized Catholic thought on the subject, his devastating critique of nuclear war and weapons introduced a much needed note of simple sanity. Moreover, it was clear that even one Merton article would almost certainly command far greater notice than more dedicated pacifists could likely win from their fellow Catholics in years of concerted effort.

Nor would it end at that. Among the many others who are probably better qualified to assess his contributions are those who could speak from a more personal vantage point, who had benefited from direct contact with him and, as a direct result of that, had found their lives changed in most dramatic fashion. Consider, for instance, the 1964 retreat conducted by him at Gethsemani on "The Spiritual Roots of Protest." Among the small and select group of retreatants were leading Protestant pacifists like A. J. Muste, John Howard Yoder, and John Heidbrink. But the names that carry greater signifiicance in the present context are Daniel and Philip Berrigan, Thomas Cornell, James Forest, and Robert Cunnane. Within the brief span of five years or less the spiritual roots tended at Gethsemani would bear fruit in active protest and prison for them all; the Berrigans for the draft board raids at Baltimore and Catonsville; Cunnane and Forest for following their leading role as members of "the Milwaukee Fourteen"; Cornell as one of the early draft card burners. In a very real sense, and strange as it may seem, what was to become known as "the great Catholic peace conspiracy" had some of its beginnings in the quiet of that Trappist retreat.

Much to my regret, I never met Merton in person though he did extend the invitation in several letters (including an invitation to that same retreat). Operating under the false assurance that a Trappist could be counted on to be on the scene at a more convenient future date, I put off going to Gethsemani until suddenly it was too late. Nevertheless we did manage through our occasional exchange of letters to share our ideas and expand our areas of agreement on what we both recognized as the most crucial moral issues facing mankind. Perhaps a personal meeting might have brought us to complete agreement, for I have always been convinced that the differences between us were semantic and not substantive. Some support for this can be found in a 1961 letter to a mutual friend in which he explained, "Technically I am not a pure pacifist in theory, though today in practice I don't see how one can be anything else since limited wars (however 'just') present an almost certain danger of nuclear war on an all out basis." Perhaps, given the changes in the official Church posture on these matters—the Vatican Council's call for an "entirely new attitude" toward war, for example— even the semantic difference might have faded away leaving Merton more ready to accept the "pacifist" designation he was so careful to avoid when it was still considered incompatible with Catholic teachings and traditions.

This would be quite consistent, in fact, with what one does find in the Merton writings, namely a definite shift of emphasis from poetic and spiritual abstractions to very precise and distinct political applications and inferences. The Merton who "burst" upon the scene in 1961 and 1962 as a vocal opponent of nuclear war was merely bringing a new perspective to many of the themes developed in his earlier contemplative works and the other books and articles which had won such popularity as "spiritual reading" when that was still in vogue. Even so, any assessment of his specific contributions to the peace movement has to begin with the flurry of publications which began to appear in those two years. The *Commonweal* article already mentioned probably deserves to be considered his first comprehensive discussion of the problem, but it did not stand alone. A few months earlier, in fact, it had been preceded by publication in *The Catholic Worker* of "The Roots of War" (October 1961), and in following months the same paper would publish "Christian Ethics and Nuclear War" (March and April, 1962) and "The Shelter Ethic" (May and June, 1962). May 1962 also brought "Religion and the Bomb" in *Jubilee*, and the English journal *Blackfriars* published "Christian Action in World Crisis" the following month. There may have been others, but these are found in Catholic periodical index listings.

"The Roots of War" was a chapter taken from *New Seeds of Contemplation* and marks the crossing-over point from meditation to political application. The major part of the book is clearly of the spiritual reading category, and it is not until the concluding pages of this particular chapter that he raises the kind of question that will characterize most of his later writings on war and peace issues. "What," he asks, "is the use of postmarking our mail with exhortations to 'pray for peace' and then spending billions of dollars on atomic submarines, thermonuclear weapons, and ballistic missiles? This, I would think, would certainly be what the New Testament calls 'mocking God'—and mocking him far more effectively than the atheists."[2] A very good question and one which probably shocked many of his readers. And, sad to say, it has lost none of its relevance even though we no longer use that "Pray for Peace" postmark.

Two other highly significant publications, which appeared in 1962 were the long poem, *Original Child Bomb*, subtitled "points for meditation to be scratched on the wall of a cave," and *Breakthrough to Peace*, a collection of essays representing "twelve views on the threat of nuclear extermination" edited by Merton and containing an introduction and a chapter ("Peace: A Religious Responsibility") authored by him.[3]

The latter volume, as it turned out, barely managed to "get under the wire." Despite the fact that, viewed from today's perspective at least, none of these writings could be considered particularly "radical" or even pacifist, they were radical enough to arouse considerable opposition—especially where it would hurt most, within Merton's own religious community. In a number of letters dating from this time, he refers to problems encountered in the course of normal internal review of his writings. The processes of censorship through which they had to pass before he received permission to publish had slowed to the point where it was necessary for him to advise prospective publishers to anticipate delays of as much as eight weeks before final approval could be expected. That first *Commonweal* article, to cite but one example, had been solicited for the Christmas issue but did not appear until February because one of the Trappist censors had turned it down. The only writings not subject to this practice and the resulting delays were those intended for small publications of clearly limited influence.

In April 1962, however, Merton was instructed not to publish anything more on the controversial topics of war and peace. Though not entirely unexpected, the ban was a grave trial and disappointment for him and a shattering blow to those of us who had welcomed the sudden emergence of so prominent an opponent of war. Material previously approved and already in the process of publication (including the *Breakthrough* volume, though he was no longer to be identified as its editor) was exempted from the ban; but henceforth, or at least until the decision was reversed, he could only circulate his views privately and in mimeographed form in much the same manner as the *samizdat* network developed by dissidents in the Soviet Union. Fortunately this was enough to assure that the setback, serious though it was, did not silence Merton altogether or destroy his effectiveness as a force for peace. He maintained his extensive correspondence, choosing some of it for two mimeographed volumes of "Cold War Letters" for private circulation and, by this means, continued to provide inspiration and encouragement to peacemongers scattered all over the country and, indeed, the world.

The ban proved to be temporary. The change in atmosphere introduced by John XXIII and the Vatican Council, coupled with changes in leadership within the Order, brought Merton back into the public debate which by now had reached new peaks of intensity under the pressures of the Vietnam war. One could say that not too much harm had been done since a few previously approved articles appeared in 1963, leaving 1964 as the year of relative silence on the issues that had come to mean so much to him. On the other hand—even assuming he ultimately managed to publish all he had intended to publish—the fact remains that any interruption at that most critical time could only serve to lessen the impact he might have had upon American Catholic thought and opinion.

Viewed from our present perspective, of course, the attempted suppression was as pointless as it was unjustified. In a decade or even less those same positions that were deemed so dangerously radical became quite respectable, so much so in fact that they have since found their parallels in the official pronouncements of popes and bishops as well as in the political activity, organized and unorganized, of the committed Catholic faithful. Merton would have taken much satisfaction from the recent Detroit Call to Action conference which, claiming to speak "in the light of consistent church teaching on modern warfare," would specifically recommend that the U.S. Catholic community "condemn, and be among those who lead in resisting, the production, possession, proliferation and threatened use of nuclear weapons and all other weapons of indiscriminate effect, even in a policy of deterrence."[3]

II

This, after all, was the issue which brought him into the debate in the first place. His *Commonweal* article had begun with the warning that "the world and society of man now face destruction" and proceeded from there to the startling accusation, "At the present moment the United States and the Soviet Union are committed to a policy of genocide." The conclusion he drew clearly anticipated Detroit by fourteen years or more: "It is pure madness to think that Christianity can defend itself with nuclear weapons. The mere fact that we now seem to accept nuclear war as reasonable is a universal scandal."

Strong words indeed for that time and place! Predictably enough, they provoked an equally strong response. One reader who worked in the Los Alamos laboratories described all opposition to nuclear arms and continued testing as "dangerous wishful thinking" and the "height of determinism, naiveté, irresponsibility, and immorality," presumably extending those characterizations to Merton himself. Merton's rejoinder stands as helpful advice and challenge to those of us who must still deal with an uncompleted task: "Meditations on a dangerous book, the Bible, have convinced me that when the human race puts itself into a major crisis, it shows a strong tendency to abdicate moral responsibility and to commit sin on an enormous scale. This is the kind of situation we face now. Unless we realize the moral and spiritual roots of the problem, our best efforts to solve it in a positive and human way are bound to be meaningless...."[6]

Merton, ever the spiritual writer and contemplative even when addressing himself to contemporary problems and political imperatives, viewed "the Bomb" and its implications for mankind in an apocalyptic and eschatological context. Writing in a Church still "triumphalist" in its approach to the world and its problems, he identified the time as a "post-Christian era" and warned that it would be "a serious error to imagine that because the West was once largely Christian, the cause of the Western nations is now to be identified, without further qualification, with the cause of God." The thought that H-bombs could be used to eliminate the Bolshevist threat, as he saw it at least, "may well be one of the apocalyptic temptations of twentieth-century Christendom. It may indeed be the most effective way of destroying Christendom, even though man may survive." But, of course, the chances were good that humankind would *not* survive, that the final result would be mutual annihilation—in which case "the free choice of global suicide, made in desperation by the world's leaders and ratified by the consent and cooperation of their citizens, would be a moral evil second only to the Crucifixion."[7]

It would be a mistake to conclude from this that Merton should be categorized as a "nuclear pacifist" in the narrow sense of being concerned only with wars in which these particular weapons would be employed. Another article. "Target Equals City," expands his concern to include the carefully planned and executed "obliteration" bombings of World War II. Reflecting upon the technological developments and strategic considerations which had laid waste so many cities of Europe, he concludes: "There is no winner, only one winner, in war. The winner is war itself. Not truth, not justice, not liberty, not morality. These are the vanquished. War wins, reducing them to complete submission."[8]

So thoroughgoing a repudiation of war—one might almost be tempted to call it "pacifist"—finds repeated expression in his writings of this period. Citing the appeals of President Kennedy, John XXIII, and Paul VI, he defines "the task of man and the Church" as nothing less than "to end all wars, to provide a satisfactory international power to police the world and subdue violence while conflicts are settled by reason and negotiation." Humankind, he finds, is the victim of a "fatal addiction to war"; like the alcoholic who can always find some reason for taking another drink, even when he knows it may destroy him, he is incapable of seeing (or seeking) a constructive alternative to war.[9] Nor is this addiction limited to those who are certifiably mad. If anything, the reverse is true as he notes bitterly in a "Devout Meditation in Memory of Adolf Eichman." "It is the sane ones, the well-adapted ones, who can without qualms and without nausea aim the missiles and press the buttons that will initiate the great festival of destruction that they, *the sane ones*, have prepared.... When the missiles take off, then, *it will be no mistake.*"[10]

But again, strange though it may seem, Merton continued to be chary of being tagged with the pacifist label. The opening statement of that same "Peace and Protest" article is a disclaimer: "If a pacifist is one who believes that all war is always morally wrong and always has been wrong, then I am not a pacifist." His lengthy and scholarly commentary on the encyclical *Pacem in Terris*[11] refers to "religious ambiguities in the term 'pacifism' [which] give it implications that are somewhat less than Catholic." Pacifist or not, however, he could not confine his writings to the purely theological discussions of traditional "just war" morality or even to the application of those principles to a hypothetical future nuclear war. For there was an actual war already in progress in Vietnam, and a goodly portion of his writings were necessarily devoted to that.

In one respect, of course, the Indochina conflict could be seen as an effective refutation of Merton's insistence upon the inevitability of nuclear escalation. After all, this was a war of more than ten years' duration, one in which a major power with the most awesome array of nuclear weapons at its disposal found itself obliged to contend with a fearfully mounting toll of casualties and little or nothing to show in the way of progress toward victory over an obviously outclassed opponent. Moreover, even when, despite all the face-saving rhetoric, the situation degenerated and defeat was imminent, the nuclear sword remained sheathed. Whether this show of restraint was due to a humane decision to spare the suffering Vietnamese the horrors and devastation that could have been unleashed (a doubtful premise when one considers the patent inhumanity of the "conventional" means that were employed) or due to the prudent fear of possible retaliation (by Hanoi's allies) upon which most theories of nuclear deterrence are based, the simple fact is that Merton's dire expectations were not validated by the fact.

Too much should not be made of this, if only because the possibility of a final and potentially fatal escalation was never excluded altogether. From time to time voices, including some prominent voices uncomfortably close to the seats of power, could be heard counseling just such action. True, the proposals usually concerned tactical weapons, those "little" battlefield atomic shells capable of carrying a destructive potential far beyond that of the "original child bomb" exploded over Hiroshima. Still, it would strain credulity to assume that there were no serious contingency plans for strategic bombings as well, designed, to use a famous general's less than felicitious phrase, to bomb them "back to the Stone Age."

It is unlikely that we will ever know for sure how close the world might have come to Armageddon had it not been for the anti-war movement and the public pressures it was able to mount against the nation's political and military leaders to dissuade them from any plans they may have had to achieve victory through annihilation. As we have already noted, Merton earned his share of credit for contributing to that movement. The Catholic "peace conspiracy" which provided such a dramatic flair to the resistance drew some of its inspiration, perhaps even some of its direction, from Merton's teachings and writings. If, as it would appear, he had some misgivings about the proliferating actions of the Fathers Berrigan and their following, there was never any question about his wholehearted support for their objective, the speediest possible end to the disastrous conflict.

His preface to a Vietnamese edition of *No Man Is an Island* stresses the difficulty of addressing a book written to deal with personal problems of individuals in a nation at peace to its new audience of readers who had already endured a quarter century and more of war. "A purely individualistic inner life, unconcerned for the sufferings of others, is unreal. Therefore my meditation on love and peace must be realistically and intimately related to the fury of war, bloodshed, burning, destruction, killing that takes place on the other side of the earth." The tragedy and the broader threat it contained were recognized as well. "Whatever may be the political issues, the rights and the wrongs, soldiers are fighting, men are killing one another, and their death tells me that 'no man is an island.' The war in Vietnam is a bell tolling for the whole world, warning the whole world that war may spread everywhere and violent death may sweep over the entire earth."[12]

There was another dimension to Merton's Vietnam concerns that cannot be overlooked. In the course of his spiritual studies and writing he had developed a profound interest in, and attraction to, the religions of the East and their practices, especially those of a contemplative nature. He became something of a specialist in Buddhism, particularly the Zen variety, and this led him into an extensive correspondence with Buddhist scholars and Zen masters. Because of this he was able to view the conflict from a perspective closer to that of the Vietnamese themselves, not only in its political meanings and manifestations (though that was important, too), but, in a more fundamental sense, in its moral and philosophical overtones for those most directly involved. A most touching expression of this spiritual affinity marks his appeal on behalf of Thich Nhat Hanh, a Buddhist monk who had toured the United States as a spokesman for a "Third Force" solution to the war. Because of this activity under pacifist auspices there was reason to fear that he would suffer severe reprisals upon his return to Vietnam. Merton's appeal praises his "brother" for "bearing witness to the spirit of Zen" and concludes

I have said Nhat Hanh is my brother, and it is true. We are both monks, and we have lived the monastic life about the same number of years. We are both poets, both existentialists. I have far more in common with Nhat Hanh than I have with many Americans, and I do not hesitate to say it. It is vitally important that such bonds be admitted. They are the bonds of a new solidarity and a new brotherhood which is beginning to be evident on all the five continents and which cuts across all political, religious and cultural lines to unite young men and women in every country in something that is more concrete than an ideal and more alive than a program. This unity of the young is the only hope of the world. In its name I appeal for Nhat Hanh. Do what you can for him. If I mean something to you, then let me put it in this way: do for Nhat Hanh whatever you would do for me if I were in his position. In many ways I wish I were.[13]

The end of hostilities in Vietnam did not completely close that particular issue. Some loose ends remain to be tied, and I am confident that Merton, if he were alive, would still be involved. There is little doubt, for instance, that he would be doing what he could to obtain full amnesty for the draft resisters and deserters forced into exile by their unwillingness to serve in a war which they, and he, considered unjust and immoral. He would welcome the support for amnesty expressed in recent statements issued on behalf of the American Catholic hierarchy; but at the same time he would deplore the cautious tone of that support and its implied limitations—to say nothing of the almost total absence of any real effort to translate that support into effective action to persuade the responsible authorities to follow through on those recommendations.

My confidence on this score is based on Merton's admiration for Franz Jaegerstaetter, the Austrian peasant martyred for his refusal to serve in the Nazi armies, and the lesson he drew from that about "the responsibility of those who help men to form their conscience—or fail to do so." As he saw it, "the real question raised by the Jaegerstaetter story is not merely that of the individual Catholic's right to conscientous objection (admitted in practice even by those who completely disagreed with Jaegerstaetter) but the question of the Church's own mission of protest and prophecy in the gravest spiritual crisis man has ever known."[14] The relevance of that question to the whole Vietnam experience and to the issue of amnesty should require no further elaboration.

The broader reference to the Church's mission of protest and prophecy does deserve some further comment however. Merton once went so far as to thank God that he (Merton, that is) was not a sociologist; yet in many respects his insights were profoundly sociological. This reference is one such case. To the sociologist Religion and the Polity (more familiarly identified in this context, perhaps, as Church and State) are two of the major social institutions and, as such, are locked into a complicated pattern of reciprocal relationships. Some of these are mutually supportive in nature; others are competitive and sometimes strain toward outright conflict. In the normal course of affairs, social peace and stability are best served when all institutions work together in friendly concert, recognizing what the Scholastic political philosophers have established as "the principle of subsidiarity." It is not surprising, therefore, that there is much in Church teaching and tradition devoted to creating and preserving that image of "right order": the emphasis given, for instance, to "obedience to legitimate authority" and, at least as the pacifist sees it, the introduction and elaboration of the "just war" morality itself.

Although, in theory at least (and occasionally in practice as well), the other side of the relationship is never dismissed completely, there is a tendency to de-emphasize or, when convenient, suspend the Church's potential as a source of dissent or even disobedience. In modern times, as the power of the secular authority has grown, religious authorities have been loath to oppose the State except when forced to resist direct intrusions upon the Church's rights and operations. What Merton is suggesting is that the religious leadership must become more sensitive to the obligation to oppose any acts of the secular power which threaten to transgress the limits of morality and violate the rights of others as well—and to be ready to marshal the faithful to effective protest in such situations.

This prophetic mission, needless to say, extended to other social issues which concerned him as well. His treatment of the racial problem in the United States and his strong protests against the economic exploitation of the underprivileged at home and abroad stressed the responsibility of Christians to take a stand against these evils. Nevertheless it is given most consistent emphasis in his writings on war and nuclear armament. It finds expression in his impatience with rigid theological formulations which justify shooting the improvident neighbor who would dare force his way into the family shelter during a nuclear attack—the impatience not so much a rejection of the principles or the reasoning but, rather, a criticism of the failure to take a more fully Christian view of the situation. "The hour is extremely grave," he wrote. "The guarded statements of moral theologians are a small matter compared to the constant deluge of irresponsible opinions, criminal half-truths and murderous images disseminated by the mass media. *This problem is going to be solved in our thoughts, in our spirit or not at all.* It is because the minds of men have become what they have become that the world is poised on the brink of total disaster. Those of us who can help in some feeble way to guide and educate consciences must take account of this fact, or also the consequences may be frightful. They may be frightful anyway, but at least we must take stock of our situation and strive as far as possible to reorientate ourselves in the light of conditions that often make theological solutions of moral cases pitifully inadequate."[15]

In what appears to have been the first major publication following the lifting of the restrictions imposed upon him, Merton addressed himself to the "black revolution" then in progress and to the world crisis. Of particular interest, however, is the introductory note in which he sets forth his justification for one committed to the monastic and contemplative state to concern himself with the problems and issues of the secular world he presumably had "left" behind. Obviously speaking for himself, he declared it was precisely his status as a monk that put him under "a solemn obligation of conscience at this moment in history to take the positions developed in the pages that follow" (most of which, it is appropriate to note, had been circulated privately in their *samidzat* version). Moreover, those obligations were derived from his monastic vows of poverty and—interestingly enough when one considers the circumstances to which he must have been referring—obedience. The key, again, is eschatological and prophetic: "The adversary is not time, not history, but the evil will and the accumulated inheritance of past untruth and past sin. This evil the monk must see. He must even denounce it, if others fail to do so."[16]

Prophecy and protest come together in what may ultimately prove to be Merton's most significant contribution to Catholic thought and behavior, his extensive writings on the theory and practice of non-violence. It should be unnecessary to stress again that *all* of Merton's writings, even those most specifically addressed to on-going social issues and controversies, were essentially "spiritual writings" in their concentration upon the development and proper applications of Christian principles and values in each particular context. If one can discern a shift of emphasis in those dealing with war and peace—the earlier articles being more heavily spiritual and theological in content than the later—it was never so complete as to risk diminishing or ignoring the moral and theological bases for the positions advanced.

There is no danger of that in the case he makes for non-violence, for the priority given to its religious and philosophical foundations is never in doubt. To Merton non-violence is first and always a matter of personal commitment and must involve the individual's total orientation to life; non-violence as tactic is a secondary, almost incidental, consideration. In this sense he is the classic Gandhian, perhaps more so even than was true of Martin Luther King and the other leaders of the non-violent civil rights movement. A little volume of exerpts from Gandhi's writings published in 1964 includes a twenty-page essay exploring in detail the relevance and meaning of the Mahatma and his works for Western humankind and Christianity. Taken by itself it provides a valuable introductory or refresher course and a corrective for some of the misconceptions that have gained currency in recent years.

As one would expect, Merton, the contemplative who devoted so much of his scholarly and spiritual attention to Eastern monastic traditions, was most impressed by the extent to which Gandhi's quest for truth had led him along the same path from the opposite direction. Gandhi neither accepted Christianity nor rejected it; instead, Merton noted, he took all that Christian thought seemed to offer of relevance to him as Hindu. The process, then, is not one of conversion but, rather, rediscovery and amplification:

> ...through the spiritual traditions of the West, he, an Indian, discovered his Indian heritage and with it his own "right mind." And in his fidelity to his own heritage and its spiritual sanity, he was able to show men of the West and of the whole world a way to recover their own "right mind" in their own tradition, thus manifesting the fact that there are certain indisputable and essential values—religious, ethical, ascetic, spiritual, and philosophical—which man has everywhere needed and which he has in the past managed to acquire, values without which he cannot live, values which are now in large measure lost to him so that, unequipped to face life in a fully human manner, he now runs the risk of destroying himself entirely.[17]

Merton, of course, did not "discover" non-violence and its implications for the Catholic Christian. For many years already, readers of the *Catholic Worker*, of which he was one, had been familiar with the contributions of other writers, Catholic and Protestant (though, regrettably, more of the latter than the former), who had dedicated themselves to bringing Gandhi's message and example to the Christian West. Merton's special contribution—and to say this is not to detract from the depth of his analysis and the profound insights he drew from Gandhi's teachings—lay in the scope and character of the audience he was able to reach. His readers were not the "ordinary" or, to use Fichter's classification, "model" Catholics; rather, they were more likely to be the type of educated Catholic whose interests ran more to spiritual readings of a more abstract and "intellectual" character than to the simpler pieties usually associated with weekly parish sermons or the instructional columns of the diocesan press. "Elitist" though the distinction may be, such readers, once they had been exposed by their own choice to the guidance and influence of Merton's writings, were more likely to carry that influence into the opinion-forming levels of the Catholic community. By the same token, others in the religious life who might have considered it "unseemly" for a monk to involve himself in public controversy on questions related to nuclear arms or other aspects of the nation's foreign or defense policies would be much more open to a treatise promoting so clearly "moral" (albeit a bit too "perfectionist" perhaps) a cause as non-violence.

In both cases Merton would be reaching informed and influential individuals and opinion leaders who would otherwise not have given much serious thought to non-violence as a *Catholic* option, however familiar they may have been with the Gandhi struggle for Indian independence or with the Quaker and other "peace church" advocates of non-violence as the way to a world without war. They may even have respected and admired both, but it required someone of Merton's acknowledged status and reputation within the Catholic community to open the doors and minds that would otherwise have remained tightly locked.

As already indicated, Merton was a "purist" in the Gandhi tradition. This meant that the necessary rediscovery of Western man's "right mind" called for much more than the tactical, media-conscious demonstrations that became the fashion in the struggles for racial justice in the South and an end to the conflict in Indochina. Like Gandhi, he was prepared to make allowance for situations in which violent resistance would be permissible as the only alternative to passive acquiescence to evil,[18] but this should not be interpreted to mean that his commitment to non-violence was pragmatically selective or weak. This is made inescapably clear in "Blessed Are the Meek,"[19] his fullest and most compelling exposition of the case for non-violence.

The perspective, again, is explicitly eschatological: "Christian non-violence is nothing if not first of all a formal profession of faith in the Gospel message that the *Kingdom has been established* and that the Lord of truth is indeed risen and reigning over his Kingdom."[20] The stress throughout is on the *positive*, non-violence as a witness to truth, rather than on the simple avoidance of violence as a means to achieve some end or as a response to violence directed against oneself. Proceeding from that fundamental principle, the essay explores seven related precepts ranging from practical instruction (the need to avoid becoming either too wrapped up in political means or being apolitical to the point of becoming ineffective or merely symbolic) to the insistence upon what might be described as ideological purity (the "absolute refusal of evil or suspect means"; openness to the adversary's point of view; perfect reliance upon Christian hope and humility) on the part of the non-violent resister.

Two points demand amplification if only because they are so crucial to Merton's position and constitute stumbling blocks to many who might otherwise be in full agreement with him. The first involves that willingness to learn from the adversary and, even more difficult in practice, the need to avoid seeing that adversary in purely negative terms—i.e., as totally inhumane, wrong, unreasonable, etc. On no account, Merton insists, is Christian non-violence to encourage or excuse hatred of a special class, nation, or social group. It follows from this that the object must never be merely to prevail or prove one's own rightness and virtue. Instead, the sincere practitioner of non-violence is obliged to deny himself "the psychological gratification of upsetting the adversary's conscience and perhaps driving him to an act of bad faith and refusal of the truth."[21]

This imposed concern for reaching the adversary and joining with him in the search for the truth (which, it may turn out, is as much his truth as ours) is not easy to achieve and maintain. To some extent it was the failure to meet that test which caused Merton to express misgivings about some acts of civil disobedience which, as he put it, "merely antagonize the adversary without making him willing to communicate in any way whatever, except with bullets or missiles." Displays which do little more than ease the personal frustration of the one protesting are to be seen as manifestations of despair, more an evidence of weakness than the moral strength non-violence requires. There is criticism, too, of those who give in to the temptation to get publicity and quick results by spectacular tricks or forms of protest. In one of his letters he scoffed at the notion of swimming out to a nuclear submarine with an anti-war banner clenched between one's teeth, and, in a much more serious vein, at one point he was ready to dissociate himself from the Catholic Peace Fellowship when a young supporter took the extreme step of immolating himself by fire in protest against the war in Vietnam. On the other hand, he supported Dorothy Day and others in their public violation of New York's civil defense regulations and was so favorably inclined toward the proposal that the U.S. and the U.S.S.R. exchange voluntary "hostages" that he would have liked to participate in that program himself if it could have been arranged.

The Berrigan-style actions, understandably enough, presented something of a personal problem because of his close association with the participants. In commenting upon them, he voiced concern that they were a sign that the peace movement was at the point of escalating beyond peaceful protest—"in which case it may be escalating into self-contradiction."[22] As far as the blood-pouring action of the Baltimore (Catonsville) Nine was concerned, he felt that line had not been crossed, but the explanation of his reasoning leaves the definite impression that he was somewhat more critical than approving. His reaction to the subsequent actions in Chicago, Milwaukee, and all the other locales is not a matter of public record. If one refers to the principles set forth in his basic essay, however, it is possible to conclude that his reaction would almost surely have shifted toward disapproval. Such actions, once they threatened to degenerate into ritual performances, would not meet the conditions developed there. "Non-violence must simply avoid the ambiguity of an unclear and *confusing protest* that hardens the war-makers in their self-righteous blindness. This means in fact that *in this case above all* [i.e. the non-violent struggle for peace] *non-violence must avoid a facile and fanatical self-righteousness,* and refrain from being satisfied with dramatic self-justifying gestures."[23]

The second of the two strumbling blocks mentioned

earlier may be even more difficult to understand and accept. It is Merton's insistence upon a detached attitude toward immediate and visible results or the prospects for success. These represent "the most insidious temptation," a "fetishism" having far too much in common with the world's fixation upon political techniques backed by force as the method by which problems of any kind are to be solved. It is not that he is totally indifferent to the outcome of non-violent efforts, but concern over success or failure must not be given precedence over the search for the truth which alone matters. Simply stated, "The chief difference between non-violence and violence is that the latter depends entirely on its own calculation. The former depends entirely on God and His word."[24]

This theme is given prominence in what proved to be his last public statement on peace, a brief message to the 1968 Tivoli meeting of the American PAX Society. The subject was "Peace and Revolution," and he took the occasion to warn against those who are "content to express our weak convictions in weak and provisional terms, meanwhile waiting for an opportunity to abandon nonviolence altogether and go over to the side of force, on the ground that we have tried nonviolence and found it wanting." His answer to this suggests a gentle rebuke to all who, however deep their commitment to the cause of social justice and peace, permitted themselves to be seduced by the temptations of success as measured in pragmatic terms and given expression in the slogan and anthem that had come to characterize the civil rights and anti-Vietnam crusades.

> Has non-violence been found wanting? Yes and no. It has been found wanting whenever it has been the non-violence of the weak. It has not been found so when it has been the non-violence of the strong. What is the difference? It is a difference of language. The language of spurious non-violence is merely another, more equivocal form of the language of power. It is a different method of expressing one's will to power. It is used and conceived pragmatically, in reference to the seizure of power. But

that is not what non-violence is about. Non-violence is not for power but for truth. It is not pragmatic but prophetic. It is not aimed at immediate political results, but at the manifestation of fundamental and crucially important truth. Non-violence is not primarily the language of efficacy, but the language of *kairos*. It does not say "We shall overcome" so much as "This is the day of the Lord, and whatever may happen to us, *He* shall overcome."[25]

III

It is obvious from what has gone before that Merton's contributions to the cause of peace are significant enough to stand by themselves. If one presumes to assess or elaborate upon them, it is not so much to add to that significance as to put them in the context of the present to determine which speak most directly to today's Christians. One issue, the war in Vietnam, has been resolved by the termination of hostilities, though, as mentioned earlier, some residues of that "overwhelming atrocity," as he put it, remain—the questions of amnesty and suitable reparations for the Vietnamese victims, for instance—and would be matters of continuing concern for him.

Other issues still await their resolution. The threat of nuclear war and the proliferation of the weapons which give that threat substance was what inspired his earliest writings in this area, and, if anything, the problem has gained new and compelling urgency in the decade since his death. That he would be active in support of groups like the Catholic Peace Fellowship and Pax Christi with their programs calling for nuclear (not to mention general) disarmament is certain. What is open to some question is whether, now that it is no longer a "scandal" to oppose these weapons since even popes and presidents have joined those demanding total abolition, this issue would still hold its position of prominence among his many concerns. After all, his would now be but one voice in a popular chorus. True, the fact that the chorus was there is due in part to his own prophetic call, but this would only be further encouragement to him to concentrate his efforts elsewhere.

One such objective worthy of his and the Church's prophetic mission was already defined in a number of his earlier writings: the total abolition of war itself. The Vietnam experience, as well as the "newer" indiscriminate forms of guerrilla war (and, of course, the equally indiscriminate forms of official reprisal) have intensified the need for a thorough and radical re-evaluation of the traditional morality of war and the veneer of credibility it lent to the concept of a "just" war. I am convinced that Merton would be in the vanguard of those involved in developing that "entirely new attitude" toward war called for by the Vatican Council and might even have overcome the reservations and reticence which kept him from endorsing a more pacifist posture. Others will protest this interpretation as the product of my own pacifist bias, but I base it on the judgment that, to all intents and purposes, he was already a pacifist—albeit a reluctant pacifist—in his later writings. Today the need to come to terms with our world of garrison states and permanent war would make it difficult indeed for him to maintain the barriers which "in theory" dissuaded him from making that fuller commitment.

However that may be, I do not think this debate either would hold top priority among his interests and concerns. Instead of devoting himself to academic considerations of if or when such a thing as a "just war" could conceivably exist, his major emphasis would be given to finding or creating viable alternatives to war. This is to say that the contribution he would rank highest were he making this assessment would almost certainly be the introduction to a broader Catholic audience of the principles and prospects of non-violence as *the* authentic Christian witness for our time. Gains have been made, of course. Non-violence as an option and especially as a tactic is recognized and respected; unfortunately, it is still not regarded as a practical or "really effective" response to violence or the threat of violence. Nor, he would be the first to insist, is its truly prophetic nature and potential understood.

In a very real sense it is here where all the strands of theological and spiritual commitment which blind all of Merton's writings, but especially those dealing with war and peace, into a consistent whole find their clearest expression: the moral indictment of our "post-Christian" era; the call for total abandonment to God's promises with full reliance upon hope, humility, and the saving power of truth; above all, the sensitivity to the eschatological implications of the moment and the behavior it asks of those who would claim to be the followers of Christ:

> The moral evil in the world is due to man's alienation from the deepest truth, from the springs of spiritual life within himself, to his alienation from God. Those who realize this try desperately to persuade and enlighten their brothers. But we are in a radically different position from the first Christians, who revolutionized an essentially religious world of paganism with the message of a new religion that had never been heard of. We are on the contrary living in an irreligious world in which the Christian message has been repeated over and over until it has come to seem empty of all intelligible content to those whose ears close to the word of God even before it is uttered. Christianity is no longer identified with newness and change, but only with the static preservation of outworn structures.[26]

By itself so grim a diagnosis could offer reason enough for despair, but Merton, of course, would have none of that. Instead, the seeming hopelessness of the situation serves to highlight other passages in his writings which give expression to the unshakable confidence that not only are the spiritual resources at hand by which those weaknesses and failings can be reversed but that, viewed from the perspective of eternal design, the contest is already over and the victory won. It is this confidence which permeates his opposition to war and his commitment to peace and non-violence and which, in the last analysis, is the essential message he has left for us:

Faith of course tells us that we live in a time of eschatological struggle, facing a fierce combat which marshals all the forces of evil and darkness against the still-invisible truth, yet this combat is already decided by the victory of Christ over death and over sin. The Christian can renounce the protection of violence and risk being humble, therefore *vulnerable*, not because he trusts in the supposed efficacy of a gentle and persuasive tactic that will disarm hatred and tame cruelty, but because he believes that the hidden power of the Gospel is demanding to be manifested in and through his own poor person. Hence in perfect obedience to the Gospel, he effaces himself and his own interests and even risks his life in order to testify not simply to "the truth" in a sweeping, idealistic and purely platonic sense, but to the truth that is incarnate in a concrete human situation, involving living persons whose rights are denied or whose lives are threatened.[27]

NOTES

1. Gordon Zahn (ed.), *Thomas Merton on Peace* (N.Y.: McCalls, 1971). For the most part quotations to be used in this essay will be taken from this volume with the title abbreviated to *TMP*. It should be noted, too, that several of the articles included in that volume were published in more than one magazine and sometimes in slightly different form.

2. Thomas Merton, *New Seeds of Contemplation* (N.Y.: New Directions, 1961), p. 119.

3. Both were published by New Directions. It is perhaps appropriate to note that one of the "twelve views" was contributed by the present writer at Merton's invitation. If memory serves, that invitation was the beginning of the correspondence that would continue sporadically between us until his death.

4. An amusing sidelight in this connection is the evidence in some of his correspondence of the time that he was quite unfamiliar with so eminent (and conservative) a peace organization as the non-denominational Fellowship of Reconciliation; later, of course, he would have close and continuing contact with the organization and its leaders and would become a sponsor of the Catholic Peace Fellowship founded under FOR auspieces.

5. Quoted by Thomas Cornell, *National Catholic Reporter* (April 8, 1977), p. 18.

6. Merton, "Nuclear War and Christian Responsibility," *Commonweal*, v. 75; 509-13; response and rejoinder, *ibid.*, 76: 84-85.

7. Merton, "Peace: A Religious Responsibility," *TMP*, pp. 114, 124.

8. *Ibid.*, pp. 94-102.

9. "Peace and Protest: A Statement," *ibid.*, p. 67.

10. *Ibid.*, p. 161. Emphasis his.

11. "The Christian in World Crisis: Reflections on the Moral Climate of the 1960's," *ibid.*, pp. 20-62.

12. *Ibid.*, p. 64.

13. "Nhat Hanh Is My Brother," *ibid.*, p. 263.

14. "An Enemy of the State," *ibid.*, p. 138.

15. "The Machine Gun in the Fallout Shelter," *ibid.*, p. 106.

16. Merton, *Seeds of Destruction* (N.Y.: Farrar, Straus & Giroux, 1967), pp. 8-9.

17. Merton, "Gandhi and the One-Eyed Giant," introduction to *Gandhi on Non-Violence* (N.Y.: New Directions, 1964), p. 4.

18. In the shelter controversy, for example, he was willing to grant that "even the proponent of nonviolence will allow that in practice a man might use force to protect the safety of his family in a fall-out shelter, assuming that he was not able to solve the problem in a legitimately nonviolent manner." *TMP*, p. 104.

19. "Blessed Are The Meek: The Christian Roots of Non-Violence," *ibid.*, pp. 208-18.

20. *Ibid.*, p. 211. Emphasis his.

21. *Ibid.*, p. 208.

22. "Note for Ave Maria," *ibid.*, pp. 231-233.

23. *Ibid.*, p. 213.

24. *Ibid.*, p. 216.

25. *Ibid.*, p. 75.

26. "Christian Action in World Crisis," *ibid.*, p. 222.

27. *Ibid.*, p. 211.

The Controversial Merton

John Howard Griffin

On the morning of February 24, 1965, Thomas Merton walked down the hill from his hermitage to the monastery to catch a ride into Louisville to see a dermatologist. He suffered from a skin condition that caused his hands to crack and open up, leaving holes that made it painful for him to work. One of the brothers in the gatehouse greeted him in Trappist sign language and told him how glad he was that the man who had come to the monastery to kill Father Merton had been subdued and taken away.

Merton learned that a visitor, outraged by the monk's writings on racism and peace, had gone berserk earlier that morning, produced a pistol and announced that he was going to assassinate Thomas Merton. Monks had disarmed him and called authorities who sent him to a mental hospital. Moments later, when Merton picked up his mail, he found several abusive letters protesting his involvement in matters of peace and justice.

The monk returned that evening to his hermitage wearing the white dermal gloves the doctor had prescribed. Alone in his cabin in the forest, he listened to rain pour against his windows and thought peacefully of death. He accepted the possibility that some madman might eventually find his way up to the hermitage and take his life. He sat at his desk and wrote in his journal with a blue fountain pen. He noted that if his life were to end in a violent way he was glad to accept it from God's hand if God would give him the grace to die in a manner pleasing to him.[1] He saw his hermitage as the place God had provided, and he wrote that he could imagine no greater joy than to have such a cabin in which to be at peace, to think and write, to listen to the wind and all the voices of the woods, to struggle with this new anguish, to prepare for his death and his exodus to the heavenly country, to love his brothers in community and all people, and to pray for the whole world—for peace and good sense among men.[2]

At the beginning of his book *Raids on the Unspeakable*, Thomas Merton cited a key passage from Gabriel Marcel: "Today the first and perhaps the only duty of the philosopher is to defend man against himself: to defend man against that extraordinary temptation toward inhumanity to which— almost without being aware of it—so many humans today have yielded."[3]

On his own, the middle-aged monk had gradually arrived at the same conclusion and had written extensively and courageously about most of the "controversial" themes that illuminated that "extraordinary temptation toward inhumanity" and the general dehumanization that resulted from yielding to that temptation. It took courage in those days to speak independently about issues such as racism, monastic reform, human rights, nuclear proliferation, and human freedom from programming—all those issues on which criticism or even analysis could and still can so exacerbate partisan emotions. Most of these were issues about which a contemplative monk might ordinarily remain safely silent, but Father Merton followed his conscience and his insights, and it cost him much in the way of esteem. True, many saw hope in his voice and viewed him as a prophetic spokesman. But many others who might admire his "spiritual" writings came to consider him a radical, a subversive, and the greatest of social sinners, "a troublemaker," because of his more controversial writing.

Merton personally disliked controversy as much as anyone I have ever known. Yet he had those remarkable insights that made him see deeper than most of us, and in conscience he had to speak out, even when it produced the hostility that hurt him deeply. Dom Helder Camara refers to such people as the "Abrahamic Minority." Dr. Viktor Frankl speaks of them as "the decent, human or humane ones who will always remain an absolute minority"—that minority of men and women throughout history who have seen deeply and who have struggled against the forces of dehumanization with a sense of overwhelming urgency precisely because so few others were aware of what was happening or cared enough to do anything about it.

In "Rain and the Rhinoceros," Merton observed: "Only the man who has fully attained his own spiritual identity can live without the need to kill, and without the need of a spiritual doctrine that permits him to do so in good conscience. There will always be a place, says Ionesco, *'for those isolated consciences who have stood up for the universal conscience'* as against the mass mind."[4]

He also said, toward the end of his life, "If you are going to be yourself, you are not going to fit anybody else's mystique." This is a most profound clue to his independence, and one of the reasons why his friends, co-religionists and even his colleagues in the Abrahamic Minority sometimes judged him incorrectly. Before you could be yourself, however, Merton felt you had to take the time alone to become yourself, to face yourself in your fundamental reality, and to peel away the accretions of mediocre or false values imposed by society, ambition and self-interest. Only then, as the overflow of such contemplation, could you find your truth and your reality. "We still carry this burden of illusion because we dare not lay it down. We suffer all the needs that society demands we suffer, because if we do not have these needs we lose our 'usefulness' in society—the usefulness of suckers. We fear to be alone, and to be ourselves, and so to remind others of the truth that is in them."[5]

I recall a young priest from Mississippi who visted the monastery of Gethsemani at the same time I did in the early 1960's. This priest spoke with Merton and me about his torment over the segregation of the churches in his area. "I know it's wrong," he said. "Sometimes I can hardly face myself in the mirror in the mornings for going along with it. What can I do?"

"Don't do a damned thing," Merton replied sympathetically. "Just take the time to become what you profess to be. Then you will know what to do."

This meant taking the time to become fully himself in all his truth before deciding on an action. The monk implied, too, that the young priest had to arrive at decisions of such gravity within himself. Having lived through the days of the Nazi oppression of Jewish people, having seen racism at close hand in this country, having witnessed the establishment's suppression and character assassination of those who opposed America's involvement in the Vietnam war as well as those involved in the struggles for human rights, Merton realized that ethics based on consensus (so easily manipulated) and expedience, rather than on principle, produced societies of a monolithic mediocrity that always sought to destroy what they could not encompass.

The decision to face reprisals for the good of those who would persecute him had to be a person's own. Merton would not make such decisions for others, nor would he judge those who simply could not make the sacrifices; and he commiserated deeply with those who attempted the sacrifice and caved in when reprisals were brought against them.

His fidelity to his particular and individual vocation was perhaps the most difficult thing for many to understand, including those whom he supported. Many activists felt that Father Louis should move out of the cloister and into the streets "where the action was" (and they could be quite obnoxious in telling him so). We were in the "real world," they seemed to think, which at least implied that the monk was not. Many activists, those of us who were in the streets, however, understood and treasured Merton's vocation—it helped us to persevere when so many were dropping away. I have often said that we could not have done what we did without dedicated souls in monasteries and convents to back us up. Merton was anchored in reality, and we looked to him to help us keep our balance and our sense of reality. Many of us, including contributors to this volume, could vouch that when desperate times came, when we seemed to be accomplishing nothing, when we were calumniated and threatened and tempted to give up, Father Louis and others like him salvaged us. We were not salvaged by the strategists or the sociologists but by men and women of highly advanced spiritual dimensions. His letter to Jim Forest,[6] quoted elsewhere in this volume, is an excellent example of his orientation in these matters. His fidelity to his contemplative vocation was therefore a critically important help to those of us in the active life to remain faithful in our vocations. Hopefully our work meshed with his. Many of us, I know, felt that we were involved in little more than emergency work to hold off a holocaust, but that the real, long-term civilizing and rehumanizing work was to be done by the artists, the thinkers, the prophets and the saints.

Alas, however, too many who made a religion of the "active life" sought to become Merton's conscience, to tell him what he ought to do and be. They wanted him to fit their own mystique. It is an understandable temptation. We were "on the scene" and knew what needed to be done and ached to have all the help in the world in accomplishing this or that good. Our temptation was to ask Merton to become less than he was by concentrating him in our area of activism, by converting him from a person of universal viewpoint to one of particular viewpoint. He saw the patterns from a greater perspective and therefore with greater wisdom. We did not always realize that.

For example, in February 1967 he received a letter from Rosemary Ruether, the theologian, challenging his solitude. Although Father Louis felt that she did not understand his vocation, he remarked that she was "very Barthian," and he felt a fundamental Christian honesty in her attitudes.

As the correspondence continued, the monk observed in his 1967 journal that Dr. Ruether was the most fiercely antimonastic person he knew, but he considered her letters an important stimulus to his thinking. He believed her antipathy for monasticism sprang from the claim, "which no monk in his right mind would make in that way," that the monk was the only true and radical Christian. He saw this as a valid problem since historically the claim had been made and supported, with certain qualifications, that lay people were good Christians insofar as they adopted a quasimonastic spirituality.

On the other hand, he wrote, Rosemary Ruether seemed to be claiming quite aggressively that she represented the true radical Christianity, and on the basis of her own authenticity "she is entitled to reject us—which makes the whole thing a little laughable."

This led him to wonder if "a special kind of hellishness" went with the very claim to be a radical and perfect Christian. He noted that history was full of examples, including monastic ones, of intolerance, heresy, cruelty and love of power—all based on the claim to radical perfection. And he found the same thing to be true often among political radicals.

If such criticism challenged and stimulated the monk, it also was felt as an intrusion, and sometimes a heavy one, on his own interior and personal freedom. He knew and experienced the existence of truths that had nothing to do with arguments, suppositions and proofs. He wearied of explaining what could not really be explained.

That night the monk sat on the porch of his cabin until darkness came. He refused, for the moment, to "rationalize anything, explain anything or comment on anything," except what was there. He was there. Fireflies, stars, darkness, the woods, the vague dark valley, "and nothing, nothing, nothing" else.

In his journal, the monk describes walking inside to his sleeping room where he knelt by the cot and gazed at the ikon of the nativity that hung on the pitted grey wall dimly illuminated by lamplight. He asked himself what there was to look for or to yearn for except all reality "here and now in whatever I am."

All of this implied a side of Merton little known or understood by his critics—his belief in the quest for true interior freedom. Freedom meant a willingness to realize and experience his life as "totally absurd" (his own expression) in relation to the apparent meaning which has been thrown over life by society and by illusion. But that could only be a starting point, he noted, leading to a deeper realization of that reality in himself and in all life. This implied the capacity to see that *realizing* and *knowing* are not the same. For Father Louis, solitude itself was the fullness of realization. He wrote: "In solitude I become *fully able to realize what I cannot know*."[7]

Dan Berrigan refers to people such as Merton as our

"readers of clues." One realizes now, over the perspective of years, that Merton could not have read the clues right if he had compromised his vision. Berrigan refers to them as the "resolute saints" in our midst, those with a simple resolve "to read things right, to tell the truth."[8] In this, Berrigan is not referring specifically to professed religious, but to those in whatever station of life who make up the Abrahamic Minority.

You had to be involved in Merton's deeds to know what he was doing—how little he lived in some alleged "ivory tower" and how deeply he lived in the sufferings of others. I once wrote publicly somewhere, and it still holds true today, that he had the deepest sense of empathy with the oppressed and the bullied that I had ever encountered. His writings on the dehumanization that occurs in all racist suppression of minorities, on the black revolution, on the plight of native peoples, on nuclear proliferation, and on the holocaust give ample witness to that.

But all of this would be only half of the picture. It would be meaningless if he had not also been concerned with the oppressors of the oppressed—the dehumanization of the oppressor groups, the terrible danger to the whole people of rationalizing injustice, the tragedy of inculcating prejudice and therefore violence in our children. His capacity to grasp all the nuances of such wounds—both to oppressors and oppressed—was very nearly infallible. He felt them with a depth I have rarely encountered.

Because he was faithful to his own vision rather than to the visions of dozens of unsolicited and self-appointed "spiritual directors" both to the right and to the left of him, he achieved a wholly unexpected renown. Yet who knows, for example, that he attempted to sell his drawings to set up a scholarship fund in memory of the bombed children of Birmingham, and succeeded with the help of his community. And who knows that he performed an "absurd" act of gratuitous charity in relation to the martyred Clyde Kennard. Very few white people know, but very many black people do. This deserves recounting briefly. Clyde Kennard was a young Mississippi-born black man who after ten years of service with the U.S. armed forces returned to Mississippi to build up a small farm into a thriving business. Having spent three years at the University of Chicago, he sought to enroll for his fourth year at Mississippi Southern University in his hometown of Hattiesburg, Mississippi. This was before James Meredith made his historic attempt to enter the University of Mississippi at Oxford. Every attempt was made by local authorities, even church people, to dissuade Clyde Kennard from this early attempt to enter an all-white university. He would be killed, they said, or at least framed into a long prison sentence. He replied that he could not turn back, explaining it would be an injustice to the children he hoped someday to have. He was arrested on a charge of buying $25 worth of chicken feed that he knew was stolen, given a mockery of a trial, and sentenced to seven years in Parchemin Penitentiary.

After three years of incarceration, we learned he was dying of an untreated cancer. Dr. Martin Luther King, Dick Gregory and I tried to make his plight public, calling it a slow and terrible form of lynching. When Kennard became terminal, he was released and at Dick Gregory's expense flown to Billings General Hospital in Chicago. Lengthy exploratory surgery revealed he was beyond medical help. I left the hospital shortly before the surgery was completed and went to Gethsemani.

Merton met me in the garden just inside the gatehouse, and without any preliminary greeting he looked directly into my face and said, "Tell me about Clyde Kennard."

He stood in the cold afternoon sunlight, dressed in his white monastic robe with a black wool pea cap on his roughly tonsured head and a faded denim jacket, his hands red and rough from work and cold. When I finished telling him, he seemed sick. "What can I do?" he asked.

"Nothing but pray, now," I said.

He left me quietly and returned inside the Abbey. I did not know until years later that he returned to his cell and wrote a brief account of our encounter in his journal. I was thinking of the judge in that Mississippi court who had sentenced Clyde Kennard, and of one of the German judges at the Nuremberg trials. The German judge, at the end, spoke with an American judge, saying, "We never knew it would lead to this horror." And the American judge replied, "It had already led to this the first time you knowingly condemned an innocent man to death."

In his journal notes for that afternoon, Thomas Merton had obviously been thinking along the same lines, for he wrote that the martyrdom of Clyde Kennard "is an evil portent for all of us." He saw it in all of its ramifications as the clue to the existence of unspeakable evil there beneath the surface of our lives.

At dusk Merton returned to my room carrying two versions of the *Hagia Sophia*,[9] one of his works that I particularly loved. One version was simply a mimeographed copy of the long poem. The other was a priceless copy of the Hammer limited edition,[10] already a collector's item. He gave me the mimeographed copy and asked me if I would take the superb Hammer edition copy to Clyde Kennard. It was in many ways a foolish gesture, an "absurd" act—to give such a treasure to a man who was already virtually dead; an act of gratuitous charity so spontaneous it carried the message not only to Clyde Kennard, but to much of the black population of the United States. The message was simple and terribly necessary: in days when racist Christians were an absolute scandal and an alienation to black people, here was a concrete exception; here was at least one who acted according to his beliefs rather than according to his prejudices.

After three years of prison, being denied everything he cherished in the way of books, Clyde Kennard received the gift and clung to it. In his short remaining agony he kept Merton's precious gift clutched to his chest, he died holding it against his chest, and he was buried with it still held to his chest. I was able to write to Father Louis, "Your gift softened his death."

If the story was virtually ignored in the white press, it was carried in detail in the black press. The resonances of this simple act spread outward and kept spreading, tempering at least a little the bitterness of a great many black people. Few other acts by any white person at that time so touched and stirred the gratitude of black America. Clyde Kennard's mother made a statement that was widely repeated throughout the land: Father Louis' gift was one of the few acts of mercy her son had known at the hands of white people during the last agonizing years of his life.

Merton was not a self-advertiser. Those of us who worked in one given area were rarely aware—at least not from him—of what he was doing in other areas. You had to be close to him in one of these areas to perceive what he really did. Thus it was quite easy for those who worked with him in the peace movements to have only an imperfect knowledge of his work in racial justice, even though he and all of us saw all of these as overlapping problems or different facets of the same massive problem of "man's extraordinary temptation toward inhumanity."[11]

If Merton understood that temptation, he also understood the other side of that temptation, mankind's temptation to "do good without God."[12] As he wrote to Jim Forest, warning him against looking for the satisfaction of results: "All the good that you will do will come not from your work or you, but from the fact that you allowed yourself, in the obedience of faith, to be used by God's love.... Think of this more and gradually you will be free from the need to prove yourself and more open to the power that will work through you without your knowing it."[13]

Certainly anyone who has tried to serve in these various areas of rehumanization recognizes a profound truth in the above observation from Merton. We have seen it proved again and again when so many of our good efforts die on the vine. We have all known the "do-gooders" who join every cause and try their hand at everything, but who constantly play out, grow tired, give up and move on to something else. Those who have persevered, battle-scarred, somehow learned fidelity to a love higher than themselves.

When I became too ill to continue work in the active life, Thomas Merton wrote that he felt our problems of social justice and peace were beyond the capacity of human beings to solve and that only God could resolve them: that it was all in God's hands. "In this light, you may now accomplish more in the proper use of your suffering than you ever accomplished in your more active life."

His attitude here was to be understood, of course. He by no means meant that we should simply give up because the solutions were beyond human help, as one reader protested when I quoted this statement somewhere in a newspaper article. He simply meant that the healing of humanity's wounds is a need so vast and complex that all of us have roles to play in any tiny progress that may be made or hoped for, and that we will have continued to contribute so long as we remain faithful to our individual vocations in the general fabric.

Nearly all of the great humanizers of our lifetime—Thomas Merton, Jacques Maritain, Dominique Pire, Gerald Vann, O.P., Catherine de Hueck Doherty, Dorothy Day; the great artists, painters, thinkers, doers; the vast numbers of "resolute saints" in every pocket of poverty, suffering and injustice (and therefore in our midst)—have somehow arrived at these fundamental truths that were clarified for us in Thomas Merton's life and writings: the tremendous necessity of first *being* and then *doing*, and the impossibility of this without the interior freedom to give ourselves entirely to our various vocations for the love of something better than ourselves.

Every single such person has been considered highly controversial and has in some way been martyred by calumny, contempt or worse for the love of fellow human beings.

The bewilderment comes from wondering: "What is controversial in any of this?"

NOTES

1. Thomas Merton, unpublished Journal, 1965, p. 188.
2. *Ibid.*, p. 187.
3. Gabriel Marcel, cited in the frontispiece to Merton, *Raids on the Unspeakable* (N.Y.: New Directions, 1965).
4. Merton, *Raids on the Unspeakable*, p. 22.
5. *Ibid.*

6. Cited in James Forest, "Thomas Merton's Struggle With Peacemaking," in this volume.

7. Merton, unpublished Journal, 1967.

8. Daniel Berrigan, *Uncommon Prayer* (N.Y.: Seabury Press, 1978), p. 24.

9. Subsequently published in Merton, *Emblems of a Season of Fury* (N.Y.: New Directions, 1963), pp. 61-69.

10. A limited edition of sixty-nine autographed, numbered copies of "Hagia Sophia" was hand-printed by Victor Hammer at the Stamperia del Santuccio press in Lexington, Ky. in 1962. They became immediate collector's items.

11. Cf. n. 3 above.

12. Cf. n. 6 above.

13. *Ibid.*

The Struggle
for Racial Justice

Gerald Twomey, C.S.P.

The entry read "Folsom Prison, September 10, 1965." The Black Muslim prisoner stirred in solitary confinement, struggling to fathom the search of another sort of "prisoner" for God. Reflecting on Thomas Merton (and the journey recounted in *The Seven Storey Mountain*), Eldridge Cleaver wrote:

> I could not keep him out of the room. He shouldered his way through the door. Welcome, Brother Merton. I give him a bear hug. Most impressive of all to me was Merton's description of New York's black ghetto—Harlem. I liked it so much I copied out the heart of it longhand. Later, after getting out of solitary, I used to keep this passage in mind when delivering Black Muslim lectures to other prisoners.[1]

Cleaver followed the entry with a throttling excerpt from Merton's autobiography,[2] mirroring plainly the solidarity and identification which Merton felt for blacks even in the 1930's. It stands as one of Merton's most powerful commentaries on racial justice, a stinging indictment of the economic and social degradation foisted upon blacks by American society.

Merton's prominence and appeal in the area of racial justice is again reflected in the words of a second black:

> The pure idealism of Merton was not expressed in simplistic dictums....He challenged one with a clear

statement of an ideal that could only be reached through agonizing spiritual work. He told us what our duty was, but gave us no formula by which to fulfill it.... Merton challenged me to be myself at a time when people demanded that I be black, but to define myself as black was to do nothing but invert the "nigger" American society had tried so hard to make me believe I was. The challenge of Merton was the perpetual struggle to vulnerability.[3]

The assessments of these two men, Julius Lester and Eldridge Cleaver, show that it would indeed have been difficult to keep "Brother Merton" out of the struggle for racial justice. Merton's penetrating vision cut through the dark cellblocks of maximum security prisons, the ivy-covered walls of universities, neat rectory parlors and convent sitting rooms, dim-lit bars and noisy coffee houses. His vision had such wide-ranging appeal and application precisely and solely because it was rooted in Truth.

Much of Merton's unique ability to empathize with the oppressed (be they Vietnamese Buddhist monks, Latin American "beat" poets, survivors of Hiroshima, or American blacks or Indians) stemmed from the fact that he never really felt completely at home or accepted anywhere in his lifetime.[4] This compassion for the oppressed was readily visible even at an early age. In a later essay, Merton tells of arguing with the head prefect of his British prep school:

> I insisted that Gandhi was right, that India was, with perfect justice, demanding that the British withdraw peacefully and go home; that the millions of people who lived in India had a perfect right to run their own country. Such sentiments were of course beyond comprehension. How could Gandhi be right when he was *odd*? And how could I be right when I was on the side of someone who had the wrong kind of skin?[5]

This concern overtook Merton, and plagued him throughout his student days. Living in New York City, he developed an acute sensitivity for the welfare of blacks, and in the pre-war era he worked actively with Catherine de Hueck at Friendship House in Harlem. However, in 1941 Merton abruptly found himself at a crossroads in his life, forced to choose between an active, apostolic life working in New York's black ghetto, and one of contemplative witness. He noted in his journal: "Anyone who believes in the Mystical Body of Christ realizes I could do more for my brothers in the world, if I were a Trappist at Gethsemani than if I were a staff worker at Friendship House."[6]

On December 10, 1941 Merton entered Gethsemani. Paradoxically, it was the evolving fruition of Merton's monastic journey which enabled him to grow in the ability to identify with (and manifest his love for) others. He later reflected: "Twenty years ago I left the world. But since that time I have learned—I believe—to look upon the world with more compassion...."[7] This developing sense of compassion moved him to speak out clearly and forcefully against trends leading to the sinful crimes of racial hatred. In the emphatic preface to *Seeds of Destruction*, written in 1964, he declared:

> It seems to me to be a solemn obligation of conscience at this moment of history to take the positions which are indicated in the following pages. These positions are, it seems to me, in vital relation with the obligations I assumed when I took my monastic vows. To have a vow of poverty seems to me illusory if I do not in some way identify myself with the cause of people who are denied their rights and forced, for the most part, to live in abject misery. To have a vow of obedience seems to me to be absurd if it does not imply a deep concern for the most fundamental of all expressions of God's will: the love of his truth and the love of our neighbor.[8]

Merton realized that as a citizen of the twentieth century, certain choices were demanded of him: "That I should have been born in 1915, that I should be the contemporary of Auschwitz, Hiroshima, Vietnam and the Watts riots are things about which, whether I like it or not, I am deeply and personally involved."[9] He believed that his choice of the monastic life was ultimately a choice for the world, his own radical acceptance of a task and a vocation in history and in time. He commented:

> And now it has become transparently obvious that mere "automatic rejection of the world" and "contempt for the world" is in fact not a choice, but the evasion of a choice. The man who pretends that he can turn his back on Auschwitz or Vietnam and act as if they were not there is simply bluffing. I think this is getting to be generally admitted, even by monks.[10]

Merton's whole worldview was conditioned by his monastic vocation. At the core of everything he said and did was his monastic experience. He perceived the charism of the contemplative as "simplicity and truth."[11] He was keenly aware that he lived in an age of crisis and struggle that cried out for the special searching and questioning which characterizes the monastic vocation: "For the monk searches not only his own heart: he plunges deep into the heart of that world of which he remains a part, although he seems to have 'left' it. In reality the monk abandons the world only in order to listen more intently to the deepest and most neglected voices that proceed from its inner depth."[12] Merton sensed that the authentic solitary is called to take on the pervasive anguish and the inescapable poverty of humankind today: "The solitary, far from enclosing himself in himself, becomes every man. He dwells in the solitude, the poverty, the indigence of every man."[13] In another place, he echoed the same theme: "Solitude has its own special work: a deepening awareness that the world needs. A struggle against alienation. True solitude is deeply aware of the world's needs."[14] He knew that the contemplative, in his most authentic witness, whether in the city or the desert, "does mankind the inestimable favor of reminding it of its true capacity for maturity, liberty, and peace."[15]

Merton continually resisted the tendency to allow the monastery to become "a snail's shell...a kind of spiritual fallout shelter into which one can plunge to escape the criminal realities of an apocalyptic age. Never has the total solidarity of all men, either in good or in evil, been so obvious and so unavoidable. I believe we live in a time in which one cannot help making decisions for or against man, for or against life, for or against justice, for or against truth. And according to my way of thinking, all these decisions rolled into one (for they are inseparable) amount to a decision for or against God."[16] It is from this basic presupposition that he defined a monk as one who assumes a critical attitude toward the world and its structures, "somebody who says, in one way or the other, that the claims of the world are fraudulent."[17]

Merton's monastic witness was grounded in the dual principles of affirmation and protest. He noted pointedly: "To adopt a life that is essentially non-assertive, non-violent, a life of humility and peace is in itself a statement of one's position....It is my intention to make my entire life a rejection of, a protest against the crimes and injustices of war and political tyranny."[18]

Perhaps the clearest statement of Merton's concerning his monastic witness marked the dedication of the Merton Collection at Bellarmine College in 1963:

> Whatever I may have written, I think it all can be reduced in the end to this one root truth: that God calls human persons to union with himself and with one another in Christ....It is certainly true that I have written about more than just the contemplative life. I have articulately resisted attempts to have myself classified as an "inspirational writer." But if I have written about interracial justice, or thermonuclear weapons, it is because these issues are terribly relevant to one great truth: that man is called to live as a son of God. Man must respond to this call to live in peace with all his brothers in the One Christ.[19]

Shortly after entering his hermitage on the grounds of Gethsemani in the late summer of 1965, Merton's passion for racial justice again showed itself, in a "Letter to a Southern Churchman":

I have publicly stated that I would no longer comment on current events. People ask why. There are many reasons, and I might as well say at once that they are reasons which may possibly be valid for me only, not for others. In any case, I did not make the decision for anyone but myself, nor would I have made it unless I had previously made my position clear in the areas of greatest urgency—race and peace.[20]

Ironically, Merton's eremitical years (1965-1968) spawned many of his most incisive social commentaries in the crucial areas of race and peace—another sign, "in the belly of a paradox." This expression of concern dovetailed with Merton's basic vision that the task of monasticism is intimately bound to "the whole question of the reconciliation of all men with one another in Christ."[21] In reflecting on the moral climate of the United States at mid-century, he reiterated the concern of Pope John in *Pacem in Terris* that human fear must give way to love, "a love that tends to express itself in collaboration."[22]

The underpinnings of all of Merton's social teaching are grounded in the fact of the incarnation of Jesus the Christ, and in the consequent resurrection destiny which all persons share:

Because God became man, because every man is potentially Christ, because Christ is our brother . . . we have no right to let our brother live in want, or in degradation, or in any form of squalor, whether physical or spiritual. In a word, if we really understood the meaning of Christianity in social life we would see it as a part of the redemptive work of Christ, liberating man from misery, squalor, sub-human living conditions, economic or political slavery, ignorance, alienation.[23]

He lamented the continuing aggravation of the racial situation, and claimed that nominally Christian America had lapsed into a "basic heresy":

It is the loss of the Christian sense which sees every other man as Christ and treats him as Christ. For, as St. John said. "We know what love is by this: that he laid down his life for us so that we ought to lay down our lives for the brotherhood. But whoever possesses this world's goods and notices his brother in need and shuts his heart against him, how can the love of God remain in him? Dear children, let us put our love not into words or into talk but into deeds, and make it real" (1 Jn. 3:16-18).[24]

In this vein, Merton believed true Christian witness to be the logical outgrowth stemming from the fact of the incarnation, rooted in a new concept of the human person which grew out of the mystery of the union of God and man or woman in Christ: "It is the full realization of man's dignity and obligations as Son of God, as image of God, created, regenerated, and transformed in the Word made flesh."[25] He elaborated on the further implications of this doctrine: "Since the Word was made flesh, God is in man. God is in *all men*. All men are to be seen and treated as Christ. Failure to do this, the Lord tells us, involves condemnation for disloyalty to the most fundamental of revealed truths. 'I was thirsty and you gave me not to drink, I was hungry and you gave me not to eat....' (Mt. 25:42)."[26]

It should be noted that this truth affected Merton profoundly even in his pre-monastic days. When he wrote of Christians and Harlem in his autobiography, he reasoned that their response would be radically different if viewed with the eyes of faith:

[They] would give up everything to go there and try to do something to relieve the tremendous misery, the poverty, sickness, degradation and dereliction of a race that was being crushed and perverted, morally and physically, under the burden of a colossal economic injustice. Instead of seeing Christ suffering in his members, and instead of going to help him who said: "Whatsoever you did to these, the least of my brethren, you did it to me," we preferred our own comfort. We averted our eyes from such a spectacle, because it made us feel uneasy: the thought of so much dirt nauseated us—and we never stopped to think that we, perhaps, might be responsible for it. And so people continued to die of starvation and disease in those evil tenements full of vice and cruelty, while those who did condescend to consider their problems held banquets in the big hotels downtown to discuss the "race situation" in a big rosy cloud of hot air.[27]

In this context, Merton echoed Berdayaev's powerful statement that the practical conclusion arising from eschatological Christianity turns into "an accusation of the age in which I live and into a command to be human in this most inhuman of ages, to guard the image of man, for it is the image of God."[28] Merton repeatedly stressed that in Christ Jesus there can be no meaning to racial divisions, no black or white. He highlighted the need to "live up to what we ourselves profess to believe, so that we may not be judged by God for mere lip-service that has (as we now begin to realize too late) reached the proportions of a world-wide scandal."[29]

Merton's voluminous correspondence and selective reading of current periodicals kept him informed of developments on the secular scene concerning the racial situation. He seldom read newspapers, and he only watched television twice in his life.[30] Yet he incisively remarked:

Events happen, and they affect me as they do other people. It is important for me to know about them too: but I refrain from trying to know them in their fresh condition as "news." When they reach me they have become slightly stale. I eat the same tragedies as others, but in the form of tasteless crusts. The news reaches me in the long run through books and magazines, and no longer as a stimulant. Living without news is like living without cigarettes (another peculiarity of the monastic life). The need for this habitual indulgence quickly disappears. So, when you hear news without the "need" to hear it, it treats you very differently. And you learn to treat it differently too.[31]

True to his artist's soul, Merton's keen sensitivity to the volatile racial situation surfaced often in his poetry. Some of the most powerful expressions of this are: "And the Children of Birmingham," "Picture of a Black Girl with a White Doll: Carole Denise McNair, Killed in Birmingham, Sept. 1963," "Plessy vs. Ferguson: Themes and Variations," and "April 4th 1968: For Martin Luther King."[32] A brief vignette from *Faith and Violence* further illustrates Merton's sharp awareness of the racial climate in America:

> In one of the big riots of 1964, the one in Harlem in mid-July, when the streets were filled with people in confusion, running from the police, when bricks and bottles were pelted down from the rooftops and the police were firing into the air (not without killing one man and wounding many others), the police captain tried to disperse the rioters by shouting through a megaphone: "Go home! Go home!" A voice from the crowd answered: "We are home, baby!" The irony of this statement and its humor sum up the American problem. There is no "where" for the Negro to go. He is where he is. White America has put him where he is. The tendency has been to act as if he were not there, or as if he might possibly go somewhere else, and to beat him over the head if he makes his collective presence too manifest.[33]

Merton accurately grasped the socio-economic basis for racial discrimination in America. He knew that the race question could not be settled without a profound change of heart on the part of the American people.

He wrote of the need for America to awaken to the blatant injustices and deep-seated problems already ingrained in the current state of affairs, which he felt would worsen before they would improve: "The only way to prevent this from generating the worst kind of race hatred and violence on both sides is to admit the existence of the problems in all their seriousness, and the consequent resolution to *share* the benefits of our society with the Negro as far as we can: that is to say, really give him equal opportunities in everything."[34] In another place, he challenged white America to live out the message which it nominally professed: "Northern liberals might admire black dignity at a distance, but they still did not want all that nobility next door: it might affect property values. Nobility is one thing, and property values quite another."[35]

Merton was incensed by the caricature of the black often still current in the United States: "What we love in the Negro tends to be, once again, the same old image of the vaudeville darkie, the quaint black mammy of plantation days, the Pullman porter with ready wit, the devoted retainer whose whole family has served a white Southern feudal tribe for generations. This is caricature of the Negro of which the Negro himself has long since grown tired, and its chief function is to flatter the white man's sense of superiority."[36] He realized that much of the racial discrimination practiced in the United States was vested in economic injustice, and he cautioned against being lulled into a false sense of black accomplishment now that small numbers of blacks were "making it" socially. He noted that while there were thirty-five black millionaires in the United States, in the larger context this was almost inconsequential: "Thirty-five out of twenty million! . . . Even when he is worth a million, a Negro cannot buy himself, in the land of the free, the respect that is given to a human person."[37] On this basis, he concluded in a pessimistic tone:

> The Negro is clearly invited to one response. He has had untold reasons for hating the white man. They are now being solidly compounded and confirmed. Even though he has nothing whatever to gain by violence, he has also nothing to lose. And violence will at least be one decisive way of saying what he thinks of white society! The result is likely to be very unpleasant, and the blame will rest squarely on the shoulders of white America, with its emotional, cultural and political immaturity and its pitiable refusal of insight.[38]

It was this type of clear-sighted vision which aroused such rank antipathy toward Merton. He was particularly threatening and offensive to certain strains of white clergy, both Catholic and Protestant, Northern and Southern. In a prominent criticism of Merton, theologian Martin Marty vigorously assailed him for daring to assume a prophetic stance on the racial question,[39] asserting that a reclusive monk had no business trying to predict an outbreak of violence in American cities. Paradoxically, Merton's wilderness perspective proved a far more accurate slant on the racial climate of America than Marty's from the streets of Chicago, and in hindsight Marty apologized for his harsh words, in a virtually unprecedented and absolute retraction.

While Merton aptly sensed the propensity for urban violence, his monastic vocation tempered his vision. He remained a monk in the true sense, and worked for unity and peace. As a contemplative critic, he affirmed: "Where minds are full of hatred and where imaginations dwell on cruelty, torment, punishment, revenge and death, then inevitably there will be violence and death."[40] Yet Merton never wavered in his personal conviction of the perduring value of non-violence as a form of affirmation and protest. At the outset of his Asian journey in 1968, he reaffirmed: "There seems to be a general impression that non-violence in America has been tried and found wanting.... I might as well say bluntly that I do not believe this at all."[41]

Merton firmly believed that non-violence was still the best tactic available for catalyzing the transformation of the present state of the world. However, he sensed the sobering reality of the deeper root of the problem, and confessed that while non-violence could continue to be used as a tactic, the days of its "real effectiveness" may well have waned substantially:

It will probably never again convey the message it conveyed in Montgomery, Birmingham, and Selma. Those days are over, and it seems that people who believed in all that was implied by non-violence will look back on those days with a certain nostalgia. For non-violence apparently presupposed a sense of justice, of humaneness, of liberality, of generosity that were not to be found in white people to whom the Negroes made their stirring appeal. The problem of American racism turned out to be far deeper, far more stubborn, infinitely more complex.[42]

Merton perceived the nub of the problem as deeply embedded within the inverted values and priorities of the American culture itself. This piercing revelation evoked Merton's strong response as a contemplative critic.

In a statement solicited by the presidential commission investigating the causes of violence in the United States, Merton grimly concluded:

The real focus of American violence is not in esoteric groups but in the very culture itself, its mass media, its extreme individualism and competitiveness, its inflated myths of virility and toughness, and its overwhelming preoccupation with the power of nuclear, chemical, bacteriological, and psychological overkill. If we live in what is essentially a culture of overkill, how can we be surprised at finding violence in it? Can we get to the root of the trouble? In my opinion, the best way to do it would have been the classic way of religious humanism and non-violence exemplified by Gandhi. That way seems now to have been closed. I do not find the future reassuring.[43]

Merton noted that at its core the problem was rooted in the contempt which many Americans exhibit for truth. He stated baldly: "I am glad that I am not a Negro because I probably would never be able to take it.... I recognize in conscience that I have a duty to try to make my fellow whites stop doing the things they do and see the problem in a different light. This does not presuppose an immediate program or a surge of optimism, because I am still convinced that there is almost nothing to be done that will have any deep effect or make any real difference."[44] Yet, despite these pessimistic overtones, Merton still upheld the overriding value of non-violence:

The current facile rejection of non-violence is too pragmatic. You point to one or two cases where it does not
seem to have gotten results and you say it has completely
failed. But non-violence is useless if it is merely pragmatic. The whole point of non-violence is that it rises above
pragmatism and does not consider whether or not it pays
off politically. *Ahimsa*[45] is defense of and witness to
truth, not efficacy. I admit that it may sound odd. Someone once said, did he not, "What is truth?" And the one
to whom he said it also mentioned, somewhere: "The
truth shall set you free." It seems to me that is what really
matters.[46]

Merton was firmly convinced of the impossibility of the
truly non-violent person to ignore the inherent falsity and
inner contradiction of a society marked with violence and
unrest:

On the contrary, it is for him a religious and human duty
to confront the untruth in that society with his own
witness in order that the falsity may become evident to
everyone. The first job of a *satyagrahi* (one who holds
onto truth) is to try to bring the real situation to light
even if he has to suffer and die in order that injustice be
unmasked and appear for what it really is.[47]

He knew that the spirit of non-violence could only spring
from a realization of the inner unity within oneself: "The first
thing of all and the most important of all is the inner unity,
the overcoming and healing of inner division, the consequent spiritual and personal freedom...."[48] In writing of
peace and non-violence Merton recognized that there could
be little peace on earth without the kind of *metanoia* which
transforms the hearts of men and women and orients them
toward the kingdom of God.

In his own journey, a figure who influenced Merton most
profoundly was Gandhi, whom he dubbed "a model of integrity whom we cannot afford to ignore.... The one basic duty
we all owe to the world of our time is to imitate him in
'disassociating ourselves from evil in total disregard of the

consequences.' "[49] He portrayed Gandhi as "one of the very few men of our time who applied Gospel principles to the problems of a political and social existence in such a way that his approach was inseparably religious and political at the same time."[50]

Merton greatly identified with Gandhi, and viewed the Gandhian witness as dedicated to adherence to a few basic claims: "...that he was not lying, that he did not intend to use violence or deceit against the English, that he did not think that peace and justice could be attained through violent or selfish means, that he did genuinely believe they could be assured by non-violence and self-sacrifice."[51] He further aligned himself with Gandhi in advocating a non-violence which sought not power, but truth: "It is not aimed at immediate political results, but at the manifestation of fundamental and crucially important truth. Non-violence is not primarily the language of efficacy, but the langauge of *kairos*. It does not say 'We shall overcome' so much as 'This is the day of the Lord, and whatever may happen to us, *He* shall overcome.' "[52]

It was this same message, which, in the 1960's, Merton perceived committed blacks articulating to white America. He railed against the myopic intransigency of the latter: "I have spelled it out for myself, subject to correction, in order to see whether a white man is even capable of grasping the words, let alone believing them. For the rest, you have Moses and the prophets: Martin Luther King, James Baldwin, and the others. Read them, and see for yourself what they are saying."[53]

Merton was both a friend and devotee of King. Both openly pledged their commitment to the doctrine of non-violence fostered by Gandhi. Merton greatly admired the tenor of the protest against civil discrimination as articulated by King and his followers: "The non-violent Negro civil rights drive has been one of the most positive and successful expressions of Christian social action that has been seen anywhere in the twentieth century. It is certainly the greatest example of Christian faith in action in the social history of the United States."[54]

Merton scored the convoluted attitude of American

whites which seemed to hold that they could learn little or nothing from blacks, and dwelt on the irony that the black person, "especially the Christian Negro of the heroic stamp of Dr. King, *is offering the white man a 'message of salvation,' but the white man is so blinded by his self-sufficiency and self-conceit that he does not recognize the peril in which he puts himself by ignoring the offer."*[55]

He recognized that from the very beginning civil rights leaders of King's stripe were actively engaged in the non-violent struggle of seeking to heal the devisive wounds of racism and to bring about unity in reconciliation. He reflected: "An absolutely necessary element in this reconciliation is that the white man should allow himself to learn the mute lesson which is addressed to him in the suffering, the non-violent protest, the loving acceptance of punishment for the violation of unjust laws, which the Negro freely and willingly brings upon himself in the white man's presence, in the hope that the oppressor may come to see his own injustice."[56]

He stressed that the struggle for black liberation was more than a battle for political rights, but a struggle for *truth*, extending beyond any political contingencies. He concluded:

The mystique of Negro non-violence holds that the victory of truth is inevitable, but that the redemption of individuals is not inevitable.... The Negro children of Birmingham, who walked calmly up to the police dogs that lunged at them with a fury capable of tearing their small bodies to pieces, were not only confronting the truth in an exalted moment of faith, a providential *kairos*. They were also in their simplicity bearing heroic Christian witness to the truth, for they were exposing their bodies to death in order to show God and man that they believed in the just rights of their people, knew that those rights had been unjustly, shamefully, and systematically violated, and realized that the violation called for expiation and redemptive protest, because it was an offense against God and his truth.[57]

Merton continually stressed that the followers of King who were committed to non-violence bore witness to the fact that there was more at stake in their protest than civil rights. He firmly believed that the survival of America itself was in jeopardy, that a house divided against itself could not stand. He sided with those who "believe that the sin of white America has reached such a proportion that it may call down a dreadful judgment, perhaps total destruction on the whole country, unless atonement is made."[58] He knew that the ramifications of the race issue deeply struck at the core of American society as a kind of lethal poison feeding into certain violence and social upheaval.

Anticipating an impending period of fear, violence, and terrorism, Merton commented:

The Black Power movement has now, in any case, re-placed Christian non-violence, and Dr. King no longer retains his position of preeminent moral authority as the greatest Negro leader. But though the Black Power movement is trying to channel the exploding energies of the Negro ghettoes in a political direction, we can see that the violence to come probably will be more and more aimless, nihilistic, arbitrary, destructive and non-amenable to reasonable control. Already it is evident that those whites who reviled Dr. King as a "communist" and rabble-rouser will have reason to regret that the guid-ance of the Negro struggle for rights has slipped from his hands into the hands of those who hold rifles.[59]

The repeatedly frustrated attempts of blacks favoring non-violent resistance inevitably led to outbreaks of uncontrolla-ble violence, fanned by more radical elements, tired of wait-ing for an all-too-slow social change. This infectious climate of violence (irrespective of racial barriers), fueled by the blind hatred of a disgruntled racist, led to King's own death in Memphis, on April 4, 1968.

Ironically, King had planned to visit his friend Merton for the first time at Gethsemani that very week,[60] but the

pressing urgency of the issues surrounding the Memphis
garbage strike lured him there instead.

> And a well dressed white man
> Said the minister,
> Dropped the telescopic storm
>
> And he ran
> (The well-dressed minister of death)
> He ran
> He ran away
>
> And on the balcony
> Said the minister
> We found
> Everybody dying.[61]

On December, 10, 1968, another minister of death
("General-Electric-brand death")[62] appeared in Bangkok,
claiming the life of Thomas Merton. Yet, like King, his life
and witness had left its imprint, and an important legacy
remains in the wake of his death. He had spoken out, clearly
and forcefully, in the areas he considered to be of greatest
importance—race and peace. And the witness of this lone
voice has begun to bear fruit.

NOTES

1. Eldridge Cleaver, *Soul on Ice* (N.Y.: Dell Publishing Company,
1968), p. 34.

2. Thomas Merton, *The Seven Storey Mountain* (N.Y.: Harcourt, Brace
and Company, 1948), pp. 344-45.

3. Julius Lester, "The Challenge of Thomas Merton," in *Callings*,
edited by Will Campbell and James Holloway (N.Y.: Paulist Press, 1974),
pp. 109-110, 121-122.

4. This insight was offered by monk and psychiatrist John Eudes
Bamberger, O.C.S.O., a long-time friend of Merton and presently Abbot of
the Genesee, in an oral history interview conducted by me at the Genesee
on November 14, 1974. From my files.

5. Merton, *Thomas Merton on Peace*, edited, with an introduction by
Gordon C. Zahn (N.Y.: McCall's Publishing Company, 1971), pp. 178-179.

6. Merton, *The Secular Journal of Thomas Merton* (N.Y.: Doubleday Image Books, 1959), p. 239.

7. Cited in Jean Leclercq's Preface to Merton, *Contemplation in a World of Action* (N.Y.: Doubleday Image Books, 1974), p. 15.

8. Merton, *Seeds of Destruction* (N.Y.: Farrar, Straus, and Giroux, 1965), pp. xiii-xiv.

9. Merton, *Contemplation in a World of Action*, p. 145.

10. *Ibid.*

11. *Ibid.*, p. 38.

12. Merton, *Contemplative Prayer* (N.Y.: Doubleday Image Books, 1971), p. 23.

13. Merton, *Raids on the Unspeakable* (N.Y.: New Directions, 1966), p. 18.

14. Merton, *Conjectures of a Guilty Bystander* (N.Y.: Doubleday Image Books, 1968), p. 10.

15. Merton, *Raids on the Unspeakable*, p. 22.

16. Merton, *Thomas Merton on Peace*, p. 257.

17. Merton, *The Asian Journal of Thomas Merton*, edited by Br. Patrick Hart, James Laughlin, and Naomi Burton Stone (N.Y.: New Directions, 1974), p. 329.

18. Merton, cited in John Eudes Bamberger, "The Monk," in *Thomas Merton/Monk*, edited by Br. Patrick Hart (N.Y.: Sheed and Ward, 1974), p. 52.

19. Merton, "A Statement Concerning the Collection in the Bellarmine College Library—November 10, 1963," in *The Thomas Merton Studies Center* (Santa Barbara, Cal.: The Unicorn Press, 1971), pp. 14-15.

20. Merton, *Faith and Violence* (Notre Dame: University of Notre Dame Press, 1968), p. 145.

21. *Ibid.*, p. 146.

22. Pope John XXIII, in *Pacem In Terris*, cited in Merton, *Thomas Merton on Peace*, p. 20.

23. Merton, *Conjectures of a Guilty Bystander*, pp. 81-82.

24. Merton, *Faith and Violence*, p. 143.

25. Merton, *Mystics and Zen Masters* (N.Y.: Farrar, Straus, and Giroux, 1968), pp. 114-115. Merton's doctrine on the human person as the image of God is treated in my forthcoming article on Merton and St. Bernard of Clairvaux in the fall (1978:3) issue of *Cistercian Studies*.

26. Merton, *Contemplative Prayer*, pp. 380-381.

27. Merton, *The Seven Storey Mountain*, p. 341.

28. Merton, *Raids on the Unspeakable*, p. 6.

29. Merton, *Faith and Violence*, p. 179.

30. *Ibid.*, p. 151.

31. *Ibid.*

32. Merton, *The Collected Poems of Thomas Merton* (N.Y.: New Directions, 1977), pp. 335-337, 626-627, 651-655, and 1006-1007 respectively.

33. Merton, *Faith and Violence*, p. 136-137.

34. Merton, *Seeds of Destruction*, p. 310.

35. Merton, *Faith and Violence*, p. 122.

36. Merton, *Seeds of Destruction*, p. 60.

37. *Ibid.*, pp. 26-27.

38. Merton, *Conjectures of a Guilty Bystander*, p. 33.

39. Cf. Martin E. Marty, "To Thomas Merton: Re: Your Prophecy," in *The National Catholic Reporter*, August 8, 1967, p. 8, for the genesis of Marty's view and his subsequent apology to Merton.

40. Merton, *Seeds of Destruction*, p. 7.

41. Merton, "Non-Violence Does Not—Cannot—Mean Passivity," in *Ave Maria*, CVIII (September 7, 1968), p. 9.

42. Merton, *Faith and Violence*, pp. 132-133.

43. Merton, *Thomas Merton on Peace*, p. 232.

44. Merton, *Seeds of Destruction*, p. 326.

45. *Ahimsa* means "non-violence as a principle" in Hindi.

46. Merton, *Thomas Merton on Peace*, p. 233.

47. Merton (ed.), *Gandhi on Non-Violence* (N.Y.: New Directions, 1965), p. 10.

48. *Ibid.*, p. 6.

49. Merton, *Seeds of Destruction*, p. 254.

50. *Ibid.*, p. 226.

51. Merton, *Thomas Merton on Peace*, p. 182.

52. *Ibid.*, p. xxix.

53. Merton, *Seeds of Destruction*, p. 70.

54. Merton, *Faith and Violence*, p. 131.

55. Merton, *Seeds of Destruction*, pp. 63-64.

56. *Ibid.*, p. 43.

57. *Ibid.*, p. 44.

58. *Ibid.*, p. 45.

59. Merton, *Faith and Violence*, p. 167.

60. Bamberger oral history interview, *op. cit.*, n. 4.

61. Merton, "April 4th 1968: For Martin Luther King," in *The Collected Poems of Thomas Merton*, pp. 1006-1007.

62. Cf. Ernesto Cardenal, "*Coplas* on the Death of Merton," in *Apocalypse and Other Poems* (N.Y.: New Directions, 1977), p. 45.

Social Concern in the Poetry of Thomas Merton

Thérèse Lentfoehr, S.D.S.

While taping a portion of his Journal for March 8, 1966, Thomas Merton digressed for a moment to say, "Now I am going to cheat a little bit, and insert some new material that I am just thinking of at the moment; though it is not in the sequence of the Journal, it fits in with it, I believe, as relevant to the idea of the solitary." Merton had been reading a book by the French phenomenologist, Gaston Bachelard, and was intrigued by his symbol of the "house," for it threw light on man's being, as related to creative memory and reflection, and the responsibility of the solitary vocation. Merton then remarked of the image of the "hermit hut" as one of the most primitive and profound:

> The image that he suggests is the image of a lonely light in the woods seen from a distance on the opposite hillside, or something, and you know that there is a man living there alone. Well, here I am with my lonely light on the hill and this is what's coming from inside the thing.[1]

The hermit is alone with God, while all around his centered solitutde there radiates a universe which meditates and prays, a universe outside the universe, which invokes the idea of a sacred universe created by the presence of a man in this particular kind of relationship with God. This is, in fact, the real universe. Merton's moving to the "hermitage" in August 1965 was, paradoxical as it may seem, a special *kairos* for some of his richest and most profound writing. This was especially true of his poetry. Because of the bulk of his prose writing we tend to forget that it was as a poet that we first came to know him. With the publication by New Directions of *Thirty Poems* in 1944, we discovered who this young poet was. A brief paragraph on the book's dust jacket informed us that he was a much traveled young man, a graduate of Columbia University, who was now a monk in the Trappist abbey of Gethsemani in Kentucky. Of the combination of a Trappist monk and so reputable a publisher as New Directions, one reviewer remarked that it was "like coming on a familiar Little Sister of the Poor in front of Penn Station dressed in the latest fashion from Fifth Avenue." Robert Lowell, in a review in *Commonweal*, called Merton "the most promising of our Catholic poets, and possibly the most consequential Catholic poet to write in English since the death of Francis Thompson." He also referred to the poems as "subtle and intense," adding: "So small and genuine an achievement is worth consideration."[2]

Five collections of poems were to follow this: *A Man in the Divided Sea* (1946); *Figures for an Apocalypse* (1947); *The Tears of the Blind Lions* (1949); *The Strange Islands* (1957); *Emblems of a Season of Fury* (1963); and two composite poetic works: *Cables to the Ace* (1968); and *The Geography of Lograire* (1969) published posthumously. In 1971 Merton's *Early Poems: 1940-1942* were published. A volume of *Collected Poems* was published in 1977 by New Directions.

Eight volumes of poetry comprise a not inconsiderable legacy to be left to the world at a poet's death, and it is unfortunate that so little recognition has been given to them in critical reviews, though they have met with a warm reception from certain groups of poets including the so-called "beats," for whom Merton had a special fondness, and the poets of Latin America.

The Merton poetry corpus includes as well early juvenalia, poems written at his prep school at Oakam (England), and others while a student at Columbia University. One of the latter, "Fable for a War," published in June 1939, in a *Columbia Poetry* anthology, won the annual Mariana Griswold van Rensselaer Prize for the best example of English lyric verse, and was reprinted in the *New York*

Times on June 18, 1939. Its themes demonstrate only too graphically that Merton was already deeply sensitive to the tragedies of war.

The poem carries a vatic note:

> Europe is a feast
> For every bloody beast;
> Jackals will grow fat
> On the bones after that;
> But in the end of all
> Only the crows will sing the funeral.[3]

Merton later remarked that the prize was one he did not deserve; nor did he include the poem in his first collection. As a student he had already published in *Chimera, Experimental Review, The New Yorker, Spirit, View,* and *Voices.* This was but the beginning, and it is interesting to note that his first writing after entering the monastery was a poem.

There is a precious manuscript extant of seven salvaged pages of a spiritual diary Merton kept as a novice, and subsequently destroyed, as he remarked in *The Seven Storey Mountain,* since he thought it more pleasing to God that he not keep it. Its first entry is dated December 13; "Entered as Postulant St. Lucy's Day." Then follows "Poem for my Friends, Dec. 12-13," beginning:

> This holy house of God
> (Nazareth, where Christ lived as a boy)
> These sheds and cloisters,
> The very stones and beam are all befriended
> By cleaner suns, by rarer birds, by humbler flowers.[4]

This poem was later published in his second collection, *A Man in the Divided Sea,* together with five other poems in the manuscript; "Cana," "St. Paul," "How Long We Wait," "Woodcutters and Harvesters" (later titled "Trappists Working"), and "The Candlemas Procession." Another poem, "The Ointment,"[5] apparently from another notebook, was never published. Interspersed with these poems are personal notes. Immediately following "Poem for my Friends," is a brief personal note "... Nothing lost. What in the world would be wasted is here all God's. All for love ... and I never hated less the world, scorned it less, or understood it better."[6] There is mystery in these lines, and that in view not only of his later writing but of his earlier writing as well.

When the so-called "Merton Room" was opened at Bellarmine College, Louisville in 1963, Merton sent a statement to the audience gathered there that afternoon, remarking: "Whatever I may have written, I think it all can be reduced in the end to this one root truth: that God calls human persons to union with himself and with one another in Christ."[7] If this rings true of all Merton's writing, it resounds with special emphasis in his poetry, since one line of poetry may sometimes carry an impact that several pages of prose cannot. Merton's poetry was a synthesis of his experience. In it he voiced mainly three areas of concern: the city (which he held responsible for "mass man" and a technological society which made humankind more and more a robot of its will); the tragedy of war; and the racial issue. In all of these he was deeply involved. Already in an early poem (*circa* 1938) he writes a "Hymn of Not Much Praise for New York City," sung by its children who "try to keep our cage from caving in./All the while our minds will fill with these petitions,/Flowering quietly in between our gongs of pulse./These will have to serve as prayers:

> But never give us any explanations, even when we ask
> Why all our food tastes of iodoform,
> And even the freshest flowers smell of funerals.
> No, never let us look about us long enough to wonder
> Which of the rich men, shivering in the overheated
>   office,
> And which of the poor men, sleeping face-down on the
>   *Daily Mirror*,
> Are still alive, and which are dead.[8]

Yet he loved New York, and when in 1964 he flew there to speak with the Zen master, Daisetz Suzuki, as the flight attendant came to ask his destination, he replied: "New

York"—"and as soon as I said that, there was a great joy in my heart because after all, I was going *home*."[9]

It was while a novice at Gethsemani that the theme of war first surfaced, as a personal tragedy—namely, the death of his brother, Sgt. John Paul Merton, R.C.A.F., whose plane came down in the North Sea. The poem titled "For My Brother Reported Missing in Action: 1943," has been much praised, reprinted, and quoted. It begins: "Sweet brother, if I do not sleep/My eyes are flowers for your tomb;/And if I cannot eat my bread,/My fasts shall live like willows where you died./If in the heat I find no water for my thirst,/My thirst shall turn to springs for you, poor traveler." Its final stanzas:

When all the men of war are shot
And flags have fallen into dust,
Your cross and mine shall tell men still
Christ died on each for both of us.

For in the wreckage of your April Christ lies slain,
And Christ weeps in the ruins of my spring:
The money of whose tears shall fall
Into your weak and friendless hand,
And buy you back to your own land:
The silence of whose tears shall fall
Like bells upon your alien tomb.
Hear them and come: they call you home.[10]

The poem was printed first in *Thirty Poems* (1944) and reprinted in *The Seven Storey Mountain*. At the time of the former, and of the latter as well, the fate of the underprivileged was much on Merton's mind; of them he had first-hand knowledge from his work at Friendship House, in Harlem, with Baroness Catherine de Hueck. In this first collection of his poems we find "Holy Communion: Harlem," later called "Holy Communion: The City," in which he addresses the children, "Here in the jungles of our waterpipes and iron ladders," and receives their answer: "Although we know no hills, no country rivers,/Here in the jungles of our waterpipes and iron ladders,/Our thoughts are quieter than rivers,/Our loves are simpler than the trees,/Our prayers deeper than the sea. . . . And Faith sits in our hearts like fire,/ And makes them smile like suns,/While we come back from lovely Bethlehem/To burn down Harlem with the glad Word of Our Savior."[11] Again, in *A Man in the Divided Sea* (1946), the poem "Aubade—Harlem" pictures their plight as "Across the cages of the keyless aviaries,/The lines and wire, the gallows of the broken kites,/Crucify, against the fearful light,/The ragged dresses of the little children."[12] And in "The Bombarded City": "Now let no man abide/In the lunar wood/The place of blood. . . . Fear far more/What curse rides down the starlit air,/Curse of the little children killed!/Curse of the little children killed!"[13]

In Merton's third collection, *Figures for an Apocalypse* (1947), an ambitious eight-part verse-drama that titles the book is based on a phrase of Léon Bloy, namely, that the world is *"au seuil de l'apocalypse."* Images of the second coming, and the destruction of the city of New York, take up the first parts of the poem, though in Part III, Merton warns his friends Robert Lax and Ed Rice "to get away while they still can":

> It is the hour to fly without passports
> From Juda to the mountains,
> And hide while cities turn to butter
> For fear of the secret bomb.[14]

The Prophet (it is thought the reference is to Marx), has failed them, who said that "Tonight is the millennium/The withering away of the state."[15] But after the catastrophe there is a marvelously healing passage. And the city that "dressed herself in paper money . . . With nickles running in her veins/And burned on her own green harbor/Higher and whiter than ever any Tyre,"[16] is beautifully transformed:

> Grasses and flowers will grow
> Upon the bosom of Manhattan. . . .

There shall be doves' nests, and hives of bees
In the cliffs of the ancient apartments
And birds shall sing in the sunny hawthorns
Where was once Park Avenue.
And where Grand Central was, shall be a little hill
Clustered with sweet, dark pine. . . . [17]

And the Heavenly City comes down—

Because the cruel algebra of war
Is now no more.
And the steel circle of time, inexorable,
Bites like a padlock shut, forever,
In the smoke of the last bomb....

Lo, the twelve gates that are One Christ are wide as
    canticles...
While all the saints rise from their earth with feet like
    light
And fly to tread the quick-gold of those streets....[18]

In Merton's fourth collection, *The Tears of the Blind Lions* (1949), there is a significant poem, which with a bit of ingenuity could be staged as a verse-drama, or performed by a verse-speaking choir. It occasions some surprise that it has received little or no attention, though not long after the book was published, the complete poem (ninety-five lines) was read over a Chicago radio station; the poem is entitled, "Christopher Columbus." In it Merton's concern is with the country "found and lost so soon":

There was a great Captain with Mary in his sails
Who did not discover Harlem or the East Side
Or Sing Sing or the dead men on the island.
But his heart was like the high mountains....[19]

In three time sequences Merton depicts his coming, his leaving and its aftermath, and our modern day. "Suddenly the great Christ-bearing Columbus rises in the sea/Spilling the

green Atlantic from his shoulders/And sees America though
a veil of waters....

  Indians come out of the brake with corn and lemons
  And he blesses the bronze gentry sitting in the air of the
    arcade:
  Thousands of Franciscans go through the fields with
    Sacraments
  And towns, towns, towns rise out of the ground....[20]

  At his leaving, "Waving, waving the little ones have
wept him out of sight...."

  When it is evening in American vespers
  Feathers of imperfect incense spend themselves
  Marking his memory on steeples.
  As fast as dark comes down town, cities,
  Returning to the virgin air
  Restore these shores to silences.
  Woods crawl back into the gulf.
  Shadows of Franciscans die in tangled wilds
  And there is just one smoke upon the plain
  And just one Indian hunter.

  What will you do, America
  Found and lost so soon?

  But the devils are sailing for your harbors
  Launching their false doves into the air to fly for your
    sands.....

  Suddenly the silences of the deep continent
  Die in a tornado of guitars....
  Break open a dozen cities! Let traffic bleed upon the land
  And hug your hundred and twenty million paupers in a
    vice without escape
  While they are mapped and verified
  Plotted, printed, catalogued, numbered and categoried
  And sold to the doctors of your sham discovery.

                    * * *

And now the cities' eyes are tight as ice
When the long cars stream home in nights of autumn.
(The bells Columbus heard are dumb).
The city's rivers are still as liquor.
Bars and factories pool their lights
In Michigan's or Erie's mirrors, now, on the night of the
    game.
(But the bells Columbus heard are dumb).
The city's face is frozen like a screen of silver
When the universities turn in
And winter sings in the bridges
Tearing the grand harps down.

But the children sing no hymn for the feast of Saint
    Columbus.
They watch the long, long, armies drifting home.[21]

In another poem, *"Senescente Mundo,"* in the same collection Merton makes reference to his priestly ministery (he
was ordained May 26, 1949) and the sad state of the world:

Yet in the middle of this murderous season
Great Christ, my fingers touch Thy wheat
And hold Thee hidden in the compass of Thy paper sun.
There is no war will not obey this cup of Blood,
This wine in which I sink Thy words, in the anonymous
    dawn!...
His Truth is greater than disaster.
His peace imposes silence on the evidence against us.
......

Suppose a whole new universe, a great clean Kingdom
Were to rise up like Atlantis in the East,
Surprise this earth, this cinder, with new holiness!

Here in my hands I hold that secret Easter,
Tomorrow, this will be my Mass's answer,
Because of my companions whom the wilderness has
    eaten,
Crying like Jonas in the belly of our whale.[22]

"To the Immaculate Virgin on a Winter Night" is a prayer:

> Lady, the night is falling and the dark
> Steals all the blood from the scarred west....
> Where in the world has any voice
> Prayed to you, Lady, for the peace that's in your power?
> Where in the world has any city trusted you?
> Out where the soldiers camp the guns begin to thump
> And another winter comes down
> To seal our years in ice.
> The last train cries out
> And runs in terror from this farmers' valley
> Where all the little birds are dead...
>
> Lady, the night has got us by the heart
> And the whole world is tumbling down.
> Words turn to ice in my dry throat
> Praying for a land without prayer.
>
> Walking to you on water all winter
> In a year that wants more war.[23]

There are several poems in Merton's fifth collection, *The Strange Islands* (1957), berating war. On the last occasion of my meeting with him—a year before his death—he suddenly broke off our conversation saying, "Sister, listen!" There was a distant thumping sound. "Those are the guns at Fort Knox," he said. "Remember my poem?" I did, with little thought that I should one day hear those guns in a personal experience. "The Guns of Fort Knox" begins:

> Guns at the camp (I hear them suddenly)
> Guns make the little houses jump. I feel
> Explosions in my feet, through boards
> Wars work under the floor. Wars
> Dance in the foundations.

Merton then speaks of trees shuddering from the root, and the hills "Not too firm even without dynamite," in shock, and even "the armies of the dead may wake . . . and do death's work once more." He then exhorts them:

> Guns, I say, this is not
> The right resurrection. All day long
> You punch the doors of death to wake
> A slain generation. Let them lie
> Still. Let them sleep on,
> O Guns. Shake no more
> (But leave the locks secure)
> Hell's door.[24]

"How To Enter a Big City" is another indictment, as "Centered in its own incurable discontent, the City/Consents to be recognized."

> The people come out into the light of afternoon,
> Covered all over with black powder,
> And begin to attack one another with statements
> Or to ignore one another with horror.
> Customs have not changed. . . .
> Everywhere there is optimism without love
> And pessimism without understanding. . . .[25]

The Tower of Babel, Part II of this collection is a morality play, a socially oriented piece, which first appeared in *Jubilee* in October 1955, and was dramatized on a New York radio station in the spring of 1957, with soloists, a chorus, and a musical score. It is based on three texts: Genesis 11:1-9, relating the building and fall of the tower; St. Augustine's *City of God* xiv, 28, which contrasts the heavenly and mundane cities, and Revelation 18:21, 23-24. Merton wrote an explanation of the drama for those preparing the radio script, stressing the towers as symbols of man's pride and self-suffering, "the worship of his own technological skill, of his own wealth, his own ambitions, his own power to crush other men and make them his slaves." In the drama Merton dramatizes their effort as an illusion, the strength of the tower as a shadow:

Everywhere the great machines of war
Stand face to face. The hunters in the sky
Bargain with life and death.
Babylon like a great star wandering from its orbit,
Unsettles the universe, dragging nations down into
     chaos.[26]

Man's true destiny is to build another city, the city of love.
The play ends with the victory of truth over falsity:

Lo the Word on the white horse
With eyes of flame to judge and fight
Mercy in his look like wine.
He alone can break the seal
And tell the conquerors His Name.[27]

The Tower of Babel is a powerful and moving work, and
should be read in its entirety.

In Merton's sixth collection, *Emblems of a Season of Fury*
(1963), so numerous are the poems that voice his social concern that their titles alone might suffice. "Why Some Look Up
to Planets and Heroes," stands first in the collection, a poem
on which Merton wrote a somewhat lengthy comment, which
was printed together with the poem when it appeared in
America, the Jesuit weekly. "The poem," he said, "is only a
partial and ambivalent statement," generated by tensions
and perplexities:

I am not disillusioned with the idea of space exploration
as such. On the contrary, this fantastic endeavor seems
to me, in spite of various abuses, to be, in the classical
sense of the word, "magnificent."... It is something
which man *should* do because he is the son of God and
the master of God's creation. And if the space man is in
all truth a sample of what the man of the future might
turn out to be, then I think I like him. I find him admira-
ble....However, that is not what the poem is about. It
has really nothing to do with the flesh and blood space
men who have made the headlines, but about the headlines themselves. It is about the image, the fabricated

illusion, the public and international day-dream of space and space men. This is less magnificent....The poem is in a minor key because it takes account of this less charming aspect of the second most enormous and second most wasteful of our great international games. The best thing about this game, however, is that it does not threaten our survival. This, at least, can be said in its favor.[28]

A few stanzas must suffice:

Brooding and seated at the summit
Of a well-engineered explosion
He prepared his thoughts for fireflies and warnings

Four times that day his sun would set
Upon the casual rider
Streaking past the stars
At seventeen thousand miles per hour

. . . .

Even when a dog died in a globe
And still comes round enclosed
In a heaven of Russian wires

Uncle stayed alive
Gone in a globe of light
Ripping round the pretty world of girls and sights

. . . .

. . . . Nobody knows
What engine next will dig a moon
What costly uncles stand on Mars

What next device will fill the air with burning dollars
Or else lay out the low down number of some Day

What day? May we consent?
Consent to what? Nobody knows.
Yet the computers are convinced
Fed full of numbers by the True Believers.[29]

But perhaps the most graphic and best known of Merton's war poems is "Chant To Be Used Around a Site with Furnaces." In a letter dated September 19, 1961, he wrote:

> I don't know what things I may have sent you lately. Probably not the Auschwitz poem that was in the Catholic Worker before it was censored. Fortunately the censor passed it. The Beats in San Francisco got it in a new magazine which is not for nuns or monks either....I don't recommend it to you. It goes a little further than N.'s teen age girls in sweaters which after all is all for the glory of God if you look at it in the right way....[30]

(The latter comment was a gentle reproof for me, because of an unfavorable remark I had made on a certain person's poem.)

Reflect upon the monotonous recitation, flat-toned, banal, bereft of any human feeling, by the keeper of the ovens, as he related his unspeakably inhuman "accomplishments":

> You smile at my career but you would do as I did if you knew yourself and dared.
>
> In my day we worked hard we saw what we did our self-sacrifice was conscientious and complete our work was faultless and detailed
>
> Do not think yourself better because you burn up friends and enemies with long-range missiles without ever seeing what you have done[31]

The poem received several reprintings and appeared in Lawrence Ferlinghetti's *Journal for the Protection of All Beings*. It is highly likely that Merton had Adolf Eichman in mind as protagonist of the poem, for at about this time he wrote a poem titled "Epitaph for a Public Servant (In Memoriam— Adolf Eichmann)," based on the trial proceedings, with Merton's editorial comment between quotations. Eichmann's words in closing:

Gentlemen Adios
We shall meet again

We shall again be partners
Life is short
Art is long
And we shall meet
Without the slightest
Discourtesy,

Repentance is
For little children.

Let the theme of peace close the topic of war with Merton's brief and beautiful poem, "Paper Cranes (The Hibakusha Comes to the Abbey of Gethsemani)," which was written for that pathetic group of scarred survivors of the Hiroshima bomb, on their Peace Tour. They came to the hermitage; he read it to them, and was deeply moved when, as they turned to go, a silent woman passing beside his table dropped on it a paper crane, the Japanese symbol of peace. The poem must be quoted in its entirety:

PAPER CRANES

How can we tell a paper bird
Is stronger than a hawk
When it has no metal for talons
Feels no hunger
And knows no hate, having no need?

Wilder and wiser than eagles
It ranges round the world
Without suspicion
And without cravings.

But the child's hand
Folding these wings
Wins wars and ends them.
Imagining the luckiest of birds

> Lights with wrens, cranes and doves
> Kind as the innocent sun
> Lovelier than all dragons.[33]

This poem was later translated into Japanese by one of the poets of the Hibakusha, and published in *Prelude* 27, 1966.

As is well known from his prose writings, one of the areas of Merton's concern was the racist issue in which he was early involved. In *Emblems of a Season of Fury*, there is a poem, "And the Children of Birmingham," in which he sets that tragedy in the framework of the story of Little Red Riding Hood, and tells it incrementally with the ironic refrain: "(And tales were told/Of man's best friend, the Law.)" Its last stanza: "And the children of Birmingham/Walked into the fury/Of Grandma's hug:/Her friendly cells ('Better to love you with.')/Her friendly officers/And 'dooms of love.' "

> Laws had a very long day
> And all were weary.
>
> But what the children did that time
> Gave their town
> A name to be remembered!
>
> (And tales were told
> Of man's best friend the Law.)[34]

Merton wrote of it, "Poem on Birmingham was in the *Saturday Review*....It is a poem I am glad about."[35]

A later, profoundly moving poem, is "Picture of a Black Child with a White Doll (Carole Denis McNair, killed in Birmingham, Sept. 1963)." It began:

> Your dark eyes will never need to understand
> Our sadness who see you
> Hold that plastic glass-eyed
> Merchandise as if our empty-headed race
> Worthless full of fury
> Twanging and drooling in the southern night
> Needed to know love.

The temptation is to quote it entire, but here is the conclusion:

> So without a thought
> Of death or fear
> Of night
> You glow full of dark ripe August
> Risen and Christian
> Africa purchased
> For the one lovable Father alone
> And what was ever darkest and most frail
> Was then your treasure-child
> So never mind
> They found you and made you a winner
> Even in most senseless cruelty
> Your darkness and childhood
> Became fortune yes became
> Irreversible luck and halo.[36]

Merton's concern and compassion was all-embracing, as witness an ironic poem, "A Picture of Lee Ying," a little girl stopped on her flight to Hong Kong, and kneeling in tears begging to be allowed to enter the city. Merton mocks the excuses of the authorities:

> *Point of no return* is the caption, but this is meaningless
> she must return that is the story
>
> She would not weep if she had reached a point of no
> return what she wants is not to return

Merton in ironic mood continues:

> When the authorities are alarmed what can you do
> You can return to China
> Their alarm is worse than your sorrow

But he comforts her, telling her not to look at the dark side, for she has "the sympathy of millions." Then the paradoxical and ironic conclusion:

As a tribute to your sorrow we resolve to spend more money on nuclear weapons; there is always a bright side.[37]

Another poignant poem is "There Has To Be a Jail for Ladies," in which Merton pleads for "ladies of the street" when "their beauty is taken from them, when their hearts are broken," and the government suggests a jail "because they are wrong." The touching last stanza:

I love you, unhappy ones....
Tell me, darlings, can God be in hell?
You may curse;
    but he makes your dry voice turn to butter. . . .
He will laugh at judges.
He will laugh at the jail.
He will make me write this song.

Keep me in your pocket if you have one. Keep me in your
    heart if you have no pocket
It is not right for your sorrow to be unknown forever.
Therefore I come with these voices:

Poor ladies, do not despair—
God will come to your window with skylarks
And pluck each year like a white rose.[38]

Though Merton knew that technology was a fact and a necessity of modern life when it becomes an end in itself, and men and women serve it instead of being served by it, it becomes a disaster. In a poem "First Lesson About Man," Merton describes the consequence:

Man begins in zoology
He is the saddest animal

He drives a big red car
Called anxiety
He dreams at night

Of riding all the elevators
Lost in the halls
He never finds the right door.

"Whenever he goes to the phone/to call joy/He gets the wrong number. . . . He therefore likes weapons/He knows all guns/By their right names/He drives a big black Cadillac/Called death. . . .

Now dear children you have learned
The first lesson about man
Answer your test

"Man is the saddest animal
He begins in zoology
And gets lost
In his own bad news."[39]

Merton's last two poetic works, *Cables to the Ace* and *The Geography of Lograire*, are composite, and of such complexity that one can but comment on them briefly here, though they merit close reading and study, so saturated are they with the social theme. In *Cables* Merton writes as an anti-poet. The work consists of eighty-eight discrete pieces of poetry and poetic-prose, arranged in what he named an "urbane struc-turalism." His concern is twofold: the failure of language as communication, the result of a mechanistic society against which the full force of his critique is aimed. Surrealistic techniques thrust the ideological content forward with great urgency, counterpointed as it is by witty parody, irony, and at times biting satire, all of which invite the reader to do some of his or her own creating. "Edifying Cables" (the work's first title) "can be made musical," says Merton, "if played and sung by full-armed societies doomed to an electric war. . . ."[40]

Since language has become a medium in which we are totally immersed, there is no longer any need to say anything. The saying says itself all around us. No one need attend. Listening is obsolete. So is silence. Each one travels alone in a small blue capsule of indignation. (Some of the better informed have declared war on language.)[41]

Merton has on occasion expressed dire concern for the computer. So one is not surprised to find in entry 8:

Write a prayer to a computer? But first of all you have to find out how It thinks. *Does It dig prayer?* More important still, does It dig me, and father, mother, etc., etc? How does one begin: "O Thou great unalarmed and humorless electric sense . . . "? Start out wrong and you give instant offense. You may find yourself shipped off to the camps in a freight car. Prayer is a virtue. But don't begin with the wrong number.[42]

Personal and descriptive entries are matchless; there is even a hope for poetry:

> I think poetry must
> I think it must
> Stay open all night
> In beautiful cellars.[43]

But if some of the entries sound frighteningly negative, there is quiet affirmation as well, for the poem's entire burden is ultimately so. What dark there is lights up from time to time with flashes of light—quotations from Eckhart, Ruysbroeck, and Dōgen. And to the final draft of the poem Merton added his own thought in like patterning and substance:

But for each of us there is a point of nowhereness in the middle of movement, a point of nothingness in the midst of being: the incomparable point, not to be discovered by insight. If you seek it you do not find it. If you stop seeking it it is there....[44]

The solution to society's ills he posits in the dimension of prayer and contemplation. In one of the lyrics Christ comes down to seek the lost and sleeping disciple, who will awaken only "When he knows history/But slowly, slowly/The Lord of History/Weeps into the fire."[45] Merton closes on a personal note, saying, "I am about to build my nest/In the misdirected and unpaid express/As I walk away from the poem/Hiding the ace of freedoms."[46]

If in *Cables to the Ace* Merton pointed to a spiritual solution, he had still more to say. That he did in *The Geography of Lograire*, part of a larger projected work which he did not live to finish, but which has its own containment. He defines the work as "a wide-angle mosaic of poems and dreams," in which he says: "I have without scruple mixed what is my own experience with what is almost everybody else's."[47] In a word, his theme is the *unity* of man. He assembles as *dramatis personae* representatives of various primitive cultures, whose dreams and desires are not too unlike our own. In his fourfold division of the world, South, North, East and West we find them all. In canto "South," Africans, Mexicans, and people from Yucatan; in "North," Merton himself holds the stage in a Joycean mix of events of his own early life in New York, and in England. Also represented in this canto are the seventeenth-century Ranters and, in a beautiful descriptive piece, an account of the ill-fated "Kane Expedition." Throughout, his method consists in much quotation from original documents with his own editing and arrangement. In "South" are portions of a fourteenth-century diary of a Moroccan Muslim, the Journal of Bronisłas Malinowski (South Sea), plus the Cargo Songs, the catechism of a movement which originated in New Guinea and Melanesia about the end of the nineteenth century. As he wrote to Naomi Burton, "I tend to find analogies all over the place, not only in Black Power, but even to some extent in Catholic renewal as practiced by some types."[48]

In the final canto, "West," Merton is back in the actual world, specifically America. In the poems, "Day Six O'Hare Telephane," and "At This Precise Moment of History," with their political and religious overtones, he is definitely there and also with the Ghost Dances of the American Indians disillusioned by unkept promises. His theme of *unity* becomes explicit in lines of "Day Six O'Hare Telephane," depicting the general confusion at the airport, and a cross-country flight, in which the narrative of flight is broken by brief texts from the *Ashtavakra Gita* addressed to the subconscious mind of the "sky-rider," or Everyman: "Having finally recognized that the Self is Brahman and that existence and non-existence are imagined, what should such a one, free of desires, say or do?"[49] Merton's answer is in the following excerpt:

> Should he look out of the windows
> Seeking Self-Town?
> Should the dance of Shivashapes
> All over flooded prairies
> Make hosts of (soon) Christ-Wheat
> Self-bread which could also be
> Squares of Buddha-Rice
> Or Square Maize about those pyramids
> Same green
> Same brown, same square
> Same is the Ziggurat of everywhere
> I am one same burned Indian
> Purple of my rivers is the same shed blood
> All is flooded
> All is my Vietnam charred
> Charred by my co-stars
> The flying generals.[50]

Together with Merton's poetry, his *Freedom Songs* should be mentioned. At the request in connection with the Christian non-violent movement for civil rights, Merton wrote lyrics for eight Freedom Songs, based on biblical themes, and "freely developed in the colloquial idiom of our time." Four of these, under title of *Four Freedom Songs*, were set to music by the Boston composer, Charles Alexander Peloquin, and arranged for baritone solo, mixed chorus, and chamber orchestra or piano.[51]

As early as 1950 Robert Speaight, the British dramatist, published Merton's works in London, in *Selected Poems*; in

1959 New Directions published *Selected Poems*, with an Introduction by Mark Van Doren, which in an enlarged edition was published in 1967. The greater number of poems from Merton's late books have appeared in such magazines as *The Atlantic Monthly, Commonweal, Epoch, Florida Quarterly, Hudson Review, Horizon, Partisan Review, Sewanee Review, Texas Quarterly*, and *Vogue*, to name a few, to say nothing of inclusion in numerous anthologies, such as *The Criterion Book of Modern American Verse*, edited by W. H. Auden; *A Controversy of Poets*, edited by Paris Leary and Robert Kelley; *Poetry for Pleasure: The Hallmark Book of Poetry*; and *A New Anthology of Modern Poetry* (Revised Edition), edited and with an Introduction by Selden Rodman, and others. For the *Harvard Vocarium Records*, Robert Speaight has recorded a number of Merton's poems.

In addition, Merton's poems have been translated into a number of European and Latin American languages, notably French, Italian, German, Spanish and Portuguese, and poems selected from *Thirty Poems* and *Tears of the Blind Lions* appear in a Greek anthology, *Exomologeseis tou anthropou eikostou aionos* (Confessions of a Man of the Twentieth Century), translated by Helen Kapita (1969).

In August 1967, in "Answers to H. Lavin Cerda," editor of *Punto Final* (Chile), under biographical data Merton wrote: "Am now living as a hermit, solitary in the forest but am in contact with groups of poets, radicals, pacifists, hippies, artists, etc., in all parts of the world."[52] Outstanding among the poets were those of Latin America, for whom he had a warm affection, and whose poetry he held in high esteem. Many of the earliest translations of Merton's writings were done in Spanish and Portuguese. In 1960 the first volume of an *Obras Completas*, containing translations of the text of seven of Merton's books, was published in Buenos Aires. In 1964 an anthology of Catholic poetry, *Antologia de la Poesia Catolica del Siglo*, was published in Madrid. There was much reprinting of his poems in Spanish and Portuguese newspapers and magazines.

The rapport between Merton and Latin poets was close, and his influence on them, and theirs on him, was great indeed. In *Thirty Poems* (1944) there appears the poem, "In Memory of the Spanish Poet Federico Garcia Lorca,"[53] by whom some of Merton's early poetry was influenced. In *Emblems of a Season of Fury* (1963), in addition to "A Letter to Pablo Antonio Cuadra Concerning Giants,"[54] Merton included five South and Central American poets, with biographical sketches, critical comment, and his own translations of a number of their poems. They are: Jorge Carerra Andrade, "one of the most appealing of the fine Latin American poets of our century"; Cesar Vallejo, "whose work can be classed with the most authentic and creative achievements of our time"; the tragic Alfonso Cortes, "who has written some of the most profound 'metaphysical' poetry that exists"; Ernesto Cardenal, a priest, and for a few years a member of the Trappist community at Gethsemani, but whose health did not permit him to remain. Merton names him "one of the most significant of the newly mature generation of Latin American poets."[55] At Merton's death Cardenal wrote a long memorial poem, "Coplas on the Death of Merton," which was published in *New Directions in Prose and Poetry, 25,* edited by James Laughlin with Peter Glassgold and Frederick R. Martin (New York, New Directions, 1972). The poem was translated from the Spanish by Mireya Jaimes-Freyre and Kenneth Rexroth. In March 1974 it was reprinted by the International Center for Integrative Studies in its *Forum* for Correspondence and Contact (March 1974). Merton also reviewed collections of poetry by a number of Latin poets, including Alberto Girri (Argentina) and Jaime Garcia Terres (Mexico) in the *Times Literary Supplement,* Dec. 6, 1958, and translated poems of Nicanor Parra from the Spanish, and poems of Fernando Pessoa from the Portuguese. He also wrote articles on the poetry of Ruben Dario and Rafael Alberti.

At a meeting of the "new" Latin American poets, together with a few young North Americans, held in Mexico City in February 1964, a "Message to Poets" from Merton was read. In it he exhorted them: "Let us obey life, and the Spirit of Life that calls us to be poets, and we shall harvest many new fruits of hope that have never been seen before. With these fruits we shall calm the resentments and the rage of man":

> Let us be proud of the words that are given to us for nothing; not to teach anyone, not to confute anyone, not to prove anyone absurd, but to point beyond all objects into the silence where nothing can be said.... Come, dervishes: here is the water of life. Dance in it."[56]

In this same "Message to Poets" Merton wrote words that are eminently applicable to himself:

> Let us then recognize ourselves for who we are: dervishes mad with secret therapeutic love which cannot be bought or sold, and which the politician fears more than violent revolution, for violence changes nothing. But love changes everything. We are stronger than the bomb....[57]

The rich testament of Merton's poetry speaks for itself.

NOTES

1. Thomas Merton, *Journal*, March 8, 1968 (manuscript).
2. Robert Lowell, *Commonweal*, 42:10, June 22, 1945, pp. 240-242.
3. Thomas Merton, *Collected Poems* (N.Y.: New Directions, 1977), p. 713.
4. *Ibid.*, pp. 90-91.
5. Thomas Merton, *Diary*, Dec. 12-13, 1941 (manuscript), p. 2.
6. Thomas Merton, *Collected Poems*, p. 777.
7. Thomas Merton, "Concerning the Collection in Bellarmine College Library" (A Statement, Nov. 10, 1963), p. 2.
8. Thomas Merton, *Collected Poems*, pp. 20-21.
9. Thomas Merton, *Journal*, June 20, 1964 (manuscript), pp. 63-64.
10. Thomas Merton, *Collected Poems*, pp. 35-36.
11. *Ibid.*, pp. 39-40.
12. *Ibid.*, p. 82.
13. *Ibid.*, pp. 75-76.
14. *Ibid.*, p. 139.

15. *Ibid.*, p 141.
16. *Ibid.*, p. 144.
17. *Ibid.*, p. 145.
18. *Ibid.*, p. 148.
19. *Ibid.*, p. 206.
20. *Ibid.*, pp. 207-208.
21. *Ibid.*, pp. 208-209.
22. *Ibid.*, p. 222.
23. *Ibid.*, pp. 218-219.
24. *Ibid.*, pp. 228-229.
25. *Ibid.*, pp. 226-227.
26. *Ibid.*, pp. 253-254.
27. *Ibid.*, p. 273.
28. Thomas Merton, *America*, March 30, 1963, p. 433.
29. Thomas Merton, *Collected Poems*, pp. 305-307.
30. Thomas Merton, *Letter*, September 19, 1961.
31. Thomas Merton, *Collected Poems*, p. 349.
32. *Ibid.*, pp. 710-711.
33. *Ibid.*, p. 740.
34. *Ibid.*, pp 336-337.
35. Thomas Merton, *Letter*, August 9, 1963.
36. Thomas Merton, *Collected Poems*, pp. 626-627.
37. *Ibid.*, pp. 322-324.
38. *Ibid.*, pp 332-334.
39. *Ibid.*, pp. 624-626.
40. *Ibid.*, p. 396.
41. *Ibid.*, p. 397.
42. *Ibid.*, pp. 399-400.
43. *Ibid.*, p. 431.
44. *Ibid.*, p. 452.
45. *Ibid.*, p 449.
46. *Ibid.*, p. 454.
47. *Ibid.*, p. 457.
48. *Ibid.*, p. 604.
49. *Ibid.*, p. 578.
50. *Ibid.*, p. 579.
51. *Ibid.*, pp. 669 ("All the Way Down"); 692 ("Be My Defender"); 701 ("Earthquake"); 711 ("Evening Prayer"); 714 ("I Have Called You"); 756 ("Sundown"); 775 ("The Lord Is Good"); 779 ("There is a Way"). (These songs have also been translated into French and Spanish). *Four Freedom Songs*, "Sundown," "All the Way," "The Lord Is Good," and "Earthquake," set to music by C. Alexander Péloquin, for Baritone Solo, Mixed Chorus, and Chamber Orchestra or Piano. Its World Premier was held August 19, 1968 (1968 Liturgical Week, Washington, D.C.). Television Premiere: October 27, 1968, (NBC-TV Sing Freedom). Published by GIA Publications, 2115 West 63rd Street, Chicago, Illinois 60636. (First drafts of the "Freedom Songs," in holograph in possession of author.)
52. Thomas Merton, "Answers to H. Lavin Cerda" (Punto Final), Chile, August 1967 (manuscript), p. 1.
53. Thomas Merton, *Collected Poems*, p. 44.
54. *Ibid.*, pp. 372-391.

55. Thomas Merton, *Emblems of a Season of Fury*, p. 116. (In addition to the Latin poets mentioned in this collection, Merton has also included translations of six poems from the French of Raissa Maritain.)

56. Thomas Merton, "Message to Poets," *Raids on the Unspeakable* (N.Y.: New Directions, 1964), pp. 160-161.

57. *Ibid.*, p. 160.

Thomas Merton:
Monk and Author

John Eudes Bamberger, O.C.S.O.

I
EARLY LIFE

Thomas Merton was born at Prades, France on January 31, 1915.[1] His father, Owen Merton, was a New Zealander and a landscape painter. His mother, Ruth, an American, was also an artist and a person with strong convictions about rearing her son not to follow fashion blindly. Both parents held views of life and of moral values that were determined much more by art than by religious persuasion, so that the young Thomas was more familiar with the world of aesthetics and artistic integrity than with prayer. He refers to his family background and its significance in the beautiful opening lines of his autobiography, *The Seven Storey Mountain*:

> ...I came into the world. Free by nature, in the image of God, I was nevertheless the prisoner of my own violence and my own selfishness, in the image of the world in which I was born....My father and mother were captives in that world, knowing they did not belong with it or in it, and yet unable to get away from it. They were in the world and not of it—not because they were saints, but in a different way: because they were artists. The integrity of an artist lifts a man above the level of the world without delivering him from it....I inherited from my father his way of looking at things and some of his

integrity and from my mother some of her dissatisfaction with the mess the world is in, and some of her versatility.[2]

Merton's early years were often unhappy. He was six when his mother died of cancer, and the frequent changes of schools caused by his father's travels and the long absences of his father as he painted in some far-off countryside brought Merton into that loneliness which haunted his spirit throughout his life. But when he was eight years old he learned to cope with his unhappiness by writing, and in that year alone he wrote three novels. He also organized a group of boys into a literary club, learning already as a child the positive uses of solitude. He felt very much an outsider, especially while a student at Montauban. He never forgot that he "grew up in dormitories" and felt deeply that he was different and not accepted by the group of boys as a whole. When his father moved to England, he enrolled at Oakham, and then went on to Clare College, Cambridge. By the time he had entered there his father had died, and this deepened his sense of being alone, leading him to an undisciplined and dissipated life in which he found little happiness. But he was a good student, and when he left England for New York he embarked upon a life of studious activity and writing with immense energy and success.

It was shortly after his father's death that he took a trip to Rome (at the age of eighteen). There he came under the influence of the ancient Byzantine mosaics of Christian Rome that made such a profound impression upon his aesthetic (and, unobtrusively, religious) sensibility.

I was fascinated by these Byzantine mosaics. I began to haunt the churches where they were to be found ...and thus without knowing anything about it I became a pilgrim. I was unconsciously and unintentionally visiting all the great shrines of Rome, and seeking out their sanctuaries with some of the eagerness and avidity and desire of a true pilgrim, though not quite for the right reason. And yet it was not for a wrong reason either. For these mosaics and frescoes and all the ancient altars and thrones and sanctuaries were designed and built for the instruction of people who were not capable of immediately understanding anything higher.[3]

The work of conversion had begun and was to continue while he was a student at Columbia in New York. There he encountered the teachings of St. Thomas Aquinas and at the suggestion of a Hindu monk began to read St. Augustine. He was baptized at the age of twenty-three, and upon terminating his studies in literature taught for a year at St. Bonaventure College in upstate New York. Though he felt a strong urge to devote his life to working among poor blacks with Catherine de Hueck at Harlem's Friendship House, he became convinced that he was called to be a Trappist monk. On December 10, 1941, at the age of twenty-six, he entered Gethsemani Abbey in Kentucky, where he lived the rest of his life. While on a trip to a conference of monks from Benedictine and Trappist communities in the Far East, he suffered a fatal accident in Bangkok, Thailand on that same date twenty-seven years later, at the age of fifty-three.

II

MONASTIC LIFE AND WORKS

Merton was a fervent and dedicated monk who lived a most stable life in the same community of Gethsemani where he entered as a young man. He began his writing career as a monk spontaneously when he found himself writing poems which seemed to flow out of his monastic experience. As an author Merton proved to be one of the most prolific in monastic history. It is quite impossible to treat here all his works, and mention shall be made only of the more influential and representative writings.[4]

Father Louis (as he was called in the community of Gethsemani) has himself described his development as an author in the monastery in the preface to A Thomas Merton Reader: "I would say that my life at Gethsemani has fallen roughly into four periods. First, the novitiate....It was a period of training, and a happy, austere one, during which I wrote little. The best Gethsemani poems belong to this period....The second period extends from 1944, my first vows, to ordination in 1949....In 1946 I wrote *The Seven Storey Mountain*, in 1947 *Seeds of Contemplation* and in 1948 *The Waters of Siloe*."[5] The first work listed here by Merton, his autobiography, was an astonishing success. It became one of the most widely read books in the United States in the years immediately following its publication, and has continued to be published and read widely until the present time. With the publication of his autobiography Merton became a famous figure in the religious and literary world, and monastic, contemplative life became American in its expression for perhaps the first time. The work provides a moving account of his early life (including the first years in the monastery) in a style that directs itself to the reader with an intimacy that is at once touching and spiritual. Merton himself realized the power and the influence of his style and refers to it in words which indicate how for him writing was part of the communion with God to which his whole life was oriented. In the preface to the Japanese edition of *The Seven Storey Mountain* he writes: "Therefore, most honorable reader, it is not as an author that I would speak to you, not as a story teller, not as a philosopher, not as a friend only: I seek to speak to you, in some way, as your own self. Who can tell what this may mean? I myself do not know. But if you listen, things will be said that are perhaps not written in this book. And this will be due not to me but to the One who lives and speaks in us both."[6]

The third period was preceded by an interval of eighteen months during which Father Louis suffered from nervous exhaustion and weak health. At the end of this moratorium he was appointed Master of Scholastics and began publishing once again. He produced *The Ascent to Truth*—a kind of summary of the whole of the spiritual life, and the most professedly theological (in the professional sense of the word) of his works. This was followed by *The Sign of Jonas*, a journal of his daily monastic life in the community of Gethsemani, containing many reflections upon his experience and upon the action of God in the life of prayer and on the revelation of God in nature. Jacques Maritain considered that the final poetic-prose passages of this work were among the finest literary writing of the present century. *No Man Is an Island*, which appeared in 1955, marks a kind of turning point for Father Louis in that it reflects broader issues of a more social and interpersonal nature without in the least, however, ceasing to stress the central place of the inner search and contemplation.

The fourth stage of Merton's monastic life began in 1955 when he was appointed Master of the Choir Novices. *Disputed Questions* and various essays on solitude, liturgy, nuclear war, and Oriental thought were produced at this time and led to a heightened influence on the American political scene as Merton published works dealing with race relations and the Vietnam war subsequent to the above-mentioned books. Even in such works of social and political focus, he continued to stress the inner life and contemplation as the dominant orientation of life.

The final period of Merton's life began when he was given permission by his Abbot to retire to a hermitage in the woods near the monastery. He lived there the last three years of his life, while continuing to give a weekly conference to the monks. In this final phase of his development he continued to rethink his experience and to explore the monastic tradition as he became increasingly interested in the spirituality of the Christian East—first, the *Philokalia*, Saint Theophane the Recluse, Saint Charbel the Syrian Hermit—but also in the Far East, and above all in Zen. During this time he published *Zen and the Birds of Apetite, Mystics and Zen Masters,* and *Conjectures of a Guilty Bystander*, a kind of journal and commentary on the events in the world as seen from the perspective of a contemplative monk.

When Merton departed on his final voyage to the Bangkok meeting where he was to die, he left two important works in manuscript. One, *The Inner Experience*, remains one of Merton's most successful attempts to describe the life of prayer in an extended discussion, and presents highly interesting material on his thinking at the very end of his life. It is also an indication that he remained deeply immersed in the teaching of St. John of the Cross as well as in Zen Buddhism. The other work has since been published under the title of *The Climate of Monastic Prayer,* and is one of the most extensive descriptions of the monastic life that he wrote. It is particularly successful in bridging the experience of modern men and women and traditional monastic practice and vocabulary. Also published posthumously was *The Asian Journal of Thomas Merton,* which contains his notes and final reflections on contributions to the contemplative life possible from the Zen and other Buddhist and Hindu traditions along with the account of his contacts with the various representatives of these traditions.

III
SPIRITUAL TEACHING

Merton's teaching is essentially the classic monastic spirituality. What accounts for its originality is the personal expression he gives to it. He was able to make a synthesis of traditional and modern values and to articulate them with force and clarity. Several basic themes are to be found constantly present in the writings of Thomas Merton at all stages of his development once he entered the monastery. However, they are treated in an ever new context as his own spiritual life and personal development evolved. In particular, his early works display a much stronger accent on separation from the world and the destructive and perverting influences of the modern technological culture and secularist values than his later works do. In the latter half of his monastic life, after his experience of teaching and giving spiritual direction to the scholastics and novices at Gethsemani had broadened his views, he became increasingly concerned with integrating values he found in the modern world with the life of prayer. This led him to comment upon problems that were currently agitating the American political scene, such as racism and the Vietnam war. He soon became an influential writer in both these realms, without, however, losing sight of the contemplative perspective. He became one of the founders of the Catholic Peace Movement, and was the recipient of a peace prize. But his own major interests were determined by the inner life and the demands of contemplative prayer and the spiritual transformation that he saw increasingly as the whole meaning of humankind's life on earth.

Merton's teaching also became increasingly focused upon experience and the concrete. This is especially apparent after his earliest works, such as *Exile Ends in Glory* and *The Ascent to Truth*, which he considered to be too much influenced by the conceptions of others about the spiritual life. He felt strong opposition to the abstract approach to life which tended to dehumanize and alienate and stultify. "We seek rather to gain a direct existential grasp, a personal experience of the deeper truths of life and faith, finding ourselves in God's truth."[7] His best writing and most personal teaching had always been characterized by this view, as is evident from his autobiography and the early poems.[8]

Because his teaching was so heavily based upon the existential and the concrete, Merton's views and opinions were in a state of continuing evolution. He did not fear to assume new positions once he received some fresh insight or underwent some further development that modified what he had earlier taught. As a result he can be cited on both sides of some issues, and it is very difficult to evaluate his thought on the basis of any single work of his, still less on any single statement.

The one word, nonetheless, that best sums up Merton's spiritual teaching is *contemplation*. He had an immense enthusiasm for the monastic life. He viewed the monastic charism as essentially ordered to the transformation of the monk, and, indeed, of every Christian who followed the way of prayer, into a true son or daughter of God. He considered the most characteristic work of the monastic life to be contemplation. Repeatedly, at all stages of his monastic life, he returned to the exploration and study of contemplative activity and its requirements and effects, and he sought to revise and restate his thoughts on it so as to communicate its meaning as fully as possible. He always associated the attainment of a fuller human life and condition with the work of contemplation, and saw contemplation as the way to greater personal freedom and purer love. Purification of the inner person and total dedication to God's will are at once the condition for contemplation and its fruit. "The monastery is a school—a school in which we learn from God how to be happy. Our happiness consists in sharing the happiness of God, the perfection of his unlimited freedom, the perfection of his love.... This is the meaning of the contemplative life...."[9]

Merton's teaching on contemplation became increasingly personal in the sense that it was ever more apparent that it centered on the person of Christ and led to the discovery of the True Self. Solitude, so important in his monastic life and teaching, was essentially a function of these two poles of contemplative activity. As he stated simply, "Solitude means *cum Christo vivere.*"[10] Solitude and contemplation became increasingly "a way of following Christ, of sharing in his passion and resurrection and in his redemption of the world.... For that very reason the dimensions of prayer in solitude are those of man's ordinary anguish, his self-searching, his moments of nausea at his own vanity, falsity and capacity for betrayal.... The way of prayer brings us face to face with the sham and indignity of the false self."[11]

Merton was to become ever more convinced that the monk's work was precisely to be present to the world through this kind of courageous dedication to contemplative union with God. "This is precisely the monk's chief service to the world: this silence, this listening, this questioning, this humble and courageous exposure to what the world ignores about itself—both good and evil."[12] Such exposure to God's truth would reveal the man's true potential to himself. It was in this realization of his own true nature, of the transcendent self that is so often emphasized in the latter part of his monastic life, that Merton's true potential was revealed, especially as he pursued his interest in Zen. But this was evidenced in his earlier years as well, as he reflected more deeply on his own experience of the sacramental life and his life in Christ.

"...My true spiritual identity is found in my identity with Christ. Then to know myself fully, I must know Christ."[13] The "void" spoken of in the Zen tradition was the way to this self-knowledge and transcendence of self.[14] But in order to complete it, a person must surrender to love: "...a man cannot enter into the deepest center of himself and pass through that center into God unless he...gives himself to other people in the purity of selfless love."[15]

On the final page of one of the last books that he wrote, Merton expressed his convictions regarding both contemplation and the place of the contemplative in the world in terms that summarize his whole monastic and spiritual teaching. "The most important need in the Christian world today is this inner truth nourished by the Spirit of contemplation: the praise and love of God, the longing for the coming of Christ, the thirst for the manifestation of God's glory, his truth, his justice, his Kingdom in the world. These are all charac-teristically 'contemplative' and eschatological aspirations of the Christian heart, and they are the very essence of monastic prayer."[16]

NOTES

1. This essay will appear in substantially this form in a forthcoming volume of the *Dictionairre de Spiritualité*, for which it was originallly written. It was revised and edited for publication here by the editor of the present volume, and appears here "by way of exception" and through the courtesy of the Board of Editors of the *Dictionairre de Spiritualité* and the kindness of Fr. John Eudes (editor's note).

2. Thomas Merton, *The Seven Storey Mountain* (N.Y.: Harcourt, Brace, 1948), pp. 3-4.

3. *Ibid.*, p. 108.

4. The full account of Merton's works would require many pages. There are altogether some forty major volumes and hundreds of essays published. His works have been translated into twenty-one languages. The unpublished material is also very considerable and contains much information concerning such matters as the early phases of the monastic renewal in the numerous letters exchanged with Dom Jean Leclercq dating from 1950 until the year of his death, correspondence with Boris Pasternak, and many aspects of the spiritual life. The Thomas Merton Studies Center at Bellarmine College in Louisville, Kentucky has the largest collection of unpublished material, including many volumes of journals, several thousand letters, some nineteen major unpublished works (dealing mainly

with prayer and the spiritual life and monastic tradition) and some six hundred and thirty-two tapes of conferences and lectures. His very considerable poetic output is published under the title *The Collected Poems of Thomas Merton* (N.Y.: New Directions, 1977). The fullest bibliographical material on Merton has recently been published in two works treating only of his published material: *Thomas Merton: A Bibliography*, by Frank Dell'Isola (Kent State University Press, 1975), and *Thomas Merton: A Bibliography* by Marquita Breit (Metuchen, N.J.: The Scarecrow Press, 1974), which treats also of works about Merton since 1956, the date of the first edition of the Dell'Isola work.

There is a plethora of writings on Merton, and they continue to emerge in the wake of his death. His influence continues to be marked, and new editions and translations of his works are being supplemented by many studies of his spiritual teaching in its various ramifications. The Thomas Merton Studies Center, entirely devoted to the preservation of Merton's works and to scholarship related to his life and work provides the fullest bibliography in its publication, *The Thomas Merton Seasonal*.

Some of the most useful works on Merton's spirituality are *Thomas Merton on Prayer* by John Higgins, S.J. (Spencer, Mass.: Cistercian Publications, 1971) and *Thomas Merton on Mysticism* by Raymond Bailey (N.Y.: Doubleday, 1976). The bibliography by Breit mentioned above gives a full list of works on Merton up to 1972. John Howard Griffin has been commissioned by the Merton Legacy Trust to write the official biography, making use of otherwise restricted private papers.

5. *A Thomas Merton Reader*, edited by Thomas McDonnell (N.Y.: Doubleday, 1962), pp. viii-ix.

6. Merton, "Author's Preface to the Japanese Edition," *Nanae No Yama (The Seven Storey Mountain)*, trans. Tudishi Kudo (Tokyo: Chou Shuppansha, 1966), p. 13.

7. Merton, *Contemplative Prayer* (N.Y.: Doubleday, 1969), p. 67.

8. Cf. *Figures for an Apocalypse* (N.Y.: New Directions, 1948) for a variety of highly personal experiences which develop some aspect or another of the contemplative life.

9. Merton, *The Seven Storey Mountain*, p. 372.

10. Merton, Preface to *Alone With God* by Jean Leclercq, O.S.B., trans. E. McCabe (N.Y.: Farrar, Straus and Cudahy, 1961), p. xxi.

11. Merton, *Contemplative Prayer*, pp. 25-26.

12. *Ibid.*, p. 27.

13. Merton, *The New Man* (N.Y.: Farrar, Straus and Cudahy, 1961), p. 170.

14. Cf. Merton, *Zen and the Birds of Apetite* (N.Y.: New Directions, 1968), p. 76.

15. Merton, *New Seeds of Contemplation* (N.Y.: New Directions, 1961), p. 64.

16. Merton, *Contemplative Prayer*, p. 144.

Destination: East;
Destiny: Fire—
Thomas Merton's Real Journey

David F. K. Steindl-Rast, O.S.B.

The moment of take-off was ecstatic. The dewy wing was suddenly covered with rivers of cold sweat running backward. The window wept jagged shining courses of tears. Joy. We left the ground—I with Christian mantras and a great sense of destiny, of being at least on my true way after years of waiting and wondering and fooling around.

May I not come back without having settled the great affair. And found also the great compassion, mahakaruna. We tilted east over the shining city. . . .

I am going home, to the home where I have never been in this body. . . .[1]

Did Thomas Merton realize the full meaning of these words when he wrote them on October 15, 1968, exactly eight weeks before his sudden death? He was setting out on a journey to India and the Far East that would afford him opportunities to see people and places he had long wanted to visit. Yet, the less than two months of this journey were merely the expression in space of an intellectual journey which had prompted this one and found its climax in it. This journey of the mind, which had begun more than thirty years earlier, was in turn only one aspect of a still more comprehensive movement, a journey of Merton's whole life toward the mysteries symbolized by the East.

The physical journey, October 15 to December 10, 1968, is well documented by Merton's own notebooks and by photographs he took. Augmented by a carefully prepared literary apparatus and appendices, these records were published under the title *The Asian Journal of Thomas Merton*.[2] Highlights of this tour were three private audiences with the Dalai Lama, on November 4, 6, and 9, various exchanges with Eastern monks, a few days of retreat near Darjeeling, and a visit to the ancient monuments at Polonnaruwa, Ceylon (now Sri Lanka). The pace of this trip was swift; its content varied; its meaning, as I see it, lay in exposure on many different levels to that reality we call the East.[3]

Merton's exposure to the East had begun much earlier, however, when as a twenty-year-old student he met a Hindu monk who called himself Dr. M. B. Bramachari (which means simply "monk"). This friendship was of decisive importance for Merton's life, since it was through Dr. Bramachari's influence that he embarked on an exploration not only of Eastern spirituality, but for the first time in his life on Western spirituality as well. Soon his fervor as a convert to the Roman Catholic Church (in 1938) and as a young monk (since 1942) blinded him temporarily to the riches of other traditions. As late as 1950, he still labeled Buddhism glibly as "quietism," "pantheism," and "absorptionism." But by that time he had begun a correspondence with Hindu scholars and was engaged in a study comparing Patanjali's system of Yoga with the mysticism of St. John of the Cross. The resemblances between the two came as a surprise. But when in 1959 Merton sent a copy of his *Wisdom of the Desert*[4] to D. T. Suzuki, it was the latter who discovered with surprised delight the parallels between the Desert Fathers and Zen Masters. This contact with D. T. Suzuki became an incentive for Merton to study Zen Buddhism and resulted in several books on this subject during the last decade of his life.

It is characteristic of Merton's approach to Eastern thought that he did not so much reach out for contact with other traditions, but rather went so deeply into his own that he could not help discovering the common roots. A strange journey indeed: the traveler, instead of going abroad, digs into the ground on which he stands, but digs so deep that he comes out in China. This is why Thomas Merton became so trustworthy a guide to other Christians. Proceeding almost with reluctance—though that is not the right expression for the joyous way he walked in his heavy boots—he never left firm orthodox ground and so moved slowly but convincingly. This is worlds removed from the spiritual faddism of others. One is reminded of St. Augustine's assertion that the doubt of Thomas does more for our faith in Jesus' resurrection than Mary Magdalene's enthusiastic belief. After all, Merton was named after the Doubter. But remember, when all the other apostles lost heart, it was Thomas who dared to follow Jesus. Not with enthusiasm, maybe, but with dedication he said: "Let us go, too, to die with him."[5] Merton, too, was willing to follow the Truth, no matter where the journey would lead. It made a difference that his mind had been launched on the journey to the East not by a mere scholar, but by Bramachari, the monk.

A geographic journey can be charted according to places and dates. The mind's journey can be traced by encounters and influences. But the heart will contend:

> I can only say, *there* we have been; but I cannot say where.
> And I cannot say, how long, for that is to place it in time.[6]

Yet the heart's journey is real to a degree unattainable on the other two levels. Reality does admit of degrees. We may go to a place and yet fail to be really present where we are. It is our mind that builds out of the raw material of the given the world that is real for us. But thought in turn is realized, and so made fully real, only by living. The journey of the heart is realization through living. For Merton, the monk, it is "our passage to eternity."[7] And eternity is not unending time; it is the very opposite of time, the Now that does not pass away. Full realization is awakening to that Now.

In an attempt to understand Merton's real journey we shall let the poet monk speak for himself, putting passages side by side rather than analyzing them. There can be no question of proving a thesis. It is merely a matter of suggestions, of pointing out a convergence of images in the hope of attuning our ears to a deeper meaning. It is as if one were to single out musical themes, intricately interwoven in a symphony. These themes are nodes in the magnetic field of the imagination, not steps in an argument. Nor shall we consider the chronology of relevant texts. The archetypal images for which we are looking are not bound by time; they surface unpredictably out of the magma of poetic imagination. The passages quoted in a given case are invitations to read the whole poem.[8] If you catch the scent, follow the track on your own. If it is the right track, it will lead you eastward, inevitably.

"Eastern mysteries of distance"

The East in Merton's mind is not a cardinal point of the compass, ninety degrees to the right of North; nor is it simply the realm of Oriental culture, as contrasted with the West. For Merton the East is an archetypal reality. It belongs to the geography of the heart, the Geography of Lograire.[9] It is a region of the poet's world, a world which is "at once his and everybody's."[10] The East is a "universal and primitive myth-dream term"[11] for an area of experience that "cannot be fully communicated,"[12] as the poet himself admits. Yet the world of images "cannot be purely private, any more than it can be purely public."[13] Thus we may venture to explore the context in which Merton's poetry speaks of the East and so begin to appreciate what kind of East it was toward which his heart journeyed.

If we listen carefully to Thomas Merton's poetic expressions, it is possible to hear the overtones which resonate when he uses the term East. We can even distinguish different octaves of meaning. One significance is brought out when the poet speaks of "eastern mysteries of distance."[14] Right away the connotation of travel is thereby linked with eastward movement. A night train, baying somewhere as if lost, occasioned that line. The homesick sound made the monks assembling for Matins in the nearness of their choir stalls marvel at the mystery of distance out there. For Merton the mysteries of distance are "eastern mysteries." He stands in an Old World tradition. In the New World one travels west for adventure. But Merton's usage is rooted in a world in which the pilgrim went east to the Holy Land and the East was the realm from which the wise men came bearing mysterious gifts. Even the explorers went West from the Old World only to search by sea for the fabled riches of the East. Steeped in this tradition, Merton speaks of his own westward departure on October 15, 1968, quite naturally as eastbound.[15]

"Eastern mysteries of distance": travel, pilgrimage, exploration. "Wide-open winds of the horizon" is a parallel image, and it makes sense that this beautiful line should have its place in a poem called "Pilgrims' Song." It makes sense also that the Pilgrims' Song should envisage a movement leading from the "dark atmosphere" of "Stepmother city" through the quite different obscurity of the mystic's "immaculate dark" to the Easter morning of a "blinding East."[16] Thus, poetic convention and usage is not the major reason why pilgrimage is inevitably eastbound for Merton. He understands his life as a movement from darkness toward the light, a nocturnal journey toward sunrise.

"Every burning morning is a prophecy"

The East as the region of sunrise suggests not only the breaking forth of light, but the daily repeated renewal of this mystery. We know from his own diaries how much it meant to Fr. Louis Merton to celebrate every morning with psalms of praise the newness of life-giving light. "The Lord God is present where the new day shines in the moisture of the young grasses."[17] The renewal of life at dawn is enriched and expanded in the poet's imagination until he sees "a whole new universe . . . rise up like an Atlantis in the East,"[18] an East which has now become the symbolic locus of ultimate cosmic renewal.

Thus, in the image of the East the archetypes of journey, of sunrise, and of renewal fuse. This fusion may have occurred at the very dawn of religion when paleolithic burial sites were oriented toward the rising sun. Are they monuments to the primordial hope of the human heart that the journey of life does not end in the darkness of death? For Thomas Merton this hope was based on his faith in "Truth greater than disaster,"[19] faith in the one who said: "I am the Truth."[20] This faith transforms the longing for cosmic renewal into eschatological hope:

> Suppose a whole new universe, a great clean Kingdom
> Were to rise up like an Atlantis in the East,
> Surprise this earth, this cinder, with new holiness![21]

The same faith makes every sunrise proclaim the one who said: "I am the light of the world."[22]

> And every burning morning is a prophecy of Christ
> Coming to raise and vindicate
> Even our sorry flesh.[23]

Faith in this cosmic prophecy transforms the very concept of the journey toward the light. It suddenly becomes a going out to meet the Bridegroom. "Behold, the Bridegroom comes! Co out to meet him!"[24] This going out, in whatever way circumstances may call for it, becomes now the touchstone for faith. This point is of crucial importance for an understanding of Thomas Merton's journey to the East.

"The madman runs to the east"

An insight that vividly brought home to Merton what it means to "go out" is reported in a chapter significantly entitled "The Madman Runs to the East."[25] (How mad the madman is remains a question. "God purposely chose what the world considers foolish to confound the wise."[26])

A book about Egypt (read in the refectory) spoke convincingly of the serenity and sanity of Egyptian life
under the Pharaohs as shown in the tomb paintings of
early centuries. Yet this serenity was not enough. The
People of God had to be chosen out of it and flung into
hunger, homelessness, anguish, and trouble. They had
to leave this placid, well-organized, pleasant life and go
into the desert. Can we believe that the civilization of
Egypt was the epitome of all that was wicked? We do not
have to. The People of God were—and are—called out of
Egypt not because it was wicked, but because they had a
more bitter and more promising destiny willed for them
by God....

...Whatever the explanation, I am struck and troubled
by the fact that if the Jews were called out of Egypt, out
of peace and into anguish, it was because God did not
will that His People should merely live productive,
quiet, joyous, and expansive lives.[27]

In order to appreciate the full impact of this passage, we must
remember that the book about the serene, joyful, productive,
and expansive life of the ancient Egyptians was read aloud
while the monks were at table. In our age of rushed lunch
hours and crowded cafeteries, it would be difficult to find a
more striking realization of the serene, joyful, productive,
and expansive life than a monastic refectory. And yet, the
whole purpose of monastic living is to attune one's ears to the
call "Go out!"

Merton was not one to mistake a change of place for the
genuine Exodus of the heart, much as he might have been
tempted, much as he kept looking for that ideal hermitage,
for that tabernacle built on the mountain of Christ's transfig-
uration. He remembered that while Peter was preoccupied
with plans for getting settled on the mountain of glory, Moses
and Elijah spoke with the transfigured Lord "about his
exodus, which he was to accomplish in Jerusalem."[28] Then,
on the way down, Jesus strictly charged the apostles: "Tell no
one of the vision you have seen, until the Son of Man is raised

from the dead."[29] Jesus still had to "go out" into his death. To go out with him through death into fullness of life, that is the genuine "going out," the exodus of the heart.

> ... The millionaires can have you, Egypt, with your
>   onion-breath!
> ... 'til we are bled from death to life,
>   ... and our escaping feet ...
> Dance on the air, and run upon the surface of the sea
> And climb us out of your dark atmosphere to face the
>   blinding East
> And conquer all skies with hell-harrowing Christ.[30]

East is the direction of this inner passage. Transformation is its essence. The great archetypal symbol of this transformation is fire.

"Clean transforming fire"

In those depths from which symbolic images emerge, the East and the transforming fire belong together. Not only poets see the sun appear "from out the fiery portal of the east."[31] Before the eyes of all the faithful the Church impressively enacts, year after year, in the Easter liturgy Christ's death and resurrection through the symbols of fire and of the rising sun. In his *transitus* Christ is the "burning Lion"[32] who leads all those who are baptized into his death "out of darkness into his own wonderful light."[33] Only in the context of this, "our passage to eternity,"[34] can we sense the full significance of those "eastward mysteries of distance where"—and this is a crucial part of the image—"fire flares."[35] In the symbols and rituals of the Easter night, fire becomes firmly associated with the transforming journey.

One has to experience the Easter celebration in a monastery to appreciate the impact of its symbolism on Merton's imagination. For that half of his lifetime which he spent in the monastery, Easter was for him the annual "taste of heaven,"[36] growing richer and richer as memories and associations accumulated. "All the Easter alleluia antiphons come back to me with rich associations of the happiest days in my life—the...Paschal seasons that I have had in the monastery."[37] "How mighty they are, those hymns and those antiphons of the Easter office,"[38] he marvels. But still more powerful is the wordless language of the Easter fire. Its primordial symbolism is as central to Merton's poetic imagery as the paschal mystery is to his life as a monk and a Christian. For Merton the monk as poet, the real journey to the East is transformation by fire.

The Easter mystery and the myth of Prometheus, the fire-bringer, together enrich the soil from which his images grow. The polarity between the two provides a powerful creative tension.

> No one was ever less like Prometheus on Caucasus, than Christ on His cross. For Prometheus thought he had to ascend into heaven to steal what God had already decreed to give him. But Christ, Who had in Himself all the riches of God and all the poverty of Prometheus, came down with the fire Prometheus needed, hidden in His Heart. And He had Himself put to death next to the thief Prometheus in order to show him that in reality God cannot seek to keep anything good to Himself alone.

> Far from killing the man who seeks the divine fire, the Living God will Himself pass through death in order that man may have what is destined for him.

> If Christ has died and risen from the dead and poured out upon us the fire of His Holy Spirit, why do we imagine that our desire for life is a Promethean desire, doomed to punishment?[39]

"The fire Prometheus thought he had to steal from the gods is his own identity in God."[40] When Christ comes to establish for good our human identity in God, he comes as the Fire-bringer. His "Heart bleeds with infinite fire."[41] This is why in Merton's Christmas poems the Christchild in the crib is already a sort of consecrated time bomb ticking towards conflagration of the whole universe.

> Here in this straw lie planned the fires
> That will melt all our sufferings:
> He is our Lamb, our holocaust![42]

The same theme is echoed in another poem:

> ...In winter when the birds put down their flutes
> And wind plays sharper than a fife upon the icy rain,
> I sit in this crib
> And laugh like fire, and clap my golden hands....[43]

Christ's infinite fire melts all our sufferings, because his Love "melts all the barriers that stop our passage to eternity"[44] and sets us free to reach the goal of the great journey.

"The whole world is secretly on fire"

Fire, in this sense, is a hidden fire, because the transformation it effects is "a secret Easter"[45]—not a date on the calendar, not the liturgical celebration of the paschal mystery, but its realization, hidden in the daily lives (and daily deaths) of those who believe in Christ and in "the Spirit of Fire Who is given us from heaven."[46] "For you have died, and your life is hidden with Christ in God. When Christ, our life shall be manifested, then you too will be manifested with him in glory."[47] "Now we will all be manifest," writes Merton in his diary the night before Easter.

> We will see one another with white garments, with palm branches in our hands. The darkness is like a font from which we shall ascend washed and illumined, to see one another no longer separate but one in the Risen Christ.

> For we must see one another. Christ must be manifest in glory. His soul is now charged with the glory of victory,

demanding a Body, and not only His own physical Body but the whole Mystical Body of the elect.[48]

We have here in his own words the theological basis for one of Merton's pivotal poetic intuitions: that the new life, which Christ's death and resurrection imparted to the world, lies hidden like fiery seed in the dark earth, waiting to become manifest; for sooner or later the fire must break forth.

In the Gospel, Jesus speaks in the same breath of the Easter event and of that sowing of fire: "I came in order to cast fire upon the earth; and would that it were already kindled!"[49] In one of his most remarkable lines Gerard Manley Hopkins spells out what must happen for Christ's fiery life to become manifest in the Church (and note the key words: "Let him easter in us, be a dayspring to the dimness in us, be a crimson-cresseted east."[50] Here Christ himself is the East. The journey to the East is in its deepest significance transformation in Christ.

For Merton the seed of our Easter life is hidden in the sacraments, especially in the Eucharist. "If Mass could only be, every morning, what it is on Easter morning!"[51] But, isn't it? Fr. Louis, celebrating Mass on some ordinary day, in some insignificant side-chapel, is aware of holding in his hands the promise of new life in the midst of an aging world. As he elevates the host, its shape suggests the Easter sunrise:

Great Christ, my fingers touch Thy wheat
And hold Thee hidden in the compass of Thy paper
    sun....
Here in my hands I hold that secret Easter.[52]

A surprise awaits us at this point of our investigation. We might have thought that in pursuing "the tracks of those wonderful fires"[53] we were worlds removed from Merton's deep social and political concerns. Yet suddenly we discover in an almost naive sounding passage of his diary the key to this monk's burning concern for the world writing in the labor pains of history:

All history has become like the Blessed Mother, in whose womb is formed the Mystical Christ and the last day will be Christmas and Easter and the Ascension: all Liturgy will be explained and enacted in one word and Liturgy will be the world's judgment.[54]

This too is an Easter entry in Merton's diary, following closely upon the one cited above, which speaks about the gradual manifestation of the risen Christ in his mystical body, the Church. In this perspective, the Christmas mystery of the incarnation does not merely precede and prepare the Easter mystery, but it expands and implants its transforming fire in the world. And what is the dynamic medium of this transformation? Liturgy.

One might have to go back to Pseudo-Dionysius or even to the Vedic experience[55] to find a view of liturgy that is at once so profoundly mystical and so explosively charged for practical action. Obviously we have to give to the term *liturgy* here the richest possible, the most dynamic meaning. For Merton the poet, the mystic, the monk who took the world to heart, liturgy is—in so many different ways—incarnation.

But once Merton's perspective of the incarnation had been broadened to include its unfolding after the resurrection, his outlook would continue to expand until, by its own inner logic, it embraced *all* of history. For history is of one piece. If the mystical Christ continues to be formed in the womb of history to the end of time, it makes sense that from the beginning of time the womb was prepared to conceive him. From here it is only a small step to realize that creation, as the substratum of history, must be included in this scheme, which now assumes cosmic dimensions. "The whole world is secretly on fire"[56] because its innermost mystery is a "secret Easter."[57]

Since the universe is of one piece, the repercussions of any historic event reverberate throughout the entire fabric of nature. In Christ's death and resurrection a secret burst forth that had been implanted in the world from the beginning of time.

For, like a grain of fire
Smoldering in the heart of every living essence
God plants His undivided power—
Buries His thought too vast for worlds
In seed and root and blade and flower,

Until, in the amazing light of April,
Surcharging the religious silence of the spring,
Creation finds the pressure of His everlasting secret
Too terrible to bear.[58]

It has to be April, the Easter month. "April is the cruelest month,"[59] for "unless the grain of wheat falls into the ground and dies, it remains alone; but if it dies, it bears much fruit."[60]

Then every way we look, lo! rocks and trees
Pastures and hills and streams and birds and firmament
And our own souls within us flash, and shower us with
    light,
While the wild countryside, unknown, unvisited of
    men,
Bears sheaves of clean, transforming fire.[61]

"Pagan and converted fires"[62]

The overtones of these passages range from allusions to the divine sparks of which Hassidic mysticism speaks, to Teilhard de Chardin's divine diaphany of matter. But the most obvious reference is to Herakleitos, whose philosophical mysticism nourished Thomas Merton for many years.

We must be very careful not to interpret Herakleitos in a material way. Fire for him is a dynamic, spiritual principle. It is a divine energy, the manifestation of God, the power of God.[63]

God's "undivided power" is easily identified by Merton with the Holy Spirit whose pentecostal tongues of fire disperse and flare up in every single flower petal of spring.

> Sparks of His Spirit spend their seeds, and hide
> To grow like irises....[64]

Fire was not only a symbol for Herakleitos. Later philosophers have derided the intuition by which Herakleitos designated fire as the "primary substance" of the cosmos—but perhaps the experience of our time, in which atomic science has revealed the enormous burning energy that can be released from an atom of hydrogen, may prove Herakleitos to have been nearer the truth than was thought by Plato or Aristotle. However, the "fire" of Herakleitos is something more than material. It is spiritual and "divine." It is the key to the spiritual enigma of man. Our spiritual and mystical destiny is to "awaken" to the fire that is within us.[65]

This "waking up" does not happen by itself. It is decision, *the* decision, the one great task in everyone's life.

> My inside, listen to me, the greatest spirit,
> the Teacher, is near,
> wake up, wake up!
>
> Run to his feet—
> he is standing close to your head right now.
>
> You have slept for millions and millions of years.
>
> Why not wake up this morning?[66]

These lines by Kabir, the Moslem-Hindu mystic, express with rare freshness a theme that runs through all of mystical literature. We are reminded of one of the earliest Christian hymns:

> Awake, thou that sleepest,
> Arise from the dead,
> And Christ will give thee light.[67]

Here the awakening is put into the context of exposure to the light of Christ, the *lumen Christi* of the Easter night ritual.[68] In an alternate version the passage just cited reads: "...and you will touch Christ"—Christ who in a celebrated apocryphal logion says: "Whosoever is near Me, near to the fire is he." St. Ephrem the Syrian, another early Christian poet, calls out to Christ: "Thou who art all fire, have mercy on me!"[69] For "who can live with the devouring fire? Who can dwell in the presence of everlasting flames?"[70] Hence Merton's anguished outcry:

> ...the whole
> World is secretly on fire. The stones
> Burn, even the stones
> They burn me. How can a man be still or
> Listen to all things burning? How can he dare
> To sit with them when
> All their silence
> Is on fire?[71]

What Merton experiences when faced with fire is the fusion of horror and attraction into religious awe. Apparently, his near-religious preoccupation with fire started early in life and never left him.

> I have seen a diary Mother was keeping, in the time of my infancy and first childhood, and it reflects some astonishment at the stubborn and seemingly spontaneous development of completely unpredictable features in my character, things she had never bargained for: for example, a deep and serious urge to adore the gas-light in the kitchen, with no little ritualistic veneration, when I was about four.[72]

> When I was a kid on a farm in Maryland (yes, even that, for a while) a barn burned down in the middle of the night and it is one of the earliest things I can remember. So burning barns are for me great mysteries that are important. They turn out to be the whole world, and it is the Last Judgment.[73]

The second quotation comes from a letter to Mark van Doren, concerning Merton's "Elegy for the Monastery Barn" that was

> ...written after the cowbarn at Gethsemani burned down, one August evening in 1953, during the evening meditation. The monks left the meditation to fight a very hot fire and the poem arrived about the same time as the fire truck from the nearest town.[74]

Merton admits with regard to the "Elegy": "Perhaps I was shy about it. As a matter of fact, it is for me subjectively an important poem."[75] And so it is, objectively, for anyone who wishes to understand the religious significance of fire in Thomas Merton's life and poetry. In a bold personification the building becomes a woman, flaunting her finery of flames—"Look how fast I dress myself in fire!"[76]—as she announces the hour of her own death. In that hour a secret is suddenly revealed; the Herakleitean fire bursts forth visibly and all familiar closeness is over. The monks stand in awe "to see her now so loved...and so feared." "She will not have us near her. Terribly, / Sweet Christ, how terribly her beauty burns us now!"

And yet, what this event is meant to reveal is more subtle than its terrible beauty. It is the secret that all those years of purposeful labor in and around that barn had no meaning in themselves; they were merely a waiting for this lavish moment of conflagration. Like fifty head of cattle in a dream all those years of hard work "come back to speak their summary" in this last hour. "This is the little minute of their destiny. / Here is their meaning found. Here is their end."

Almost unnoticed this poem has turned into a momentous statement about monastic life and its meaning. A story from the Desert Fathers conveys the same message:

> Abba Lot came to Abba Joseph and said: "Father, according as I am able, I keep my little rule and my little fast, my prayer, meditation, and contemplative silence; and according as I am able I strive to cleanse my heart of thoughts: now what more should I do?'

The old man, rising, held up his hands against the sky, and his fingers became like ten torches of flame. He said: "Why not be totally changed into fire?"[77]

"If Christ will burn me clean" [78]

If the essence of the journey to the East is transformation by fire, all of monastic life is a journeying on that road. But the road is rough and rugged. Merton had few illusions in this regard. Where there is fire, there is also smoke. Another story from Merton's *Wisdom of the Desert* applies this truth in a homespun fashion to the spiritual life. It's a story about Abbess Syncletica, a timely reminder that there were great women among the "Fathers" of the Desert.

Abbess Syncletica of holy memory said: "There is labour and great struggle for the impious who are converted to God, but after that comes inexpressible joy. A man who wants to light a fire first is plagued by smoke, and the smoke drives him to tears, yet finally he gets the fire that he wants. So also it is written: Our God is a consuming fire. Hence we ought to light the divine fire in ourselves with labour and with tears."[79]

The journey is a tearful one, but the goal is "the burning promised land,"[80] "our blazing heaven,"[81] "the sacred, unimaginable tabernacles/Burning upon the hills of our desire."[82] One can, one must, prepare for this "first-last hour of joy."[83] Yet the event itself is never brought about or earned by any effort. It is pure gift.

In *Thomas Merton's Asian Journal* we find an entry which describes, if description is possible, this gift, this "flash of mighty intuition by which multiplicity is suddenly comprehended as basically one—penetrated through and through by the logos, the divine fire."[84] Having followed him this far, we should be attuned to the key words Merton uses in this remarkable passage concerning his experience at Polonnaruwa, especially the lavish accumulation of words like *clean, clear, clarity*, words suggesting purification.

I was knocked over with a rush of relief and thankfulness at the *obvious* clarity of the figures, the clarity and fluidity of shape and line, the design of the monumental bodies composed into the rock shape and landscape, figure, rock and tree. And the sweep of bare rock sloping away on the other side of the hollow, where you can go back and see different aspects of the figures.

Looking at these figures I was suddenly, almost forcibly, jerked clean out of the habitual, half-tied vision of things, and an inner clearness, clarity, as if exploding from the rocks themselves, became evident and obvious.... All problems are resolved and everything is clear, simply because what matters is clear. The rock, all matter, all life, is charged with dharmakaya...everything is emptiness and everything is compassion. I don't know when in my life I have ever had such a sense of beauty and spiritual validity running together in one aesthetic illumination. Surely, with Mahabalipuram and Polonnaruwa my Asian pilgrimage has come clear and purified itself...clear, pure, complete.[85]

Having been granted this "beautiful and holy vision," Merton wonders, "I don't know what else remains." The implicit question is full of tragic irony. What should remain for one who can say, with all the weight with which Merton said it, "I know and have seen what I was obscurely looking for....I have now seen and have pierced through the surface and have got beyond the shadow and the disguise"?[86] A man who can say this has nothing left to do. And that is liberation.

In a Zen koan someone said that an enlightened man is not one who seeks Buddha or finds Buddha, but simply an ordinary man *who has nothing left to do.* Yet mere stopping is not arriving. To stop is to stay a million miles from it and to do nothing is to miss it by the whole width of the universe. As for arriving, when you arrive you are ruined. Yet how close the solution is: how simple it would be to have nothing more to do if only—one had really nothing more to do. The man who is unripe cannot get there, no matter what he does or does not do. But the ripe fruit falls out of the tree without even thinking about it. Why? The man who is ripe discovers that there was never anything to be done from the very beginning.[87]

What Merton said—only a few minutes before his death—about the Buddhist notion of nirvana seems to apply also to the preceding paragraph: "This kind of view of reality is essentially very close to the Christian monastic view of reality. It is the view that if you once penetrate by detachment and purity of heart to the inner secret of the ground of your ordinary experience, you attain to a liberty that nobody can touch."[88] Quite clearly, we can also discover this concept of liberation within the poetic context of the Journey to the East and transformation by fire: Elias, the archetype of the monk, the prophet who called fire down from heaven and was taken up to heaven in a fiery chariot—

Elias becomes his own geography
(Supposing geography to be necessary at all),
Elias becomes his own wild bird, with God in the center,
His own wide field which nobody owns,
His own pattern, surrounding the Spirit
By which he is himself surrounded:

For the free man's road has neither beginning nor end.[89]

"Bring me my chariot of fire!"[90]

"The ripe fruit falls out of the tree without even thinking about it."[91] Toward the end of his life, Merton had been much preoccupied with Rilke's poetry.[92] The ripe fruit falling is Rilke's image for death. Not death in general, but one's own unique death. Not the death known in our hospitals, the "little death" that hangs in us like sour fruit, still green at harvest time. Of that alienated dying Rilke says in *The Book of Hours*:

What makes our dying alien and shakes us
Is that it's not *our* death, but one that takes us
Only because we've not matured our own;
Therefore there comes a storm and down we're blown.[93]

But the "great death," as Rilke understood it, is the death
with which we live serenely in deep familiarity from child-
hood on. It is that death whose abiding presence lies at the
core of one's life, nurtured by every longing and aspiration
with all the ardor of our hearts and brains.

For, we are just the leaf and just the skin.
But that great death which each one has within,
That is the fruit around which all revolves.[94]

"*A subitanea et improvisa morte libera nos, Domine!*"[95] This
invocation, which Merton chanted every Easter night in
choir, is echoed and made more specific in Rilke's fervent
line: "O Lord, grant everyone the death that is his very
own!"[96] Though sudden and unforeseen, Thomas Merton's
death on December 10, 1968 was his very own death indeed.
His journey did not merely come to an end; it reached its
destination. On three distinct levels of meaning, this destination was "the East."

Bangkok, where Thomas Merton died, was the original
goal of his journey to Asia, although other stops en route
there had been added to his itinerary. It was in order to give
the address he delivered that morning that his abbot had
given him permission to travel to the East. This task accomplished, he retired to his room, where he was found an hour
or two later "lying on the floor. He was on his back with the
electric fan lying across his chest. The fan was still switched
on, and there was a deep burn and some cuts on his right side
and arm.... It was evident that he was already dead."[97] The
letter from which these lines are taken was signed by representatives from Australia, India, Indonesia, Japan, Hong
Kong, and New Zealand, who attended that gathering of
monastic leaders from throughout the eastern hemisphere.

The paper which Merton delivered at the Bangkok Conference was entitled "Marxism and Monastic Perspectives." It focuses on a double polarity which had occupied his mind for more than half his lifetime: the polarity between Marxism and monasticism, and, within monasticism, the polarity between the Buddhist and Christian traditions. There is little doubt that Merton himself would have wanted to revise the transcript of this talk in which he had departed rather offhandedly from his not too well prepared notes. Yet the key note rings through with unambiguous clarity:

> There is an essential orientation that goes beyond this or that society, this or that culture, or even this or that religion... East and West. We accept the division, we work with the division, and we go beyond the division.[98]

Merton was by now "thinking along lines that are going to change both Western and Eastern society and create the world of the future."[99] Affirming and yet transcending the polarities even of East and West, his mind turned toward the direction of a new and different dawn.

If our tracing of Thomas Merton's real journey to the East did not go too far wrong, we might expect to find in his last public statement some confirming evidence. And indeed we do. His last words contain two of the clearest expressions he ever attained regarding liberation and transformation as essential features of his monastic quest:

> The monk belongs to the world, but the world belongs to him insofar as he has dedicated himself totally to liberation from it in order to liberate it.[100]

> What is essential in the monastic life is... this business of total inner transformation. All other things serve that end.[101]

As we draw out the lines of liberation and transformation, we find them converging toward that ultimate East which Herakleitos called "the 'death of fire,' a passage from darkness into greater light, from confusion into unity."[102]

"There was a deep burn . . . on his right side and arm," said the official report. It noted also that in death his "face was set in a great and deep peace, and it was obvious that he had found Him whom he had searched for so diligently."[103]

Those who die the death of fire—the death which Christianity was to call martyrdom, and which Herakleitos definitely believed was a "witness" to the Fire of the Logos—become superior beings. They live forever. They take their place among the company of those who watch over the destinies of the cosmos and of men, for they have, in their lives, entered into the secret of the Logos. "They who die great deaths rise up to become the wakeful guardians of the living and the dead."[104]

NOTES

1. Thomas Merton, *The Asian Journal of Thomas Merton*, ed. Naomi Burton Stone, Brother Patrick Hart, and James Laughlin (N.Y.: New Directions, 1973), pp. 4-5.
2. *Ibid.*
3. Cf. David Steindl-Rast, O.S.B., "Exposure: A Key to Thomas Merton's Asian Journal?" in *Monastic Studies* (1974).
4. Merton (trans.), *The Wisdom of the Desert: Sayings of the Desert Fathers* (N.Y.: New Directions, 1960).
5. Jn. 11:16.
6. T. S. Eliot, *Four Quartets* (N.Y.: Harcourt, Brace, and World, 1971): "Burnt Norton," II:68f.
7. Merton, "Freedom as Experience," in *The Collected Poems of Thomas Merton* (N.Y.: New Directions, 1977), p. 187.
8. All applicable citations to Merton's poetry will refer to the exhaustive volume of *The Collected Poems of Thomas Merton* cited above (editor's note).
9. Merton, "The Geography of Lograire," cited *ibid.*, pp. 455-610.
10. *Ibid.*, p. 459.
11. *Ibid.*, p. 460.
12. *Ibid.*, p. 459.
13. *Ibid.*
14. Merton, "The Trappist Abbey: Matins," cited *ibid.*, p. 46.
15. The airport in San Francisco is located southeast of the city. Having taken off there many times in different directions, I have studied the

various possibilities carefully, and have come to the conclusion that Merton's plane could hardly have "tilted east" over the city, as he claimed. What he meant was that the plane tilted in the direction of "the East," but that was actually west. The slip seems significant.

16. Merton, "Pilgrim's Song," in *The Collected Poems*, p. 190.

17. Merton, *The Sign of Jonas* (N.Y.: Harcourt, Brace, & Co., 1953), p. 346, one of many passages devoted to the sacred joy of early morning.

18. Merton, "Senescente Mundo," in *The Collected Poems*, p. 222.

19. *Ibid.*

20. Jn. 14:6.

21. Merton, "Senescente Mundo," in *The Collected Poems*, p. 222.

22. Jn. 8:12.

23. Merton, "The Trappist Cemetery: Gethsemani," in *The Collected Poems*, p. 116.

24. Mt. 25:6.

25. Merton, *Conjectures of a Guilty Bystander* (N.Y.: Doubleday Image Books, 1968), pp. 275-350. (The following Zen koan suggests the title of this section: "The madman runs to the East/and his keeper runs to the East;/ Both are running to the East,/Their purposes differ.")

26. 1 Cor. 1:27.

27. Merton, *Conjectures*, p. 310.

28. Lk. 9:31.

29. Mt. 17:19.

30. Merton, "Pilgrim's Song," in *The Collected Poems*, p. 189.

31. Merton, "Prometheus: A Meditation," in *The Behaviour of Titans*, cited in *A Thomas Merton Reader*, edited by Thomas McDonnell (N.Y.: Doubleday Image Books, 1974), pp. 343-44.

32. Francis Thompson, "Orient Ode."

33. 1 Pet. 2:9.

34. Merton, "Freedom as Experience," in *The Collected Poems*, p. 186.

35. Merton, "Trappist Abbey: Matins," cited *ibid.*, p. 45.

36. Merton, *The Sign of Jonas*, p. 297.

37. *Ibid.*, p. 99.

38. Merton, *The Seven Storey Mountain* (N.Y.: Harcourt, Brace & Co., 1948), p. 401.

39. Merton, "Prometheus," pp. 343-344.

40. *Ibid.*, p. 341.

41. Merton, "A Christmas Card," in *The Collected Poems*, p. 184.

42. *Ibid.*

43. Merton, "Holy Child Song," cited *ibid.*, p. 655.

44. Merton, "Freedom as Experience," cited *ibid.*, p. 186.

45. Merton, "Senescente Mundo," cited *ibid.*, p. 221.

46. Merton, "Prometheus," p. 341.

47. Col. 3:3f.

48. Merton, *The Sign of Jonas*, p. 297 (Easter 1950).

49. Lk. 12:49—The following verse speaks of the passion of Jesus as a baptism in which he has to be immersed.

50. Gerard Manley Hopkins, "The Wreck of the Deutschland" (line 276).

51. Merton, *The Sign of Jonas*, p. 298.

52. Merton, "Senescente Mundo," in *The Collected Poems*, p. 221.

53. Merton, "St. John's Night," cited *ibid.*, p. 171.

54. Merton, *The Sign of Jonas*, p. 297.

55. Raimundo Panikkar, *The Vedic Experience: Mantramanjari: An Anthology of the Vedas for Modern Man and Contemporary Celebration* (Berkeley, Cal.: University of California Press, 1977).

56. Merton, "In Silence," in *The Collected Poems*, p. 280.

57. Merton, "Senescente Mundo," cited *ibid.*, p. 221.

58. Merton, "The Sowing of Meanings," cited *ibid.*, p. 187.

59. T. S. Eliot, "The Wasteland," I: The Burial of the Dead.

60. Jn. 12:24.

61. Merton, "The Sowing of Meanings," in *The Collected Poems*, p. 187.

62. Merton, "St. John's Night," cited *ibid.*, p. 171.

63. Merton, "Herakleitos the Obscure," cited in *A Thomas Merton Reader*, p. 261.

64. Merton, "The Annunciation," cited in *The Collected Poems*," p. 284.

65. Merton, "Herakleitos," p. 258.

66. Robert Bly, trans. *The Kabir Book* (Boston: Beacon Press, 1977).

67. The paradox of this exposure is expressed in T. S. Eliot's lines, "We only live, only suspire/Consumed by either fire or fire": *Four Quartets*, Little Gidding IV:212f. William Empson, in "Missing Dates," alludes to the same paradox: "The complete fire is death. From partial fires the waste remains and kills." Merton himself contrasts in a similar sense "fire" and "Flame" in "The Annunciation." Compare also Merton's "Freedom of Experience," a poem that should be read in light of Gerard Manley Hopkins' "That Nature Is a Heraclitan Fire, and of the Comfort of the Resurrection." An exploration of the message common to these and related poems, e.g., Fyodor I. Tyutchev's "Nak nad gorjačeju zoloj," would deserve a separate study. See in this context also an entry in Merton's Journal, March 10, 1951: "I nearly set the whole forest on fire yesterday..." in *The Sign of Jonas*, p. 324.

68. *Ibid.*

69. Gerald Vann, O.P., *The Water and the Fire* (London: Collins, 1953), p. 82.

70. Is. 33:14.

71. Merton, "In Silence," in *The Collected Poems*, p. 280.

72. Merton, *The Seven Storey Mountain*, p. 5.

73. Merton, *The Selected Poems of Thomas Merton* (N.Y.: New Directions, 1967), p. xi.

74. *Ibid.*

75. *Ibid.*

76. This and the following quotations are from Merton's "Elegy for the Monastery Barn," found in *The Collected Poems*, pp. 288ff.

77. Merton, *The Wisdom of the Desert*, p. 50 (translation slightly altered here).

78. Merton, "Canticle for the Blessed Virgin," in *The Collected Poems*, p. 160.

79. Merton, *The Wisdom of the Desert*, p. 55.

80. Merton, *The Sign of Jonas*, p. 345.

81. Merton, "Evening: Zero Weather," in *The Collected Poems*, p. 174.

82. Merton, "St. John's Night," cited *ibid.*, p. 171.

83. Merton, "Elegy for the Monastery Barn," cited *ibid.*, p. 288.

84. Merton, "Herakleitos," p. 264.

85. Merton, *The Asian Journal*, pp. 233-36.

86. *Ibid.*, p. 236.

87. Merton, *Conjectures*, p. 282.

88. Merton, *The Asian Journal*, Appendix VII, "Marxism and Monastic Perspectives: A Talk Delivered at Bangkok" (December 10, 1968), p. 342.

89. Merton, "Elias: Variations on a Theme," in *The Collected Poems*, p. 240. Note especially Part II of this poem, in which the hermit's surroundings in the Kentucky woods begin to glow from within the light borrowed from the Bible stories about Elijah—e.g., "Where the woods are cut down the punished/Trailer stands alone and becomes/(Against all the better intentions of the owner)/The house of God/The Gate of Heaven/("My chariot of fire")."

90. *Ibid.*, Part II.

91. Merton, *Conjectures*, p. 282.

92. In a private note, dated March 19, 1966, Merton referred to Rilke as "an especially interesting poet in whom one can find a great deal of relevant material...not only about poetry, but about the spirit of modern man, etc., etc., also modern man's attitude to religion and so forth....Rilke has intriguing and characteristic problems."

93. Rainer Maria Rilke, *The Book of Hours* (N.Y.: New Directions, 1968), III, Of Poverty and Death (translation slightly altered here).

94. *Ibid.*

95. "From sudden and unprepared death, deliver us, O Lord!" (From the Litany of All the Saints).

96. Rilke, *Book of Hours* III:6 (my own translation).

97. Merton, *The Asian Journal*, Appendix VIII: "Letter to Abbot Flavian Burns, December 11, 1968," p. 345.

98. *Ibid.*, Appendix VII, p. 340.

99. *Ibid.*, p. 328.

100. *Ibid.*, p. 341.

101. *Ibid.*, p. 340.

102. Merton, "Herakleitos," p. 270.

103. Merton, *The Asian Journal*, p. 345.

104. Merton, "Herakleitos," pp. 270-71.

A Witness to Life: Thomas Merton on Monastic Renewal

Patrick Hart, O.C.S.O.

It is not without significance that Thomas Merton should have entered the Abbey of Gethsemani at a time when Frederic Dunne was Abbot. I have often reflected on this stroke of Divine Providence in bringing Merton's first Abbot from a family of professional printers in Zanesville, Ohio (coincidentally from the same town where Ruth Jenkins, Merton's mother, was born). The fact that Abbot Frederic Dunne had been a book printer and binder by profession made him profoundly sensitive to the importance of the printed word. To the young Thomas Merton, arriving at Gethsemani on December 10, 1941, to begin his novitiate training, the Abbot was predisposed to be appreciative of his gifts. At the time Abbot Frederic confided enthusiastically to one of the brothers: "We have a *real* poet and writer in the novitiate."[1]

The Abbot, as a consequence of his great desire to make the Trappist-Cistercians known in this country, encouraged Fr. Louis (the name he was known by in the community) soon after his novitiate to translate biographies of early Cistercian saints from Latin and French. Since Merton knew Latin well, and had majored in modern languages at Cambridge and Columbia, he was well equipped for just this sort of work. Thus, long before Vatican II and its emphasis on monks and religious returning to the sources, to study the works of their founders and early saints, Fr. Louis was busy translating obscure lives of Cistercian saints and thus becoming acquainted not only with the Cistercian Fathers of the twelfth century, but going back to our monastic ancestors, the pre-Benedictine dwellers of the Egyptian desert, to the early

173

Benedictine monks of Gaul and Italy, as well as the Irish monks and hermits of the fifth and sixth centuries.

My earliest recollections of Thomas Merton when I entered Gethsemani a decade later, in June 1951, were shortly after Merton had been made Master of the Students. He had access to the old vault (where all the valuable manuscripts and rare books were stored) as an office and counseling room for the students. It was a room close to the Guest House refectory in the front wing of the old quadrangle of the monastery. Each time he came walking jauntily down the hall to his vault cell, he pulled out an enormous key, nearly a foot in length, making great gestures as he unlocked the big iron inner doors of the fireproof vault. He usually had a student with him, or one might be waiting outside the door, doubtless for spiritual direction. He gave one the impression of being a happy and spontaneously friendly monk.

As Master of Students at Gethsemani, Fr. Louis very soon began to emphasize the need for more opportunities for solitude and to help the young monks in their desire for contemplative prayer. With about two hundred monks in the community at the time, it was difficult enough to find a quiet place to be alone, since we were only permitted outside the relatively small enclosure if work in the fields or the vast woods brought us there.

During the course of an official visitation from the Abbot General of the Order, Fr. Louis made a strong plea to have the enclosure extended to include a small wooded knoll on the east side of the enclosure wall. To everyone's great surprise, he was successful in this attempt, and thus on Sundays and feast days the students were allowed to go out to the woods for several hours of prayer or *lectio divina* or simple relaxation in this beautiful natural setting. Not long afterward the novices were likewise given a similar permission, and a wooded area and lake south of the enclosure wall was reserved for them.

This was meant to give the young monks more opportunities for solitude and thus restore the contemplative dimension to the monastic life which had been obscured formerly by an overemphasis on penance and work and an overly ornate liturgy.

Aside from his gifts and abilities as a translator, his knowledge of French, German, Spanish and Italian put him in contact with many of the new currents of thought in monastic and theological circles long before others in the community were aware of their existence. He kept abreast of all the finest journals emanating from Europe at this time. As it developed, Merton began to initiate his own monastic renewal at Gethsemani in the early 1950's by giving conferences on the Cistercian Fathers. This work brought him into direct contact with the four great "Cistercian evangelists": St. Bernard of Clairvaux, William of St. Thierry, Guerric of Igny and Aelred of Rievaulx, as well as many lesser-known monastic writers. He went far beyond De Rancé and the Reform of La Trappe to the earliest Cistercian Fathers of the twelfth century. Naturally, this was received as a breath of fresh air for the community at Gethsemani, and soon spread to other monastic communities in this country and abroad.

In 1955 Thomas Merton was appointed Master of Novices, after having been Master of the Students for just four years. He was to hold this responsible position for another ten years. During this period he had a tremendous influence on the lives of the young men who entered the monastery, and along with the Abbot he was actually responsible for their monastic training and formation. This enabled him to view, sometimes critically, certain methods used in the past, and thus he launched a novitiate training program of his own.

Merton delved into the monastic sources, studying the Cistercian Fathers with the novices and discussing them in open dialogue. Thanks to his insistence, more time was given to *lectio divina*, although manual labor was not neglected. Merton felt, however, that in the past too much emphasis had been placed on manual labor, to the detriment of a fruitful *lectio divina*, meditative reading, study and personal prayer.

Notes of the talks and conferences by Father Louis were subsequently typed up, mimeographed and circulated to many other communities, once the monastic grapevine spread the word of Merton's pioneering efforts at Gethsemani. Thus, before long, copies of the notes on "monastic orientation" which covered the years from 1951 to 1955 were bound in six volumes and circulated to Benedictine and Cistercian houses in this country and abroad. Beginning with his first year as Novice Master, there were the "Lectures on Cassian" which were soon followed by his own commentary on the Rule of St. Benedict. About this time his introductory course on the Scriptures in the monastic tradition (especially St. Paul) was given and two volumes of notes on the "Liturgical Seasons" appeared. In 1961 he launched a series of conferences on "Ascetical and Mystical Theology" and in 1963 began a course on "The Cistercian Fathers and Their Monastic Theology." Conferences during 1963 and 1964 were on "Pre-Benedictine Monasticism," including the Celtic monastic tradition that he found so fascinating. This gives some idea of the broad terrain covered by Merton in these monastic conferences.

Thomas Merton at the very outset of any discussion on monastic renewal was careful to make the proper distinctions in regard to a renewal that was appropriate for monastic communities in contrast to that which was more proper for active religious congregations and societies. In a memorandum on monastic renewal, which was published posthumously, he made this point quite clear: "In monastic reform, care should be taken first of all to maintain or restore the special character of the monastic vocation. The monastic life must not be evaluated in terms of active religious life, and the monastic orders should not be equated with other religious institutes, clerical or otherwise."[2] He went on to stress the point that the monastic community does not ideally exist for the sake of any apostolic or educational work, even as a secondary end. "The works of the monk are not justified by their external results but only by their relevance to his monastic life alone with God. They are meaningful insofar as they are appropriate to a life out of this world, which is also a life of compassion for those who remain in the world, and of prayer for the salvation of the world."[3]

When discussing monastic renewal, Merton always pointed out the fact that the doors (and windows) of the cenobitic monastic community must be opened out onto the desert. He believed strongly that there must be room for those monks who felt a growing need for a greater measure of silence and solitude in their lives as they matured in the monastic life. "Monastic superiors should be ready to see and encourage in their subjects any exceptional and genuine desire for a deeper life of prayer and for a return to a simpler monastic way."[4] Merton pointed out that it was the Abbot's responsibility to foster the spiritual growth of each member of his community. "The Abbot is responsible to God for the development and true sanctification of his monks. When therefore they believe they should seek a simpler, more solitary and more fervent life of prayer, they should not be prevented from investigating reasonable possibilities of doing so . . . but should be helped in various ways to test their abilities and prove the reality of their higher vocation."[5]

Thus Merton saw the possibility of a more solitary life within the context of the traditional monastic community as an important point in renewal. It was a matter of giving precedence to the personal charism of an individual monk over that of the institution. In other words, a true eremitical vocation that might develop and grow within the cenobitic community should be encouraged if it were considered authentic by a monk's spiritual director and his superior. Merton wrote a number of articles on the history of eremitism within the *ordo monasticus*, showing clearly that from its very beginning some monks of the Cistercian Order, after many years in the community, in later life became hermits and solitaries. This was even in evidence at La Trappe during the time of Rancé. These published pleas for a renewal of the ancient tradition paved the way for an eventual approval by the General Chapter of the Order allowing monks this option after being well-tried in the community, and with the Abbot's approval, as St. Benedict in his Rule provides.

Merton's Abbot, Dom James Fox, during the General Chapter of 1965 successfully presented the issue of the possibility of hermits within the Order. His efforts bore fruit, and within a few years Dom James himself resigned his office as Abbot of Gethsemani and became a hermit on the property of Gethsemani. Consequently, the hermit vocation is accepted in monastic communities, although it will always remain a rare calling and few will leave the ranks of the community for the solitary combat of the desert.

One may legitimately ask the question: How was Merton able to keep in touch with all the various monastic experiments and efforts at renewal in other areas of the world, isolated as he was in his monastery in the hills of Kentucky? In actual fact, if one examines his voluminous correspondence over the years, one sees a large segment directed to monks and nuns of Europe and America, Benedictines, Camaldolese, Carthusians and of course Cistercians. For example, his correspondence with the eminent Benedictine scholar and historian, Father Jean Leclercq of Luxembourg, dates back to 1950 and continued unabated until the time of Merton's death in Bangkok, Thailand in 1968. The early letters are full of questions about new experiments in the foundations in Africa and Asia.

In this country the experiment of Dom Damasus Winzen at Mount Savior near Elmira, New York, impressed Merton deeply. Mount Savior symbolized for him what was best in the early monastic experiments in this country in the early 1950's. Dom Damasus believed in a simple type of Benedictine monastery, without parishes or a school and/or seminary attached. Dom Damasus, however, held firmly to traditional monastic hospitality and consequently provided for a large guest house. But he believed it essential that monks earn their living by their own hands by farming, with their life centering around a simple but beautiful vernacular liturgy. And above all, he envisioned only one class of monks. (This idea eventually found favor with other Benedictines and the Cistercian Order as a whole, when their General Chapters abolished the two classes of monks, thus unifying their respective communities.)

It was the policy at Mount Savior to ordain only enough priests to take care of the liturgical needs of the community, unlike the prevalent custom in Trappist-Cistercian monasteries at that time. A number of Merton's letters to a monk of St. John's Abbey, Collegeville, touch on the subject of monks remaining simple monks, rather than clerics destined for the priesthood almost automatically. Writing to Father Ronald Roloff concerning monks not seeking ordination to the priesthood, in a letter dated November 13, 1962, he observed: "Already for some time we have been insisting that the important thing in the choice of vocations for our choir monks was the monastic vocation, not the call to the priesthood. Also, many of the novices have freely admitted that they really prefer to be simple monks and not priests."[6] He pointed out to his correspondent that until a few months previous we had not tolerated this, but since the recent General Chapter it was agreed to try it as a part of the new monastic program. He went on to say: "Hence, we now have a half-dozen newly professed who are going ahead with the explicit intention of remaining simple monks and not becoming priests. They are the best in the house actually. I do not know if they will all manage to have their desire; some may have to be ordained later, just because they do have qualities that make for superiorship, etc. But for my part I would personally support such a one all the way and would encourage him to remain a simple monk insofar as it was possible."[7]

Another subject treated in this same letter was that of a new approach to monastic formation at Gethsemani. It spanned a longer period than in the past, and was geared more specifically for monks, rather than seminarians or priests in the secular ministry. In other words, these studies would concentrate on subjects germane to the monastic vocation: Scripture, patrology and a kind of monastic theology tailored specifically for monks. Instead of three years of simple vows, the Order began to allow for as much as six years. He explained: "After the novitiate, all the choir monks, whether they will eventually go on to the priesthood or not, *continue their purely monastic formation.* This is what we all here consider to be the really important point. They will not begin clerical studies for at least three years after the novitiate."[8] Merton then outlined a pet plan of his own to develop a monastic pre-philosophy course which would have nothing to do with the manuals, "but will be a sort of *lectio divina* of texts from St. Anselm, St. Augustine,

Boethius, and so on. This would be a very interesting course and very important. This would not be until the third year. Before that they will take nothing but Scripture, monastic history, the Fathers and a language."[9]

Personal relationships within the monastic community were another very important consideration in Merton's view of renewal. Writing on the subject of "Openness and Cloister" he concluded that in the past the structures of the contemplative life had acquired too much rigidity and uniformity. He felt there was too much emphasis placed on exterior regularity and on uniform observance which tended to stifle personal development and did not take sufficient account of a monk's personal needs. "Contemplative openness must develop not only in relation to the outside world, but also, and above all, within the community itself. Free and spontaneous contacts between the religious themselves are absolutely necessary. Religious must communicate frankly and sincerely in a personal way and not only in the set of formalized relationships which have been favored in the past."[10] Merton went on to stress the importance of relationships being more "natural" and human, which inevitably would result in a greater freedom and openness in communicating with one another.

But as in so many other cases, Merton balanced this very well with an insistence on a measure of solitude and silence for those whose spiritual growth demanded more of this: "On the other hand, to balance this freedom of communication, the legitimate needs of individual religious for greater solitude and silence must also be respected." He felt that a monastic community (or any community for that matter) which is growing in charity and self-understanding will spontaneously recognize the special needs of its members, and in a spirit of charity strive to accommodate them. Merton added that the mature contemplative (who may not always necessarily be the most brilliant or gifted person in the community) "can contribute a great deal to the common life by his or her silent and solitary prayer. Even those who are not yet fully formed need the experience of periods of solitude and silence in order to grow in the life of prayer. Contemplative communities should recognize the value of encouraging these personal aspirations."[11]

Turning for a moment to Merton's poetry, his early Gethsemani poems celebrate monastic life in all its aspects: "Trappists, Working," "Trappist Abbey: Matins," and "Evening: Zero Weather." One realizes the profound effect that the liturgical life had on this young monk, and how it was intended to transform the entire life of the monk. These poems reflect the early Merton perfectly at peace in his natural setting in the hills of Kentucky. In "A Practical Program for Monks," one of his later poems (written about 1958, consequently after he had been four years Master of Juniors and two years as Master of Novices), the poet complains about the attention accorded to externals, not without a bit of humor. The poem is a protest against an overemphasis on rules and regulations which tend to distort the simple contemplative life of solitude and prayer. Merton's frustration shows through in this poem as he ironically contrasts the highly structured, regimented life with the ideal contemplative life:

Plenty of bread for everyone between prayers and the
    psalter: will you recite another?
Merci, and *Miserere.*
Always mind both the clock and the Abbot until eter-
    nity.
Miserere.

Details of the Rule are all liquid and solid. What canon
    was the first to announce regimentation before us?
Mind the step on the way down![12]

Another area of monastic renewal about which Merton wrote and spoke was traditional monastic hospitality. Before ecumenical dialogue became fashionable, Merton began to see small groups of non-Catholic seminarians and college students, as well as artists, poets, intellectuals, and pacifists, including non-Christians. Among the latter were Zen Buddhist monks, Sufis, Jewish rabbis and a host of others. Merton felt that it was important for monks to have some contact with these people, who in turn would influence others of their own group and beyond. Actually, he began meeting with groups of Baptist and Episcopalian and Disciples of Christ seminarians in the late 1950's and early 1960's. He made himself available to them, usually giving them an address of welcome, telling them something of the monastic life, and then opening the forum to discussion, which was always quite lively. He became very popular in this area, and as a consequence after several years had to call for help from some of the other monks. Having come from a non-Catholic background himself, and with his tremendous interest in Eastern monasticism, he was able to empathize with these groups in a way many other monks could not, which helps to explain his singular success.

Merton summarized succinctly his thought in this matter in "Letter to a Priest," which was published in *Seeds of Destruction*, concerning the Rahnerian diaspora situation: "What I am trying to say about the monk is perhaps too paradoxical and too outrageous to be clear, let alone acceptable: but I think the monastic state should be one of complete liberty from the pressures and confusions of 'the world' in the bad sense of the word, and even from the more 'worldly' side of the Church, so that the monk, isolated and at liberty, can on the one hand give himself to God and to the Word of God, attain to a truly Christian understanding of the needs and sufferings of the men of his time (from his special vantage point of poverty, labor, solitude and insecurity) and also enter into dialogue with those who are not monks and not even Christians."[13]

He constantly stressed the need for monks in their efforts at renewal to examine and return to the sources of their tradition. Writing on the subject of ecumenism and monastic renewal, Merton was later to explain: "The problem of monastic renewal, at the deepest level, is theological, and it is at this point that the monks are finally coming face to face with Luther's challenge. In 'returning to the sources' they are only doing in a more thorough and systematic way what Luther himself did by reexamining his vocation in the light of the Gospel and the Pauline Epistles."[14] Merton then pointed

out that monks and nuns today, studying the original monastic sources, seen in their historical and cultural contexts, must
begin to ask themselves much more disturbing questions
than simply those which are endemic to their monastic observance: "It is no longer just a matter of recovering a genuine
understanding of monastic enclosure, silence, worship, fast-
ing and trying to adapt these to a modern situation. The very
concept of a vowed and cloistered life, of a life devoted to
prayer apart from the world, of silence and asceticism, has to
be reexamined."[15]

Merton then sounded a warning to facile proponents of
renewal, fearing that those not well grounded in a solid
monastic tradition would end up discarding things of peren-
nial value, thus impoverishing and trivializing monasticism:
"Let us admit that quite possibly if we are too ready to
sacrifice silence, solitude, etc., we may quickly find ourselves
deserted by vocations."[16] On the other hand, he believed a
certain amount of adaptation was necessary to meet the needs
of the time, thus making the monastic life viable for many
who would not otherwise be attracted to this way. "But also if
by relinquishing my own favorite interpretation of what the
perfect life of silence and contemplation ought to be and
submitting to certain adaptations I can make the monastic life
possible for others who would not otherwise be able to live it,
then it would seem that charity itself ought to tell me that this
"need" of others is an appeal to my own generosity, in a way
very different from that which I anticipated when I made my
vows."[17]

Speaking about the monastic dialogue with the world
and the relevance of monastic life for the future, Merton
insisted that everything depended on the *quality* of the lives
of the monks today, and the seriousness with which they
examined their witness in terms of the ensuing generations
of monks: "Monastic life will remain relevant to the future,
specifically in the next two generations, insofar as
monasteries open themselves to dialogue and exchange with
the intellectual community. But for this dialogue to be meaningful, the intellectual community must find in the
monasteries both a monastic reality (people of depth and

simplicity who have acquired the values of monasticism by living them) and openness to social reality of the twentieth century."[18]

Again, Merton emphasized the need for inner transformation, for without a real and deep spiritual renewal, the exterior changes would avail but little. He saw this combining of real monastic depth and openness to the living intellectual and cultural forces of our times as requiring a special charism. In the thought of Merton, a charism was a gift one must struggle with to deserve as well as preserve. He felt the most basic and important monastic charism is the essential calling to prayer and renunciation and inner transformation. Toward the end of his life, Merton became more and more concerned with the subject of transformation of consciousness, which was in current usage at that time.

If monks were not genuinely authentic and deep men of prayer and at the same time men of compassion and concern for the anguish of the world, Merton felt their witness would be of little value and perhaps cause more harm than good to those coming to seek their counsel and help. He suggested in this context: "If our monasteries are truly centers of deeply experienced monastic life, those who are most alive in the outside world will spontaneously come to share our silence and discuss with us their own fruitful insights. It is this exchange and participation which I believe to be of decisive importance for monasteries. But it all depends on solitude and prayer."[19]

Writing on the necessity of the individual monk to begin where he found himself, and not depend on or wait for communal renewal, Merton stated realistically that what one needs to do is start a conversion and a new life oneself, insofar as one can. "My work for renewal takes place strictly in my own situation here, not as a struggle with the institution from which I am relatively free now as a hermit, but in an effort to renew my life of prayer in a whole new context, with a whole new understanding of what the contemplative life means and demands. Creativity has to begin with me and I cannot sit here wasting time urging the monastic institution to become creative and prophetic...."[20]

This realistic approach was typical of Merton in his later

years, after many of his earlier idealistic illusions evaporated. In the last analysis it all depended on how each monk personally responded to his call, his special graces of vocation. The point was well made in the following passage: "What each one of us has to do, and what I have to do, is to buckle down and really start investigating new possibilities in our own life; and if new possibilities mean radical changes, all right. Maybe we need radical changes for which we have to struggle and sweat some blood. Above all we must be more attentive to God's way and God's time, and give everything when it is really demanded. But, on the other hand, let these be real changes and not just neurotic upheavel."[21]

The essential monastic experience, as Merton saw it, was centered on love. He knew from monastic tradition, and especially from the Cistercian twelfth-century writers like St. Bernard of Clairvaux and William of St. Thierry, that ideally the monastic life was considered a "school of love" or "charity's own school." He resonates the teachings of the Cistercian Fathers in the following passage: "Love alone is enough, regardless of whether it produces anything. In the so-called contemplative life, love is sufficient to itself. It does of course work, it does of course do things; but in our life the emphasis is on love above everything else, on faith above everything else. Especially faith above works."[22]

As Merton grew older and wiser in the monastic life, he depended more and more on the mercy of God, as he often confessed. That is why he loved so much the English mystic, Julian of Norwich, whom he preferred in his later years to the Spanish mystics, St. John of the Cross and St. Teresa of Avila, with whom he was so taken in his early monastic life. "The characteristic of our life is that it makes us realize how much we depend directly on God by faith. How much we depend directly upon the mercy of God, how much we depend upon receiving everything directly through Him, and not through the mediation of our own activity. So that while we continue to act, we act in such a way that this consciousness of dependence on God is greater, more continual, more all-embracing and more satisfactory than it is in the active life. This is what we really seek."[23]

After the appearance of a provocative article in the *Na-*

tional Catholic Reporter in December 1967 by Colman McCarthy, Merton wrote a letter to the editor early in 1968 in which he said: "The monastic charism is a charism of freedom: including the freedom not to count in the world and not to get visible results in it. The freedom not to have to talk if you don't want to. Not to have to pronounce judgment on anything. Or contrariwise, to speak out without hesitation when you think something has to be said."[24]

Merton then spelled out the implications of the monk's charism of freedom: "Above all the monastic charism is a freedom from set routine official tasks, a freedom from the treadmill of putting out a superfluous religious magazine, of preaching retreats that are driving nuns stark mad, of bullying married couples...."[25] Rather, Merton got to the heart of the monastic vocation by saying that a monk does not have to do any of these things, not simply because he has a secret nobody else possesses, but rather "because he is liberated from the need to produce anything by which to justify himself in the eyes of other men. He is not accountable to them for his life because it is something that cannot be drawn up on a balance sheet for anybody's inspection. The 'solitude' of the monk is the loneliness of being accountable directly to God for something he does not quite understand himself."[26]

At the root of this emphasis on the solitude of the monk, the person of contemplative prayer, was Merton's firm conviction that it was more important for the monk *to be* than to do or to act, especially when he was speaking of the monastic ideal in a time of renewal and change. He wanted to be sure that critics of renewal kept this in mind. He disagreed with many critics of monasticism who would have monks abandon their monastic solitude and become more involved in the active ministry, and thus open the doors of the monastery to the world, taking a much more cautious view. He did, indeed, see a need for more openness than in the past, so that guests could come to the monastery for retreats or perhaps to obtain help in their prayer life by those qualified among the monks to advise. But he was opposed to the idea of turning the monastery into a counseling center or a mini-parish church. The monastery had its own particular function in the mystical body of Christ, the Church, and as long as it was faithful to this charism, the more profitable it would be for the Church and the world.

Thomas Merton certainly believed that renewal must come from the ranks of monks and nuns, the grassroots, rather than from the higher echelons. Writing on the Council and monasticism shortly after the close of Vatican II, Merton stated: "While the major superiors and the competent Councils and Chapters must of course finally decide what adaptations are to be put into effect, in accordance with the Rule and Constitutions, it is nevertheless essential that all the members should actively participate in such tasks as: estimation of the meaning and value of their vocation, clarification of the relevance of their particular religious ideal for themselves and their time, evaluation of the contribution they might make to the understanding and aid of the contemporary world, defining the relevance in a present-day context of certain observances belonging to the past, and bringing to the attention of Superiors the real everyday needs and problems of subjects."[27]

The theological implications were clear to Merton who saw this approach as not only pragmatic, but in accord with the new perspectives on the Church. Indeed, we must recognize that "all true renewal must be the work of the Holy Spirit and that the Holy Spirit cannot be said to work exclusively 'from the top down,' manifesting the will of God only to higher superiors and, further down, granting to subjects no light but only the strength and grace to accept this will, as it comes down the chain of command, with total obedience and blind faith. The new emphasis in the theology of the Church sees the Holy Spirit working *in the collective* and 'collegial' effort of all, each in his own sphere and according to his own function in the Church."[28]

Those who knew Thomas Merton very well recognized that they were faced with a complex personality, and his statements on various subjects sometimes tended to be contradictory at first glance. Monastic renewal was no exception, and in reading some of his remarks on the subject, one feels that there was a certain ambiguity which he himself failed to face squarely. For example, Merton spoke passionately of the need for renewal: "Renewal is something deeper and more total than reform. Reform was proper to the needs of the Church at the time of the Council of Trent, where the whole structure of religious life had collapsed, even though there was still a great deal of vitality among religious. Today the structure and organization is firm and intact: what is lacking is a deep and fruitful understanding of the real meaning of religious life."[29] He went on to define renewal as a restoration of authentic meaning to forms and acts that must recover their full value as sacred signs. Yet in a talk he gave to some rather conventional nuns in Calcutta shortly before his death, he deplored some trends in renewal in the United States, such as "a collapse of formal structures that were no longer properly understood; a repudiation of genuine tradition, discipline, contemplation, trivializing the monastic life."[30]

These are rather strong statements for a proponent of renewal in the monastic world. Again, one must consider the audience to whom he was addressing himself. Merton accommodated himself easily to his audience, and began where he found people. It is certainly true to say that his tone was quite different when speaking to a group of revolutionary students in Santa Barbara at the Center for the Study of Democratic Institutions.

It must be admitted that basically Thomas Merton was a man of tradition, which he knew well and loved. Yet, he was not a monk who believed in preserving the past for the sake of preservation. Perhaps only someone steeped in authentic monastic tradition as Merton was can really speak out meaningfully on the subject of monastic renewal. Needless to say, he did this without hesitation, but here he minces no words: "Certain structures need to be shaken, certain structures have to fall. We need not be revolutionaries within our institutions.... But on the other hand, we don't want to go to the other extreme and just simply be ostriches refusing to see that these institutions are in many respects outdated, and that perhaps renewal may mean the collapse of some institutional structures and starting over again with a whole new form."[31]

Speaking of the spirit of openness to renewal in religious circles, which Merton considered most important in any renewal of religious life, he went on to say: "This means that observances which are 'closed' and incomprehensible even to the religious themselves will almost inevitably generate a spirit of pretentiousness and artificiality which is incompatible with the true Gospel simplicity. Such observances must either be re-thought so that they recover a living meaning, or they must be discarded, and if necessary replaced by others that fulfill the function which they have ceased to fulfill."[32]

In studying the various statements made by Thomas Merton over the years on the subject of monastic renewal, one realizes that he was functioning as a critic, showing several sides of an issue, pointing out weaknesses on both sides of a question. This is apparent in dealing with the delicate subject of the monk's withdrawal from the world, his need for a certain *distance*. In the opening pages of *Contemplation in a World of Action*, Merton writes: "It is certainly true that this special perspective necessarily implies that the monk will be in some sense critical of the world, of its routines, its confusions, and its sometimes tragic failures to provide other men with lives that are fully sane and human. The monk can and must be open to the world, but at the same time he must be able to get along without a naive and uncritical 'secularity' which blandly assumes that everything in the world is at every moment getting better and better for everybody."[33] He admits this critical balance is often very difficult to achieve, but it is something the monk must strive for. "For the monastic life has a certain prophetic character about it: not that the monk should be able to tell what is about to happen in the Kingdom of God, but in the sense that he is a living witness to the freedom of the sons of God and to the essential difference between that freedom and the spirit of the world."[34]

Merton was conscious of the fact that God so loved the world that he gave his only-begotten Son, but he also knew well that the Son of God came into a world that refused to receive him, a world that opposed and rejected him. Merton summed up his position in these moving words: "The monastic life then must maintain this prophetic seriousness, this wilderness perspective, this mistrust of any shallow optimism which overlooks the ambiguity and the potential tragedy of 'the world' in its response to the Word. And there is only one way for the monk to do this: to live as a man of God who has been manifestly 'called out of the world' to an existence that differs radically from that of other men, however sincere, however Christian, however holy, who have remained in the world."[35]

Dom Jean Leclercq in his excellent introduction to *Contemplation in a World of Action*, published after Merton's death, ends by quoting a letter from Thomas Merton which bears repeating here. In this letter accepting the invitation to come to Bangkok, Thailand, where he was to meet his death, Merton wrote to Leclercq: "The great problem for monasticism today is, 'not survival, but prophecy.' "[35] And those words are as true today as when they were written, a decade ago.

In his later years, Merton often compared the monk to the social critic, and as an example he pointed out that the earliest monks fled the secular society of Rome and sought solitude and silence and purity of heart in the desert of Egypt. It was the monk's way of renouncing the culture of his day, and his withdrawal from society was his personal criticism of the world as he viewed it. In his address at Bangkok, a few hours before his death, Merton referred to a young French revolutionary student who had made the statement some weeks earlier at the Center for the Study of Democratic Institutions at Santa Barbara: "We are monks, too." Merton was deeply impressed by these words, and he reflected: "The monk is essentially someone who takes up a critical attitude toward the world and its structures, just as these students identify themselves as people who have taken up a critical attitude toward the contemporary world and its structures."[37] The criticism was quite different, as Merton pointed out. Yet he was saying something that was important for the monk to hear: "However, the student seemed to be alluding to the fact that if one is to call himself in some way or other a monk, he must have in some way or other reached some kind of critical conclusion about the validity of certain claims made by secular society and its structures with regard to the end of man's existence. In other words, the monk is somebody who says, in one way or another, that the claims of the world are fraudulent."[38]

In this respect Merton was closer to Karl Rahner and his "diaspora" Christian than to the vapid optimism of some of the followers of Teilhard de Chardin. Reflection on the atrocities of the twentieth century, especially the "holocaust" of six and a half million Jews by the Nazis and our own ignominious performance in Vietnam, made him very much a sober realist; yet he remained a person of Christian hope in the ultimate victory of Christ, despite human shortcomings.

During the course of his Asian journey, Merton gave a number of talks at the Temple of Understanding in Calcutta, to the Jesuit scholastics near Darjeeling, and of course his last conference at the meeting of Asian monastic leaders in Bangkok. Reading over these texts, some of which have been published as appendices to *The Asian Journal,* we see again the same balanced position between the extreme right and the reactionary left in renewal matters. Speaking of the irrelevance of monks in an informal talk in Calcutta, he asks the rhetorical question which he then proceeds to answer: "Are monks and hippies and poets relevant? No, we are deliberately irrelevant. We live with an ingrained irrelevance which is proper to every human being. The marginal man accepts the basic irrelevance of the human condition, an irrelevance which is manifested above all by the fact of death."[39]

Ironically, Merton then spoke of death and the marginal person, the monk, the displaced person, the prisoner, as a witness to life in these deeply moving words: "All these people live in the presence of death, which calls into question the meaning of life. He [the monk] struggles with the fact of death in himself, trying to seek something deeper than death; because there is something deeper than death, and the office of the monk or the marginal person, the meditative person or the poet is to go beyond death even in this life, to go beyond the dichotomy of life and death and to be, therefore, a witness to life."[40]

If anything can ultimately be said about Thomas Merton, it must be that he was "a witness to life." May his great spirit remain with us as we continue our renewal. In some sense the monastic life, like the Church itself, will always be renewing itself, and the wisdom and insights of Thomas Merton can assist us not only today, but especially in the years to come.

NOTES

1. Personal recollections of a monk of Gethsemani.
2. Thomas Merton, *The Monastic Journey*, edited by Brother Patrick Hart (Mission, Kan.: Sheed, Andrews, and McMeel, 1977), p. 165.
3. *Ibid.*
4. *Ibid.*, p. 167.
5. *Ibid.*
6. Merton, "An Exchange of Letters on Monastic Questions," (Gethsemani, Ky.: Abbey of Gethsemani, 1963), p. 24.
7. *Ibid.*
8. *Ibid.*, p. 25.
9. *Ibid.*
10. Merton, *Contemplation in a World of Action* (N.Y.: Doubleday, 1971), p. 141.
11. *Ibid.*, pp. 141-42.
12. Merton, *The Collected Poems of Thomas Merton* (N. Y.: New Directions, 1978).
13. Merton, *Seeds of Destruction*, (N.Y.: Farrar, Straus and Giroux, 1964), p. 319.
14. Merton, *Contemplation in a World of Action*, p. 182.
15. *Ibid.*, p. 183.
16. Merton, *The Monastic Journey*, p. 131. Cf. also Br. Patrick Hart (ed.), *Thomas Merton/Monk* (N.Y.: Sheed and Ward, 1974), pp 173-93.
17. Merton, *The Monastic Journey*, p. 131.
18. Merton, *Contemplation in a World of Action*, p. 223.
19. *Ibid.*, p. 225.
20. *Ibid.*, p. 338.
21. *Ibid.*
22. *Ibid.*, p. 374.
23. *Ibid.*, pp. 374-75.
24. Merton, Letter to the Editor, *National Catholic Reporter*, January 11, 1968, "Regaining the Old Monastic Charism," p. 11.
25. *Ibid.*
26. *Ibid.*
27. Merton, "The Council and Monasticism," in *The Impact of Vatican II*, edited by Jude P. Dougherty (N.Y.: Herder, 1966), p. 51.
28. *Ibid.*, pp. 51-52.
29. *Ibid.*, p. 49.

30. Merton, "A Conference on Prayer," in *Sisters Today* XLI (1970), pp. 449-56.

31. Merton, *Contemplation in a World of Action*, p. 337.

32. Merton, "The Council and Monasticism," p. 54.

33. Merton, *Contemplation in a World of Action*, p. 8.

34. *Ibid.*, pp. 8-9.

35. *Ibid.*, p. 9.

36. *Ibid.*, p. xx; cf. *Thomas Merton/Monk*, pp. 93-124.

37. Merton, *The Asian Journal of Thomas Merton*, edited by Brother Patrick Hart, Naomi Burton, and James Laughlin (N.Y.: New Directions, 1973), p. 329.

38. *Ibid.*,

39. *Ibid.*, p. 306.

40. *Ibid.*

"To Be What I Am": Thomas Merton as a Spiritual Writer

Elena Malits, C.S.C.

For about seven years I have been using Thomas Merton's books, especially his various autobiographical writings, in many of the religious studies courses I teach in a Catholic college. I am both surprised and not surprised at the responses. These students of the 1970's certainly come from an experience of Catholicism very different from mine in the 1950's, yet they appear no less fascinated by Merton than I was at their age. Some of them tell me they can better relate to their parents, not to mention the institutional Church, for having read *The Seven Storey Mountain*. More importantly, Merton continues to do for this generation of undergraduates what he did for mine—open to them a whole new world of religious meaning. I can remember feeling unsettled, prodded, awakened, enlivened when I first began reading Thomas Merton. He raised unsuspected questions and uncovered hidden yearnings in me. Now I find my students describing the effect Merton has on them in terms I poignantly recognize. For more than just a few of them he becomes a vital presence shaping their lives, as he did—and still does—mine. Through reading Merton these young people embark upon the journey of discovering themselves and the God within their own depths. They join quite a number of us in that on-going quest upon which Thomas Merton launched us.

In this essay on Merton as a spiritual writer, I am consciously beginning where Merton has taught me to start the

194

process of religious reflection—getting in touch with my own experience, remarking what happens inside and around me, positioning myself in the world where I live. That is precisely what Thomas Merton himself did so skillfully—and what he empowered his readers to respect, and enabled some to try doing.

Merton's Particular Gifts

Merton was gifted with a capacity for discerning and describing the action of God in the concrete circumstances of his everyday life. Poet that he was, he had learned how to observe, how to allow things to impress themselves upon him, and how to recast imaginatively his experience into communicable form. Writing about himself and the ordinary (and not-so-ordinary) events of his monastic life was for Merton both an ascetic discipline and an aesthetic passion. Indeed, such writing was a psychological and a spiritual necessity for his continuing development and it played an essential role in his sustained effort to work out his vocation. He sensitively captured what autobiographical writing meant for him in a 1949 journal entry:

> And yet it seems to me that writing, far from being an obstacle to spiritual perfection in my own life, has become one of the conditions on which my perfection will depend. If I am to be a saint—*and there is nothing else that I can think of desiring to be*—it seems that I must get there by writing books in a Trappist monastery. If I am to be a saint, I have not only to be a monk, which is what all monks must do to become saints, but I must also put down on paper what I have become. It may sound simple, but it is not an easy vocation.

> To be as good a monk as I can, and to remain myself, and to write about it: to put myself down on paper, in such a situation, with the most complete simplicity and integrity, masking nothing, confusing no issues: this is very

hard, because I am all mixed up in illusions and attachments. These, too, will have to be put down. But without exaggeration, repetition, useless emphasis. No need for breast beating and lamentation before the eyes of anyone but You, O God, who see the depths of my fatuity. To be frank without being boring. It is a kind of crucifixion. Not a very dramatic or painful one. But it requires so much honesty that it is beyond my nature. It must come somehow from the Holy Ghost.[1]

It was a demanding task, to be sure, but Thomas Merton loved as well as dreaded it! He was endemically an autobiographical writer, not only producing a formal autobiography in his early thirties, but publishing several journals and many autobiographical essays throughout his life.[2] Even his topical essays, e.g., on literature, social issues, or theological controversies, usually had an autobiographical dimension. Merton wrote about what was happening "out there" only insofar as he sifted things through his own consciousness. What he offered his readers was never presented as an "objective account" of anything, but simply as Thomas Merton's reading of events, Thomas Merton's responses, Thomas Merton vis-à-vis this or that. His preface to *Conjectures of a Guilty Bystander* summed up the characteristic Merton mode:

These notes add up to a personal version of the world in the 1960s. In elaborating such a version one unavoidably tells something of himself, for what a man truly is can be discovered only through his self-awareness in a living and actual world. But these pages are not a venture in self-revelation or self-discovery. Nor are they a pure soliloquy. They are an implicit dialogue with other minds, a dialogue in which questions are raised. But do not expect to find "my answers." I do not have clear answers to current questions. I do have questions, and, as a matter of fact, I think a man is known better by his questions than by his answers.[3]

Merton's questions were never isolated from his personal experience of living. They arose not merely from cerebral speculation, but from the very struggles within his own soul to affirm the power of God in a sinful world and within his sinful self. As he put it toward the end of that same preface:

> There are many other concerns appropriate to an age of transition and crisis, of war and racial conflict, of technology and expansion. Above all, there are the day-to-day impressions, the simple conjectures, of a man in his own world with its own challenges. It is a monastic world, and doubtless strange to those who have no experiences of any such thing. Yet it is, I think, open to the life and experience of the greater, more troubled, and more vocal world beyond the cloister. Though I often differ strongly from that "world," I think I can be said to respond to it. I do not delude myself that I am not still part of it.[4]

More than any other contemporary religious writer, I think, Thomas Merton taught us to appreciate the technological potential of asking one's own authentic questions. He reintroduced and legitimized using the "I" in religious inquiry—not the "I" which merely asserts various opinions, theological or otherwise, but the probing "I" seeking to discover God in the self, in others, in all creation. The literary context for articulating that "I" is, of course, autobiographical narrative. Merton expressed his questions as he described the circumstances of his life in which they were generated. That is to say, he was constantly engaged in a process of telling his story. Augustine had done it, and Thomas Merton returned us to autobiography as a form of theological discourse. It appears to me that such is Merton's real significance as a "spiritual writer."

His story was one of on-going development or continuing conversion. Aside from *The Seven Storey Mountain*, Merton recounted that story only in bits and snatches, not in any one continuous narrative. But that was typically Thomas Merton; he would leave to his readers the task of discovering the "hidden wholeness" of his life. He himself wrote about living as he experienced it: disparate, unsystematic, disjunctive, paradoxical. And he wrote about himself not as one instance of a general type, but simply as *this* man in all his specificity and particularity.

The Individual in God's Hands

In his autobiographical writings Merton reveals himself as a human being with richer possibilities than most of us (extraordinary combinations of talents and interests), and undoubtedly with more realizations. He stands before us— occasionally tempted to pose—as contemplative monk (person of mystical prayer, cenobite, Master of Novices, hermit); versatile writer (poet, novelist, commentator, critic, mediator-on-paper); passionate intellectual (probing art, literature, theology, philosophy, history, psychology, the traditions of many cultures); committed seeker of justice (for the minorities, the underprivileged, the oppressed, the rejected, the ignored and forgotten ones); lover of peace (among nations, races, religious traditions, and within the individual heart). But Thomas Merton never put himself forth as a paradigm; he does not offer us a model—but "only" himself.

He was adamant, in fact, that he be taken neither as a paradigm of virtue nor as a pattern for vocation. Sometimes people misunderstood and tried to make him into one or the other or both. Sometimes Merton inadvertently fostered those tendencies. That may have been the inevitable consequence of so powerful a personality and such a remarkable gift for expression.

Not only in the autobiography, but in writings throughout his life, Merton considered himself a sinner. And like all those who grow in the spiritual life, he pronounced himself even more guilty as his sense of God's goodness and mercy deepened. For Thomas Merton (as for Paul, Augustine, and John of the Cross), such testimony is itself a measure of growth. The epilogue of *The Sign of Jonas*, for instance, written almost ten years after his entrance into Gethsemani, is a classic statement of a growing awareness which, while intensifying the sinner's sense of his failure, shifts the emphasis to

God's forgiving love. Merton imaginatively projected the voice of God in Paradise saying to him:

"What was vile has become precious. What is now precious was never vile. I have always known all the vile as precious: for what is vile I know not at all.

"What was cruel has become merciful. What is now merciful was never cruel. I have always overshadowed Jonas with My mercy, and cruelty I know not at all. Have you had sight of Me, Jonas My child? Mercy within mercy. I have forgiven the universe without end, because I have never known sin."[5]

A man acutely conscious of having been transformed and always undergoing transformation by the creative power of a loving God, Merton sought to focus his attention on God rather than himself. But that attempt was eminently paradoxical, for Thomas Merton could know God only in and through coming to know himself.

For all his criticism of introspection as fatal to the contemplative life, Merton was preoccupied with his own inner workings to an extraordinary degree. Except for Soren Kierkegaard, one could scarcely find a religious personality more disposed to self-reflection or more given to articulating his own inwardness. Merton's self-consciousness, nonetheless, cannot simply be equated with psychological introversion. While he certainly exhibited intense interest in his own interior processes and (disclaimers to the contrary) obviously obtained emotional satisfaction from such activity, Merton was neither a withdrawn personality nor fixated upon himself. Undoubtedly there were neurotic and egotistical elements in his make-up, but in the main Merton's type of self-consciousness appears psychically and morally sound. The lightsome quality of his later personal writings even suggests that contemplative solitude relieved him of taking himself too seriously.

In his exquisite little autobiographical piece, "Day of a Stranger," Merton revealed himself as a man sufficiently at home with himself to quit worrying about whether he was or was not "being himself." In fact, he poked fun at the current imperative:

> In an age where there is much talk about "being your-self" I reserve to myself the right to forget about being myself, since in any case there is very little chance of my being anybody else. Rather it seems to me that when one is too intent on "being himself" he runs the risk of impersonating a shadow.[6]

Of course, there was no danger that Thomas Merton could forget about "being himself" in the sense of trying to discover and be faithful to his authentic identity.

To call Merton "self-conscious" is not to accuse him of being mired in a passive state of perception regarding himself. Rather, his self-consciousness should be thought of as an activity, the activity of attempting to articulate what he was undergoing or doing. Merton was constantly engaged in a process of exercising the skill of saying what was going on in his life.[7] He was committed to the task of "spelling out" his involvements, at least to himself, although he shared much of what he discovered through publishing his journals. But the point of all his journal writing was precisely this: to say as unambiguously as possible what he understood himself to be experiencing or undertaking in the events of his life.

Merton was not only reciting an account of what happened to him and how he responded to the situations in which he found himself. Indeed, he *was* doing that, for all forms of autobiographical writing entail such description. In his journals and personal essays Merton was explicitly attending to the *significance* of events and deeds in his life as he apprehended it. He was telling the story of his own unique self-consciousness. In the most literal sense, the activity of writing about himself embodied Merton's sense of his own identity and gave it intelligible form. He came to know who he was and what he might become primarily through the effort of articulating the self he experienced in its multiple engagements. Thus his autobiographical efforts could be said to be both expressive of himself and constitutive of himself. Thomas Merton would not have been who he was apart from the labor to tell himself (and us) whom he understood himself to be and what he took his life to mean.

The Discipline of Autobiographical Writing

Autobiographical writers need to be self-conscious persons, of course, or they would not undertake such a venture of communication. Still, some are more intensely self-conscious than others—and that is not an unmixed blessing. While it is wholesome, even essential, for the development of an integrated self to "spell out" what the person understands himself to be doing, it is also a dangerously seductive enterprise. The greater the facility for articulation, the easier may someone be snared into endless "explanations" to himself concerning his behavior. Psychology calls it "rationalizing," and ethics terms it "self-justification." Merton often enough got caught in those rounds.

Nonetheless, Thomas Merton still appears a fundamentally honest human being who tried to face the reality of himself *through* writing about himself. In the activity of formulating what he grasped about himself he would recognize the truth and be able to acknowledge it. Thus Merton's autobiographical writing not only was the way he came to insights into himself and his behavior, but it provided an occasion for making choices to change, modify, discard, or appropriate certain aspects of himself. In this sense such writing was an essential element in his on-going development.

Merton's practical decisions were quite literally worked out in his notebooks. Sometimes he consciously tested a course of action by writing about its implications before he undertook it in fact. More often, he simply reflected on what he was already doing by writing about what he did. That was an activity of assessment, and it led Merton to make some significant changes in his life. Writing *The Secular Journal* helped him to decide to enter the monastery, writing *The Sign of Jonas* helped him learn how to live with the paradox of his vocation as a monk-writer, and writing *Conjectures of a Guilty Bystander* helped him to make up his mind regarding how to assume social and political responsibility.

But such writing accomplished still more than sharpening his clarity about himself and fostering decisiveness. Autobiographical writing affected—and in some measure effected—Merton's character as a religious person. The task of telling his story served to monitor Merton's pretensions and laid bare any claim to righteousness. It poignantly disclosed to him the disjunction between his aspirations and his real achievements. Writing goaded Merton into humility, not only in the moral sense of non-assertiveness, but in the religious sense of acknowledging all one has as having been received. Thomas Merton's appreciation of his life as pure gift, as mercy, was not incidental to his continual effort to articulate his experience and shape it into a story.

The genuinely religious character of the man was expressed in that rich and variegated narrative. It is there for us to encounter and to measure by Merton's own affirmation that what he sought was simply "to be what I am." That sums up, as well as anything he wrote, how Thomas Merton conceived who he was and where he was going. He phrased it this way:

> My task is only to be what I am, a man seeking God in silence and solitude, with deep respect for the demands and realities of his own vocation, and fully aware that others too are seeking the truth in their own way.[8]

This language is the very antithesis of what Merton regarded as cheap talk about "being yourself." We have already noted that he ridiculed the advice to "be yourself." For Merton that was a distortion of authentic humanism and, worse, inimical to the Gospel. It conveniently overlooks the facts of evil, sin, suffering, and death in the world and in oneself. That easy recommendation trades on the illusion that we know who we are from the outset, and that life is but a matter of letting the lovely reality of ourselves unfold. It feeds on the deception that we are free without being liberated, that we stand in no need of redemption. Merton knew better.

When Thomas Merton describes his task as "to be what I am," he is explicitly invoking the language of Christian faith which reveals to the believer that he is both sinful and freed from sin, guilty but forgiven, radically unworthy before God yet loved so much that his Son assumed flesh and died to save him. Thus the task of Merton "being who he was" entailed accepting himself as a sinner. It meant recognizing the shadows still—always—present within himself and acknowledging his real vulnerabilities. But it also meant affirming that he had been liberated from his sinful past by God's loving kindness, and that he was called to continual transformation. "To be what I am," as Merton employed the formula, appealed to the Pauline view of the "new man" in Christ, the Augustinian theology of redemption as reformation of the image of God in man, and the Kierkegaardian understanding of what goes into "becoming a Christian."

Merton's description of his life-task as "only to be what I am," then, suggests a deliberate appropriation of his own sinfulness and a deliberate acceptance of the liberation wrought in him by grace. To appropriate deliberately one's personal sins is to announce, admit, and acknowledge responsibility for one's destructive deeds or culpable failures. Deliberately to accept one's own liberation by grace is to praise God for what he has done in one's life and to pledge oneself to live in fidelity to that transforming power which is at work, Augustine brought together these two meanings in naming the account of his life *Confessions*. Thomas Merton did something analogous. His autobiographical writings are not the tales of a hero, but "confessions" in the Augustinian style. Therein lies, I think, a clue to Merton's significance as a contemporary religious figure.

A Story of Continuing Conversion

There is a certain structural similarity between Merton and Augustine worth noting. These two personalities were alike in temperament, modes of consciousness and expression, and conviction regarding the ingredients of religious conversion. Both Augustine and Merton were profoundly reflective and intensely passionate men. For each the quest for understanding had an existential bearing, and the living out of that search offered the content for reflection. Both were essentially autobiographers—persons who articulated their self-understanding in, through, and by telling the story of their lives. It was Augustine, of course, who gave us the genre of autobiographical writing that has so deeply affected Western culture, and who provided the model of a conversion story that integrates personal testimony and reflective theology in a coherent unity. Thomas Merton is not great in Augustine's measure. Certainly, he is not so original a thinker nor so great a theological genius as the Bishop of Hippo, though Merton is nonetheless a religious autobiographer, a "spiritual writer," of the same type.

Augustine had cast his life story in the form of a journey into his innermost depths: a recovery of the self at the point of one's being wherein God dwells—a return to the Source. The central metaphor of Augustine's *Confessions* is "the heart." He structured his narrative according to the stages of what his heart desired: lust, wisdom, rest in God. It is a movement from disintegration, to partial integration, to unity within the self—in God.[9]

Merton, too, told his life story as an interior journey. That story, as we have seen, was told in fragmentary fashion in many journals, essays, and poems. His autobiography proper *was* a unified narrative; however, it was written too early to tell the whole life story, and from a perspective relatively too immature to reflect a genuinely personal and integrated theology. The very image Merton had invoked for the title of his autobiography was, after all, borrowed from Dante. And viewed from the perspective of Merton's entire life and total autobiographical output, his story of climbing the mountain of purgation represents but a beginning. Perhaps even more significantly, that metaphor suggests a relatively external quest. Merton's "ascent up the mountain" is not, therefore, the structural equivalent of Augustine's metaphor of the transformation of his "heart's desire" for expressing the true dimensions of Merton's interior journey. Rather, the monk's language of "being who he is" really comes closer to that. It is this language, in all its metaphorical variations, which functions to articulate Merton's most properly personal theological understanding of his own life. It is "being who I am" that is the linguistic key to reading Merton's entire life as an inner search for God who reveals himself in the utter uniqueness of each individual human being. To "be who he is" Thomas Merton had to tell his story as a journey into the unknown, for one's "true self" is known only in God. That is to say, for Merton, as for Augustine, the self as image of God participates in the ineffable mystery of the divine.[10]

In my estimation, the importance of Thomas Merton as a vital religious personality and profoundly influential spiritual writer lies precisely in his fidelity to the task of "being who he was" and communicating the awareness of his particularity to the rest of us. Another way of putting that is to remark that Merton has given us an authentic account of the Christian life as continuing conversion. Merton's story testifies to the effectiveness of God's creative Word informing a person's life so that he or she seeks to be only himself or herself and by that process actually transcends himself or herself.

There is an inescapable paradox in writing about one's religious experience, as there is in living it: the more "universal" one presumes to be, the less he attains universality. The individual who would play everyman is really nobody. The person who tries to follow many religious paths ends up following none at all. On the other hand, the more a person is faithful to his or her own particularity, the more is he or she able to reach others different from himself or herself and to communicate with them in the common humanity which all share. Or the more authentically a religious person lives according to the specific commitment that his or her particular faith elicits, the more can he or she appreciate another's aspiration toward the divine, though it may have a form quite different from his or her own.

Merton said it better: "At the center of our souls we meet together, spiritually, in the infinite sources of all our created lives."[11] It is by "being ourselves," our "true selves," however, that we arrive at that point. The authentic realization of one's individuality is the meeting place. The person who has found himself or herself can recognize who others are:

> Our task now is to learn that if we can voyage to the ends of the earth and there find *ourselves* in the aborigine who most differs from ourselves, we will have made a fruitful pilgrimage. That is why pilgrimage is necessary, in some shape or other. Mere sitting at home and meditating on the divine presence is not enough for our time. We have to come to the end of a long journey and see that the stranger we meet there is no other than ourselves—which is the same as saying that we find Christ in him.[12]

We might say that the paradox of genuinely reaching others through really being oneself is a manifestation of the law of Christian incarnation. For the Word became a human person, this human person, Jesus of Nazareth. God's love is disclosed in him and through his utterly specific life with its concrete events, especially those which give his life its definitive shape: his cross and resurrection. Through this man and this life, humankind is redeemed. What God has done for human persons and what men and women can become through the power of that saving love is made known *as a story*.

Identity as Fidelity

Thomas Merton understood the paradox and appreciated stories. His writings are effective because they make a good story about this very particular life. They are able to touch the lives of others—many different kinds of people—because they reflect the experience of one man, a man who took seriously the task of "being who he was." Just as it is the story of *Augustine's* heart (his concrete, unique story) that moves us, so it is Merton's expression of his individuality in the narrative form of his own story which is most compelling.

That story reveals Merton as a person able to grow continuously by integrating into himself the intellectual, moral, and religious values others had to offer, without surrendering those which he had personally appropriated as his own. Nearly twenty years after writing his autobiography, Merton affirmed the basic choices that had shaped his life through his religious conversion and monastic vocation, indicating how he was both faithful, yet open to change:

> The occasion of a new preface invites the author to reflect once again on the story, his own story, and the way he has told it....In its present form, which will remain its only form, it belongs to many people. The author no longer has an exclusive claim upon his story.
>
> But if the story remains what it is, has the author changed?
>
> Certainly I have never for a moment thought of changing the definitive decisions taken in the course of my life: to be a Christian, to be a monk, to be a priest. If anything, the decision to renounce and to depart from modern secular society, a decision repeated and reaffirmed many times, has finally become irrevocable. Yet the attitude and the assumptions behind this decision have perhaps changed in many ways.
>
> Since that time, I have learned, I believe, to look back into that world with greater compassion, seeing those in it not as alien to myself, not as peculiar and deluded strangers, but as identified with myself. In breaking from "their world" I have strangely not broken from them. In freeing myself from their delusions and preoccupations, I have identified myself, none the less, with their struggles and their blind, desperate hope of happiness.[13]

That capacity—to remain true to one's fundamental decisions without being locked into the stage of development from which they emerged—is the mark of a genuinely integrated self. From the time of his conversion to Catholicism onward, Thomas Merton was possessed of an identity he recognized as *his*, though it would take a lifetime to realize and to articulate it fully.

Such an actualized identity belongs to the person who has attained what Merton, borrowing from Reza Arasteh, a Persian psychoanalyst, called "final integration." Merton explained it thus:

> The man who has attained final integration is no longer limited by the culture in which he has grown up. "He has embraced *all of life*....He has experienced qualities of every type of life": ordinary human existence, intellectual life, artistic creation, human love, religious life. He passes beyond all these limiting forms, while retaining all that is best and most universal in them, "finally giving birth to a fully comprehensive self." He accepts not only his own community, his own society, his own friends, his own culture, but all mankind. He does not remain bound to one limited set of values in such a way that he opposes them aggressively or defensively to others. He is fully "Catholic" in the best sense of the word. He has a unified vision and experience of the one truth shining out in all its various manifestations, some clearer than others, some more definite and more certain than others. He does not set these partial views up in opposition to each other, but unifies them in a dialectic or an insight of complementarity. With this view of life he is able to bring perspective, liberty and spontaneity into the lives of others. The finally integrated man is a peacemaker, and that is why there is such a desperate need for our leaders to become such men of insight. [14]

Though ostensibly explicating Arasteh's idea, Merton might have been describing himself. In fact, that characterization of the fully realized human personality is not far from Merton's account of his experience in the garden of Polannaruwa in the last week of his life. In one of his last journal entries, Merton shows himself to us as someone who has "embraced all of life" and has attained a "unified vision." He was looking at some statues of the Buddha in an ancient temple ruins:

I am able to approach the Buddhas barefoot and undisturbed, my feet in wet grass, wet sand. Then the silence of the extraordinary faces. The great smiles. Huge and yet subtle. Filled with every possibility, questioning nothing, knowing everything, rejecting nothing, the peace not of emotional resignation but of Madhyamika, of sunyata, that has seen through every question without trying to discredit anyone or anything—*without refutation*—without establishing some other argument....

Looking at these figures I was suddenly, almost forcibly, jerked clean out of the habitual, half-tied vision of things, and an inner clearness, clarity, as if exploding from the rocks themselves became evident and obvious.... The thing about all this is that there is no puzzle, no problem, and really no "mystery." All problems are resolved and everything is clear, simply because what matters is clear. The rock, all matter, all life, is charged with dharmakaya...everything is emptiness and everything is compassion. I don't know when in my life I have ever had such a sense of beauty and spiritual validity running together in one aesthetic illumination.[15]

Merton was a man whose horizons were constantly enlarged. But he was able to move to new vantage points precisely because he actually stood somewhere. He reflected upon his standpoint at every stage of his life's journey, and thus was able to develop without being uprooted. Having learned to "see" differently through the Zen discipline and understanding the vision of reality which Buddhism offers, Merton nonetheless remained a Christian. He encountered the wisdom of the East and became a more enlightened Christian. Having shared the anguish of those in the front lines of the struggle for peace and justice in the world, Merton kept faithful to his contemplative vocation. He "went out" to a suffering world by "staying in" monastic solitude. From his conversation with the world, Merton "returned to himself" more converted to his particular task in the world as a monk. He learned to "be who he was" through fidelity to his continuing quest to discover that reality in God:

> To reach one's "real self" one must, in fact, be delivered by grace, virtue and asceticism, from that illusory and false "self" whom we have created by our habits of selfishness and by our constant flights from reality. In order to find God, whom we can only find in and through the depths of our own soul, we must therefore first find ourselves. To use common figures of speech, we must "return to ourselves," we must "come to ourselves."[16]

I think it not exaggerated to say that Father Louis was more a priest for being an autobiographical writer. That writing functioned, in fact, as his ministry to men and women, and as the means by which it was possible for Thomas Merton to "return to himself" as this individual person. And perhaps Merton was never more a priest, i.e., a mediator between God and humankind, than when he was telling his life story. For that story displays what, according to the author of the letter to the Hebrews, goes into making a true mediator—on the model of Jesus himself:

> It was essential that he should in this way become completely like his brothers, so that he could be a compassionate and trustworthy high priest of God's religion, able to atone for human sins. That is, because he has himself been through temptation he is able to help others who are tempted (Heb. 2:17-18).

The matter might be put another way. Merton's life story articulates an affirmation at the heart of the Christian revelation. Augustine testified to it, but it was formulated much earlier by another inherent autobiographer, Paul of Tarsus:

I shall be very happy to make my weakness my special boast so that the power of Christ may stay over me, and that is why I am quite content with my weaknesses, and with insults, hardships, persecutions, and the agonies I go through for Christ's sake. For it is when I am weak that I am strong (2 Cor. 12:9-10).

Merton's account of "being who I am" is a story of a person made strong in weakness. Facing the paradoxical truth of Christianity entails a real journey into the unknown, for nobody "knows" that truth except by living it out. Merton made the journey and made it into a story that can profoundly affect us. He is a great spiritual writer because he has communicated the lively tale of his own quest for God. He comes through as one who has trod the path—gone before us and found that which he sought. We believe Merton, and are empowered to undertake our own journey.

His books on various aspects of the spiritual life—prayer, penance, solitude, suffering, peace, joy—are most effective when placed in the context of Merton's own lived experience. But it is his autobiographical writings themselves, I have insisted, that are his richest legacy to us. In these most of all Merton speaks to us and helps those who read him discerningly to take a few steps inward. His life, and the story which narrates it, quietly announces the presence of the transforming Word made flesh. And a real power, the power of his Spirit, spurs us on through the flesh-and-blood story of Thomas Merton.

NOTES

1. Thomas Merton, *The Sign of Jonas* (New York: Image Books, 1956), pp. 228-29.

2. Merton's published journals include *The Secular Journal of Thomas Merton* (New York: Farrar, Straus and Cudahy, 1959); *The Sign of Jonas* (New York: Harcourt, Brace and Company, 1953); *Conjectures of a Guilty Bystander* (New York: Doubleday, 1966); *The Asian Journal of Thomas Merton* (New York: New Directions, 1973). To mention but a few of his autobiographical essays: "As Man to Man," *Cistercian Studies IV* (1969), pp. 90-94; "Day of a Stranger," *Hudson Review XX* (1967-68), pp. 211-18; "Learning To Live" in *University on the Heights,* ed. E. Wesley First (New York:

Doubleday, 1969); "My Campaign Platform for Non-Abbot and Permanent Keeper of the Present Doghouse," *Unicorn Journal* I (1968), pp. 95-96; "Rain and the Rhinocerous," *Holiday* (1965), pp. 8-16; "The White Pebble" in *Where I Found Christ*, ed. John A. O'Brien (New York: Doubleday, 1950).

3. Merton, *Conjectures of a Guilty Bystander*, p. 5.

4. *Ibid.*, p. 5.

5. Merton, *The Sign of Jonas*, pp. 351-52.

6. Merton, "Day of a Stranger," in *A Thomas Merton Reader* (revised edition), ed. Thomas P. McDonnell (New York: Image Books, 1974), pp. 431-32.

7. A contemporary philosopher, Herbert Fingarette, has usefully developed this model of self-consciousness: "To become explicitly conscious of something is to be exercising a certain skill. . . . The specific skill I particularly have in mind as a model for becoming explicitly conscious of something is the skill of saying what we are doing or experiencing. I propose, then, that we do not characterize consciousness as a kind of mental mirror, but as the exercise of the (learned) skill of 'spelling out' some feature of the world as we are engaged in it. Like its model—language skill proper—this skill is ubiquitous among men, though in both cases the subtlety, the range, and the aptness of the exercise of the skill varies markedly among individuals." Fingarette explicates this notion in detail in his insightful book, *Self-Deception* (London: Routledge & Kegan Paul, 1969), pp. 38-39.

8. Merton, "What Missionary Aim Does a Monk Have?" *Contemplation in a World of Action* (New York: Doubleday, 1971), p. 231.

9. Saint Augustine, *Confessions*, Bk. II, 1-2; III, 4; I, i.

10. Merton, "Image and Likeness," *The New Man* (New York: Mentor-Omega Books, 1961), p. 37

11. Merton, "The Second Adam," *ibid.*, p. 86.

12. Merton, "From Pilgrimage to Crusade," *Mystics and Zen Masters* (New York: Delta Books, 1967), p. 112.

13. Merton "Author's Preface to the Japanese Edition," *Nanae No Yama (The Seven Storey Mountain)*, trans. Tadishi Kudo (Tokyo: Chuo Shuppansha, 1966).

14. Merton, "Final Integration," *Contemplation in a World of Action*, p. 212.

15. Merton, *The Asian Journal of Thomas Merton*, pp. 233-34.

16. Merton, "Image and Likeness," *The New Man*, p. 44.

Merton and History

Jean Leclercq, O.S.B.

The title of this essay is not "Merton the Historian" because Merton was not a historian, nor did he ever pretend to be one. Yet, poet and writer that he was, this thinker-monk grasped the importance of history and the utility of knowing the past in order to understand the present. He had more the sense of tradition than of history. Tradition does not identify with the past but comes down to us through it. Nor is tradition strictly speaking knowledge of the past, although it does suppose this knowledge. Merton's ideas on history could be sifted out from his immensely extensive works in which he dealt with so many subjects. Possibly he said less about history than about other topics. Yet, even though it may not be explicitated, the conception he had of it is one of the keys to understanding him. Here I will mainly deal with the practical use he made of history, and my chief source will be certain letters he wrote to me from 1950 up to the year of his death, 1968.[1] When this correspondence is published, the extracts I am going to quote from it can then be set in a living context. Here I can only mention in passing certain facts. But at least this cursory reminder will help us to see how Merton tried to learn from what historians had to say, anxious as he was to get back to the sources of tradition, so that their message might become, in his own time, both present and prophetic. In other words he tried to find out the facts, and then to discern their meaning so that the permanent values in them might catalyze the present, orienting it to the future.

I

LEARNING THE PAST

I think that we may distinguish two phases in Merton's knowledge of those who witness to Christian thought and to the spiritual experience of past centuries. The first of these periods covers roughly the years of his conversion to monastic life and his formation in it. It goes up to approximately 1950 and is attested to mainly by *The Seven Storey Mountain* and his first books. Traces are still to be found in later years in *Conjectures of a Guilty Bystander* and elsewhere. As a young monk beginning his first studies he was not satisfied with the prevalent theological manuals and textbooks. He instinctively went to great authors and great books such as Gilson in *The Spirit of Medieval Philosophy*, and Maritain, whose *The Degrees of Knowledge* inspired the title of his own work *The Ascent to Truth*. Merton's thought is deeply marked by Maritain's *Art and Scholasticism* which, though only a small book, had a powerful impact on the European Catholic generation of the 1920's. To this we may add Fr. Martin C. D'Arcy's *The Mind and Heart of Love*, as well as *Eros and Agape* by Anders Nygren, and so many other of those books which captivated our youth. There is scarcely any difference between the way in which these works were loved by any young high school lad such as myself in 1928 and in the following years, and that enthusiasm shown by the adult convert Merton some ten years later. Such are the years when one has neither time nor preparation for acceding to authors themselves. One is happy to be introduced to them by thinkers, who have assimilated them and transmitted their message in an attractive manner.

One can understand these bursts of enthusiasm if, as was my own experience ten years before Merton, one has also undergone them. Having had the privilege of being Gilson's student (and later his friend, in the 1930's and 1940's) and having frequented Maritain before and after the Second World War, I realize that they had the ability to enchant one with all that they had to say and write. For the young man Merton their works were already sources of inspiration. These masters had worked on the texts and Merton handed on some of their results to a wide American audience. In particular, he began a first synthesis (which though bookish was nevertheless already definitive) of the different contributions made to the history of thought and religious experience. These contributions were made by ancient Greek philosophers, Fathers of the Church, Thomists, and the Carmelite school, which was represented for Merton by its most eminent witnesses—St. Teresa of Avila and St. John of the Cross. However, when we talk of "Merton's sources" we must always carefully distinguish between those authors of whom he had second-hand knowledge, people like Plato and Plotinus, and those whom he knew from having read their texts. Whatever this genial young monk may have had to say about the former, at a time when he had hardly finished his theological studies, inevitably contains a certain amount of simplification. But this was not true, even then, for the authors he had read for himself, and whom he had studied and was already beginning to comment on either orally or in writing. This personal frequentation of the sources which were at the origin of his second period of formation began toward the close of the 1940's. It was then that Merton began to read assiduously the Fathers—St. Bernard and many others. And it was then that he saw that they had a message which was not reserved for him alone, but which he felt compelled to share with his milieu and his times. The first letter I have kept is dated April 22, 1950. In it we read a decisive passage which contains the germ of a whole program:

> We have just remodeled the vault where our rare books are kept and have extended its capacities to include a good little library on Scripture and the Fathers and the Liturgy—or at least the nucleus of one. Here I hope to form a group of competent students not merely of history or of texts but rather—in line with the tradition you so admirably represent—men competent in all-round spiritual theology, as well as scholarship, using their time and talents to develop the seed of the word of God in their souls, not to choke it under an overgrowth of use-

less research as is the tradition in the universities of this country at the moment. I fervently hope that somehow we shall see in America men who are able to produce something like *Dieu Vivant*. Cistercians will never be able to do quite that, I suppose, but we can at least give a good example along those lines. Our studies and writing should by their very nature contribute to our contemplation at least remotely, and contemplation in turn should be able to find expression in channels laid open for it and deepened by familiarity with the Fathers of the Church. This is an age that calls for Augustines and Leos, Gregorys and Cyrils!

It was in this perspective that he maintained a constant interest for the great witnesses of the past. In the same letter I have just quoted, he shows that he takes the study of history quite seriously, including what it may suppose in the way of techniques. There is mention of a microfilm of a manuscript of St. Bernard in the library at Gethsemani which I had asked him to send to me. In his turn he asked me to send him offprints of the articles I was publishing at the time on the Cistercian manuscripts to be found in European libraries. He inquires, too, about an edition of the works of Aelred of Rievaulx which I had mentioned in one of my letters to him. He shows particular interest—and this is already revelatory of one of his major preoccupations in life—for Aelred's *Rule for Anchorites*, a sort of handbook for hermits. He showed interest in the progress of my research work preparatory to the critical edition of the works of St. Bernard, asking questions about the difficulties I came across, my discoveries and the results.

When the Camoldolese monks asked me to write several books on Blessed Paul Giustiniani, a humanist from Venice who lived at the beginning of the sixteenth century and became a hermit, Merton immediately wrote me a letter in which it is obvious that these witnesses to the past were for him still very living:

Above all I want to thank you for your *Dottrina del B.P. Giustiniani*. I find it most useful and am glad to have it, particularly because it would otherwise be quite impossible for me to make the acquaintance of his personality and ideas. You have given us a valuable source. I hope books will appear on all the great Camaldolese figures. Dom Giabbani sent me some pictures of Camaldoli and it is both beautiful and inspiring to me....I would be interested in having some pictures of it as I may perhaps do an article on the Camaldolese—by way of exception, since I do not write for magazines any more. This would be in the hope of helping them make a foundation in this country. They are needed. (Aug. 21, 1953)

As I go through these letters in chronological order I notice that they mention Ambrose Autpert, an eighth-century Italian Benedictine; Dom Calmet, a seventeenth-century commentator on the *Rule of St. Benedict;* Abbot Vital Lehodey, a French Trappist and spiritual writer in the first years of the twentieth century whose biography had just been written by I. Vallery-Radot; and, Grimlaic, the author of a monastic rule in the ninth century. Merton also mentions the millennary of Mount Athos (on which occasion 1 had given a talk during a congress at Venice on monastic hospitality).

I have read with great pleasure the wonderful article of P. McNulty and her collaborator on the Orientale Lumen in the Commemorative Athos volume. It is really magnificent and it will help me a little in my work on recluses. I am keeping on patiently and quietly in this, and will I hope eventually begin to get something on paper about Grimlaic. I also enjoyed the magnificent quote on the Athos hermits, by a fifteenth-century Italian traveler, quoted in the article on the Amalfitan community of Athos. (Holy Saturday, 1964)

As I had told him about the lectures I was giving to young monks in Rome, later published as *The Love of Learning and the Desire for God,* and also about my collaboration in the *History of Christian Spirituality,* he continually offered encouragement as he often did when I was writing a book. I always received from him the stimulus of a man who draws profit from existing works, however imperfect they may be. Anyone who knows how depressing the criticisms which scholars hand out among themselves are will realize how comforting is the appreciation given by persons who, though they may be less learned, are more intensely alive.

Merton opened up more and more to traditions which were outside Benedictine or Cistercian monasticism. He was interested, for example, in more recent Orders such as the Franciscans. He greatly appreciated the works of I. Hausher on the Hesychast tradition of Eastern Christianity, and he had a growing interest for the non-Christian Eastern spiritual traditions such as Buddhism and Islam:

> ...I wonder if I could borrow an offprint of a piece you did on monasticism in Islam in order to summarize it. There is another study on pilgrim monasticism in Islam which is published in Morocco and which I hope to obtain from Toumliline, unless you have a copy you can lend me. I would be most obliged if you could let me have at least your article, for the chronicle. Though I never got permission to go to Japan, I am getting a lot of books on Zen from different sources and this will provide interesting material. (April 2, 1965))

II
DISCERNING THE TRADITION

As Merton notes in the text just cited, any information about the past was simply "material" which gave him food for thought. For him, learned books and articles were like the "dry bones" which we read about in the book of the prophet Ezekiel, and to which the Spirit gave new life. Tradition is something more and better than a mere knowledge of the past. Tradition is certainly something that exceeds an obsession with the past, when that is considered the best possible thing to be reproduced in the present. Any "archeological restoration" of this sort only leads to "traditionalism," which results in some period of the past (usually the recent past, taken to be privileged) being set up as an absolute standard and lasting value. In such cases "tradition" is confused with traditions. Whereas the former is the lifestream issuing from Christ and his Spirit, which he sends to vivify the Church in every age, the latter are only passing, limited and provisory periods which, if taken out of the mainstream of time and life, lose any significance. Nothing could be further removed from Merton's attitude. For him it was not enough to have read, identified, dated, studied and understood a text. All this was only a springboard from which his mind leapt forward into projective thinking. He kept his judgment open. This is evidenced in an extract from a long letter in which Merton spoke of his personal reactions to Jean Daniélou's interpretation of Origen and Gregory of Nyssa and the relationship between those two patristic authors and St. Bernard, as well as the *Thoughts* of a thirteenth-century Carthusian, Blessed Guigo, and Louis Bouyer's presentation of St. Anthony the Great:

> I liked Bouyer's Saint Antoine. Still, I wonder if he does not overdo his interest in the fact that in the early ages of the Church people were so clearly aware that the fall had put the Devil in charge of material things. Fr. Daniélou's *Signe du Temple*, in its first chapter, gives a good counterpoise to that view—for heaven still shone in creation and God was very familiar with men in Genesis! (October 9, 1950)

This gradual broadening of Merton's views was not symptomatic of any dilettantism by which he would be hopping superficially from one subject to another with amateurish enthusiasm. He very markedly avoided any provincialism and struck out for universality:

> I believe it is good for me to work on the *monastic* ideal as a whole, and not to be a "propagandist" for any one Order. Instead I think the more we work for unity among ourselves, the better it will be. (Dec. 7, 1953)

Parallel with his study of the tradition of the Church, Merton continued to deepen his knowledge of the New Testament texts upon which this tradition is based:

> I am teaching a course on the theology of St. Paul and I have Bonsirven, Cerfaux, Allo etc....Do you know of anything especially good in the way of new books on St. Paul? (Jan. 8, 1954)

Lastly, the best proof of his desire to insert his own destiny into the uninterrupted flow of tradition is the way in which he was careful to set his own eremetical vocation in the eremetic trend dating back to the origins of monasticism. He came to perceive more and more clearly that he was called to be a hermit. We can ask whether this calling was "traditional." How did he have to carry it out and where? What lessons can be drawn in this respect from the monastic hermits of the past? It was for him, and for others like him, that I set about studying seriously the solitary life in monastic history and published some of my findings. Merton followed the work with vital interest. He had no intention of restoring the past in archeology, but he wanted to be sure that in following this call to solitude he was not giving way to a personal whim. He wanted to relive an experience which belonged to the Church, and he was humble enough to learn from history. Thus it was that his project slowly matured, first in himself, then in his superiors and his milieu:

> I was interested to hear there was a hermit at La Trappe under De Rancé. I value your prayers in this time of mystery and searching. It is more and more evident to me that someone must go through this kind of thing. By the mercy of God, I am one of those who must pass through the cloud and the sea. May I be one of those who also reach the promised land. Whatever happens, I shall certainly write much less and I have no desire to become a "literary hermit." I feel that God wills this solitude in American monasticism, even if someone has to leave

America temporarily to find it. Let us remain united in the Holy Spirit. (June 3, 1955)

I have stopped writing, and that is a big relief. I intend to renounce it for good, if I can live in solitude. I realize that I have perhaps suffered more than I knew from this "writing career." Writing is very deep in my nature, and I cannot deceive myself that it will be very easy for me to do without it. At least I can get along without the public and without my reputation! Those are not essentially connected with the writing instinct. But the whole business tends to corrupt the purity of one's spirit of faith. It obscures the clarity of one's view of God and of divine things. It vitiates one's sense of spiritual reality, for as long as one imagines himself to be accomplishing something he tends to become rich in his own eyes. But we must be poor, and live by God alone—whether we write or whatever else we do. The time has come for me to enter more deeply into that poverty. (Aug. 11, 1955)

The witness of monks in the past was for him not merely a matter of abstract or scientific learning:

Meanwhile for my part I am happily lecturing on Cassian. What could be better material for my situation? Although I cannot live like Abbot Isaac, Nesteros, or Piamon, I feel that they are my fathers and my friends. (Dec. 3, 1955)

As times goes on it seems that I grow closer to the state in which nothing at all is written. I have not attempted anything like a book since I became novice master. But with the inveterate itch of the writer I have turned some novitiate conferences into a pamphlet. Of this, too, I shall soon be cured. I have spent the year teaching a course on Cassian, on the *Cistercian Consuetudes*, and now on St. Bernard—I am just beginning. I am eager to see your lectures given at San Anselmo, which you said would probably be published. What I am doing is nothing at all, just an introduction for novices, and very superficial.

I do hope this winter to be able to set several things aside and apply myself to the study of Clement and Origen, and the Alexandrians, and the Fathers of Egypt, and the sources of monastic spirituality in general. Is there anything new on this, in the last year or so? More and more I feel attracted to Evagrius. The new *Sources Chrétiennes* re-edition of Diadochus de Photike is to me delightful and nourishing. I have become very fond of it and am almost inseparable from it. I like Diadochus very much.

The question of solitude is no longer any kind of a question. I leave everything in the hands of God and find my solitude in his will, without being theatrical or glowingly pious about it. I am content. But the right kind of contentment is a perfect solitude. When one is more or less content with the "nothing" that is at hand, one finds in it everything. I do not mean "nothing" in a tragic, austere sense, but the plain nothing which is the something of everyday life. The life of a Benedictine does not require all the fierce strippings of a St. John of the Cross, but the common way without exaltation (even in nothingness) is enough. (1956)

Along with Cassian, Bernard, the early Christian Fathers or the medieval hermits—especially those from Cluny which I had studied and which Merton mentions in several of his letters—Blessed Paul Giustiniani remained a constant source of inspiration:

Returning to the question of the Giustiniani book—I believe an English translation would be very desirable and you might be able to interest an American publisher in the idea. (Feb. 6, 1956)

And in fact he wrote a very fine preface to the English translation of this book. He put much of himself into this text (which is reproduced in the first of his posthumous writings, *Contemplation in a World of Action*).

The result of his patient struggle for the eremetical life is expressed in a few lines from a letter written in 1965, more than ten years after we began studying this deeply rooted monastic tradition:

> Yes, I was a bit surprised that the General Chapter even officially and publicly admitted that a Cistercian could become a hermit without the Order collapsing. It seems definite that I will be able to do this, and I am in fact spending most of my time in the hermitage. (July 5, 1965)

And more than a year later he wrote again, this time from the total peace of his hermitage:

> Jacques Maritain was here in October and we had a fine visit. He is very much a hermit now, and his latest book has added a hermit voice to the contemporary harmony (or disharmony). *Le Paysan de la Garonne* is I think very fine. I think you would like it. I have heard from your friend Dom Gregory in Tanzania and will write him soon. Also we had a true Sufi master from Algeria here. A most remarkable person. It was like meeting a Desert Father or someone out of the Bible. He invited me to come to talk to his disciples in Algeria, but I told him this would be quite impossible. Yet I would love to talk to them in fact, and also to see some monasteries in Africa. But I suppose that will never be allowed. No matter. The woods are all I need. (Nov. 18, 1966)

III
INSERTING TRADITION IN THE PRESENT

So, as we have seen, history was put into harness for the benefit of tradition, and it was this that opened Merton's receptiveness to actuality, giving him a key to understanding it. This attentiveness to the present is stressed more and more in the letters of the last years of his life. Here is just one example dating from 1965:

Many thanks for the offprint on African Monasticism and for your letter from Togo. I am convinced, by both of them, that the purity of life there must be something very inspiring. Of course God will bless them more than other countries in so far as they are much poorer, much more dependent on Him, much closer to the nature He has made. I do not mean to imply by this that technology has something bad about it, but nevertheless I think that in the big and prosperous nations the problems of monasticism will be otherwise complex. To begin with I am becoming more convinced that true simplicity, in the depths of the heart, is almost impossible for an American or for a European. Certainly they may be subjectively sincere and mean well, but the fact they come from a society that divides man from the very start and fills him with conflicts and doubts must mean something. I am impressed by the fact that what *aggorniamento* has meant here has been doubt. And that is perhaps healthy, or healthier than the old rigid refusal to admit even the possibility of anything being questioned. (July 5, 1965)

So Merton continued to be optimistic despite his realistic viewpoint. Two years after the letter just quoted, he wrote to me, saying:

With Rome as it is, renewal will always be a slow struggle. The whole conception of authority all down the line is not favorable to a really spontaneous renewal, but we can be glad that things are as good as they are and not worse. The dead concepts will continue for a while to usurp the place belonging to life, but I do not think it will really matter much—except that some monasteries may finally be closed down. Perhaps that will be for the better. (Feb. 17, 1967)

A good example of the knack Merton had for using knowledge of tradition to respond to contemporary aspirations and needs is seen in the short essay he wrote in June 1966 on "Franciscan Eremitism" for the review *The Cord*.

From the outset of the essay he states a principle in his method:

At the present moment, when there is a revival of eremitism in the monastic setting, it might be interesting to consider Franciscan hermits in their historical perspective. To do this, we have to understand the very important pre-Franciscan movement of itinerant and preaching hermits in the tenth and twelfth centuries.[2]

The development which he then gives is based on the best studies on the subject. He begins by establishing the fact that "St. Francis was in the direct line of the earlier hermit tradition." Then, with the ability he had of going straight to the core of any document, he brings out the novelty that there was in "the special statute or instruction composed by St. Francis for those retiring to hermitages":

The importance of the document lies in the spirit which it exhales—a spirit of simplicity and charity which pervades even the life of solitary contemplation. It has been noted that the genius of sanctity is notable for the way in which it easily reconciles what seems at first sight irreconcilable. Here St. Francis has completely reconciled the life of solitary prayer with warm and open fraternal love.

Merton was also fond of picking out piquant details in a text:

In the struggle to preserve the primitive spirit of poverty and utter Franciscan simplicity, the hermitages played the part that may be imagined. It is interesting, incidentally, that when St. Bonaventure was made a Cardinal he received the news while he was washing dishes in a hermitage.

It is not hard to understand that in periods of reform the ideal of solitude has had an important part to play in renewal of the Franciscan life and apostolate. This is especially clear when we study St. Leonard of Port Maurice and the Franciscan revival in Italy in the eighteenth century. St. Leonard himself got his vocation while listening to the Friars chant Compline in the *Ritiro* on the Palatine, and his promotion of the *Ritiro* movement is both characteristic and important in his life as a reformer.

After a few historical considerations on this movement, and the similarities between this *solitudine* and the "Carmelite 'desert,' " he proposes a practical suggestion about the renewal of a particular observance:

In all the forms of religious life we are asking ourselves today whether the accepted methods of renewing our fervor are quite adequate to present-day needs. Certainly the prescribed eight-day retreat has its value. But the new generation is asking itself seriously whether this rather formalistic exercise really produces any lasting fruit. Is it simply a tightening of nuts and bolts on machinery which is obsolete? Modern religious who feel the need of silence generally seek it not merely for the purpose of self-scrutiny and ascetic castigation but in order to recuperate spiritual powers which may have been gravely damaged by the noise and rush of a pressurized existence. This silence is not necessarily tight-lipped and absolute—the silence of men pacing the garden with puckered brows ignoring each other—but the tranquility of necessary leisure in which religious can relax in the peace of a friendly and restful solitude and once again become themselves. Today more than ever we need to recognize that the gift of solitude is not ordered to the acquisition of strange contemplative powers, but first of all to the recovery of one's deep self, and to the renewal of an authenticity which is twisted out of shape by the pretentious routines of a disordered togetherness. What the world asks of the priest today is that he should first of all be a *person* who can give himself because he has a self to give. And indeed, we cannot give Christ if we have not found Him, and we cannot find Him if we cannot find ourselves.

These considerations might be useful to those whose imaginations and hopes are still able to be stirred by the thought of solitude, and of its important place in every form of the religious and apostolic life, in every age, especially our own.

IV
A PROPHETIC PREPARATION FOR THE FUTURE

Merton's knowledge of the past and his attentiveness to contemporary history gave him, on many points, an anticipatory attitude. "Truth will set you free," said the Lord. It would be possible to give multiple variations on this inexhaustible theme. We could, for example, embellish it with a statement such as "History will set you free from the past" or "Tradition will set you free from traditions." When he went back to the sources, Merton shook off the hampering shackles of the very recent past which grew out of the nineteenth century, and he did much in the way of liberating his immediate background from such various confines. He preferred theology and spirituality to the usages which had come down from this period of formalism. To theology and spirituality, which are always appropriate for any period, he added the witness of the great men of ancient, medieval and Renaissance times. In this way he taught an important lesson to his contemporaries. Today, what many people lack is a correct knowledge of history and tradition. Certainly psychology, sociology, linguistics and such other new disciplines are very useful, and they offer immediate satisfaction to the inquiring mind because they deal with the immediate. However, without some familiarity with what went on in days long ago, there is every risk of being no more than "the man of the immediate," as Kirkegaard puts it. Merton was able to distance himself from this "immediate." In this way he did not become enslaved to it and was therefore able to judge the times more equitably. Such a distance between Merton and the immediate was the fruit of his solitude and his study of tradition. He survived transitory fads and is already being ranked with the great witnesses of the continued presence and action of God throughout the ages, including our own. A present-day exponent of doctrine and methodology recently placed Merton alongside other men and women who, in narrating their own life, help us to comprehend God's work in the world:

> Could contemporary Catholic theology take up this autobiographical material, leave aside the extraordinary elements and—within the framework of a personalist understanding of revelation—study to advantage how remarkable men and women like Augustine, Teresa of Avila, Thomas Merton and Dietrich Bonhoeffer came to know Christ's revealing himself in their lives and traced through their writings the progress of that salvific relationship of revelation?[3]

Merton himself, a few months before his death, sketched out his theology of what he called "The Historical Consciousness," in an essay which begins:

> God has revealed Himself to us in history by becoming man. Christ, the Man-God, is the Lord of History. Awareness of Christ implies therefore some awareness of history, not in the abstract, academic sense, but in the concrete: an awareness of the crisis of our times' relation to Christ's plan for the salvation of man. A Christian consciousness is therefore a special kind of historical consciousness: an awareness of kairos (the providential time of crisis and judgment) and of choice. The choice for Christ and against his enemy is not simply an interior rectification of intention ("I do this for love of you"); it should also be a choice made in the context of historic crisis.[4]

After this introductory passage, Merton goes on to give examples of some of the problems posed in the ecclesiastical, social and political spheres. He then adds:

> Should contemplatives know about these problems? Obviously they cannot try to follow them in detail. Even experts are baffled by the situation. But the contemplatives should have a genuine and a deep historical consciousness, since Christ is in fact manifesting Himself in the critical conflicts of our time.

In other words, a certain amount of *information and identification* will add a much needed dimension of reality to our contemplative lives. We tend to live in a kind of historical vacuum, as if nothing had changed since the sixteenth century—or the nineteenth (most of our customs reflect the historical situation of those days). But an historical consciousness of the poverty of the modern world will help us to take a more realistic view of the comparative comfort and security in which we live in our cloisters. In this way our prayer, informed by the deep sense of contemporary human anguish, will become more real with the reality of genuine compassion.

Whether we understand them or not, the conflicts of our times will have an effect on us anyway. We can choose: either we will be afflicted by vague rumors and horror stories, fantasies and nightmares, violence, or we will acquire a mature human and Christian awareness of the *kairos* in which the Church herself is deeply involved. She faces an historical changeover of decisive importance. The domination of Western and European culture is at an end, and for better or for worse a whole new world is in formation. Do we know what this means for Christ and for Christians? Is our prayer informed by this awareness?

These last words are important because they show that for Merton everything, including the knowledge of history, past or present, should lead to prayer and, through prayer, to conversion. It is his encounter with the Eternal which allowed him to link up the past, present and future. On many points he seemed to anticipate on solutions which have since proved to be the obvious ones. History has already corroborated the aptness of more than one of his intuitions. After I had procured an invitation for him to talk at the first Pan-Asian monastic meeting in Bangkok at the end of 1968, he sent me a letter back saying:

> Those who question the structures of contemporary society at least look to monks for a certain distance and critical perspective, which alas is seldom found. The vocation of the monks in the modern world...is not survival but prophecy. We are all busy saving our skins.

He did not play the prophet, but was a member of a body—monasticism—which, because it does not aim at immediate action, can look far ahead, foresee and foretell. He felt that this was not restricted to Christian monasticism. In other religious traditions, what interested him was not so much the lofty and subtle doctrines, as the monks themselves, those who today, as in the past centuries, live according to these doctrines, thus attesting to their practicality. In such action fired by contemplation, Merton discerned an energy capable of changing the course of history. He spent the last weeks, even the last hours of his earthly life, serving this God-given dynamism. All along the road, from Kentucky to Thailand, via California, Alaska, India, and Ceylon, he sowed the seeds of ideas which others were to cultivate and bring to fruition. During the second Pan-Asian monastic meeting at Bangalore, in 1973, reference was constantly made to Merton's intuitions, and the preparations for the third meeting in 1978 are again taking inspiration from him.

On the morning of December 10, 1968, he placed on the podium the text of the paper which he had written on "Marxism and Monastic Perspectives."[5] Then, from the abundance of thought which it had required, from the depths of the silence in which he had lived, he improvised a talk, which though it encompassed the thoughts contained in his script, extended beyond them and orientated them toward the practical applications called for in each country. A prophet is a person of neither vague ideas nor ready-made solutions. He or she is a person who, by reason of the vigor of his or her concepts and the intensity of his or her contemplation, compels other persons to act, giving them worthy reasons for doing so. Because he was a person of vision—not of "visions"—and a powerful catalyst, Merton was a prophet, and there is nothing to say that he was the last of the prophets.

That a country like the United States should produce someone of such wealth, and continue to listen attentively and so broadly to his message, augurs well for the future of the Church and the world. Is there any reason not to hope that God will raise up at all times other such witnesses of his own eternal contemplative action, Love?

NOTES

1. I must apologize for speaking so often in the first person, for a monk should always withdraw and leave room for the truth that he or she is writing about. But Gerry Twomey asked me for a personal witness, and I could hardly refuse.

2. I am taking the extracts for this article from the typed manuscript which Merton sent to me. (The essay later appeared in Merton, *Contemplation in a World of Action* (N.Y.: Doubleday, 1971), pp. 273-281.

3. Gerald O'Collins, S.J., "A Neglected Source for the Theology of Revelation," *Gregorianum* 57 (1976), pp. 759-760.

4. For the selections used in this essay, I used the text that I borrowed from Br. Patrick Ryan, and I acknowledge my debt to him.

5. The text of this talk is contained in an appendix of Merton, *The Asian Journal of Thomas Merton*, edited by Br. Patrick Hart, Naomi Burton, and James Laughlin (N.Y.: New Directions, 1973), pp. 326-343.

By His Death

(In Memoriam: Thomas Merton, 1915-1968)

By his death we are not diminished.
He has entered
into the space of thought,
he walks on the light
and serves where he serves.
In his death
surely we have no cause for dismay,
being not diminished.

When, in this little after hour,
death sounds our summons,
we too shall walk on the light,
if our cup is rinsed,
and serve where we serve,
with him in our Lord
joined in perpetual act of creating.

By his death and ours
surely we are increased,
we are not diminished.

John Moffitt

Notes on the Contributors

Brother Patrick Ryan, O.C.S.O. is a Trappist monk of the Abbey of the Genesee, Piffard, N.Y. He has published several poems about Merton and numerous articles on monastic spirituality and history. He recently completed graduate studies at the Institute for Cistercian Studies at the University of Western Michigan, and is an authority on William of St. Thierry, the twelfth-century Cistercian Father. One of his special interests is the relationship of the Western Christian monastic tradition to the native African and Asian spiritual traditions.

Gerald Sean Twomey, C.S.P., a member of the Paulist Washington Community, is presently completing studies in theology and Church history at the Catholic University of America, and undertaking a study of the spirituality of Isaac Thomas Hecker, founder of the Paulist Fathers. He is particularly interested in Cistercian Monasticism and has published articles on Thomas Merton and monastic spirituality in *Cistercian Studies, Monastic Exchange,* and *The Social Studies.* He conceived and edited the present volume on the prophetic concerns of Thomas Merton.

James Forest, a noted peace activist, was the editor of *Fellowship* magazine and now serves as international general secretary of the Fellowship of Reconciliation, headquartered in The Netherlands. He attributes much of the formation of his peace consciousness to the writings of Merton. Their extensive and rich correspondence in the early 1960's is one of the most significant primary sources available in assessing and appreciating the facets of Merton's social witness.

Gordon Zahn, professor of sociology at the University of Massachusetts, Boston, has been a leading spokesperson of Catholic pacifism for the past forty years. A long-time correspondent with Merton, he is the author of several books, including *German Catholics and Hitler's Wars, Conscience and Dissent,* and *In Solitary Witness.* He has written and lectured widely on Merton.

John Howard Griffin, of Fort Worth, Texas, was one of Merton's dearest friends, and has been designated by the Trustees of the Merton Legacy Trust to write the authorized biography. Their friendship is chronicled in, *A Hidden Wholeness: The Visual World of Thomas Merton.* Griffin is a world-renowned writer, best known for the narrative, *Black Like Me.*

Sister Thérèse Lentfoehr, S.D.S. is a poet of distinction and a member of the Congregation of the Sisters of the Divine Saviour. She currently resides in Racine, Wisconsin. Her friendship with Merton dates from 1939, and she possesses perhaps the most extensive private collection of Mertoniana in existence. She has written and lectured extensively about Merton, and has recently completed a critical study of his poetry entitled *Beautiful Cellars.*

Brother David Steindl-Rast, O.S.B., a monk of Mount Saviour Monastery in Pine City, N.Y., was born in Vienna, where he studied art, anthropology, and psychology. He has written and lectured widely on Merton, studied and practiced Zen at the Zen Studies Society in New York City, and organized the Center for Spiritual Studies in Trumbull, Conn.

Brother Patrick Hart, O.C.S.O. is a monk of the Abbey of Gethsemani, and former secretary to Merton. The executor of the Merton Legacy Trust, he edited *The Asian Journal of Thomas Merton, Thomas Merton/Monk,* and *The Monastic Journey.* He presently serves as the Abbey's representative on Merton affairs.

Sister Elena Malits, C.S.C. is the chairperson of the department of theology at St. Mary's College, Notre Dame, Ind. Her doctoral dissertation at Fordham University is on Merton's spirituality, and she has lectured and written extensively on Merton.

Father John Eudes Bamberger, O.C.S.O. was elected Abbot of the Genesee in 1971. For many years a monk of Gethsemani (and doctor/psychiatrist there), he was chosen Secretary-General of the Cistercians in the late 1960's and entrusted with the responsibility of implementing the *aggiornamento* of Vatican II within the Order. His studies on Merton have appeared in *Continuum, Sobornost,* and the *Dictionnaire de Spiritualité.*

Dom Jean Leclercq, O.S.B., the distinguished monastic scholar, is a Benedictine monk of the St. Maur Abbey in Luxembourg. The foremost authority on St. Bernard and the first generation of the Cistercians, he is especially noted for his studies in monastic spirituality, comparative religion, and psychohistory. He wrote the introduction to *Contemplation in a World of Action,* and enjoyed an extensive and provocative eighteen year correspondence with Merton (presently being edited for publication), terminating with Merton's death in 1968.

John Moffitt, an accomplished poet and literary critic, is poetry editor of *America,* and presently lives in Unionville, Va. He is especially interested in the East-West dialogue, and was present at the Bangkok Conference where Merton died. He is the author of several poems and essays about Merton.